Autonomy and Judaism

SUNY Series in Jewish Philosophy

Kenneth Seeskin, Editor

Autonomy and Judaism

The Individual and the Community in Jewish Philosophical Thought

Edited by

Daniel H. Frank

State University of New York Press

Published by
State University of New York Press, Albany

For information, address State University of New York Press,
State University Plaza, Albany, N.Y., 12246

Production by M. R. Mulholland
Marketing by Dana E. Yanulavich

Library of Congress Cataloging-in-Publication Data
Autonomy and Judaism : the individual and the community in Jewish
    philosophical thought / edited by Daniel H. Frank.
        p.   cm. — (SUNY series in Jewish philosophy)
    Revised papers from the 10th Annual Conference of the Academy for
Jewish Philosophy, held June 4-5, 1989 in Philadelphia at the
Reconstructionist Rabbinical College and at Temple University.
    Includes bibliographical references and index.
    ISBN 0-7914-1209-1 (CH : acid-free). — ISBN 0-7914-1210-5 (PB :
acid-free)
    1. Autonomy (Philosophy)—Congresses. 2. Philosophy,
Jewish—Congresses. 3. Judaism—20th century—Congresses. I. Frank,
Daniel H., 1950-   . II. Academy for Jewish Philosophy (U.S.).
Meeting (10th : 1989 :   Philadelphia, Pa.) III. Series.
B5802.A89A97 1992
181' .06—dc20   91-37943
                                                                   CIP

10 9 8 7 6 5 4 3 2 1

Dedicated to the Memory of
Steven S. Schwarzschild
Teacher
Colleague
Friend

Contents

Preface

This volume began life as a set of working papers presented at the tenth annual conference of the Academy for Jewish Philosophy. The conference, "Autonomy and Judaism," was held June 4–5, 1989 in Philadelphia at the Reconstructionist Rabbinical College and at Temple University. In light of the discussion at the meetings, all the essays included herein have been revised. None has been published previously.

The editor is grateful to those individuals who, in one way or another, are particularly responsible for the appearance of this volume, namely, Norbert Samuelson, Kenneth Seeskin and Jacob Staub. In addition, all the participants at the conference owe a debt of gratitude to the Reconstructionist Rabbinical College and to Temple University for the excellent facilities which they provided. One debt, alas, cannot be repaid, at least now. It is owed to Steven Schwarzschild, a founding member of the Academy, in gratitude for his sustained forthrightness, collegiality and friendship. It is entirely fitting that this volume, *Autonomy and Judaism*, be dedicated to his memory.

Introduction

Philosophical reflection on autonomy is modern. The problem of autonomy as manifested in the tension between individual rights and the correlative duties entailed by membership in a civic community arises with the development of the natural rights tradition in European thought in the seventeenth century, a tradition associated with the writings of Grotius, Hobbes, Locke and others. As such, this problem enters Jewish thought at a later date, with emancipation and deghettoization at the end of the eighteenth and the beginning of the nineteenth centuries. Simply put, before Jews became citizens of modern states, reflection on autonomy in this political sense did not, indeed could not, arise among them. Associated with this political debate is the epistemic and, ultimately, religious worry of whether autonomous human reason, reason by itself, can (or cannot) provide the grounding or foundation for morality and religion. This discussion, most prominently associated with Kant at the end of the eighteenth century, entered Judaism almost simultaneously. As both the political and the religious side of the modern discussion concerning autonomy make clear, the entire issue focuses upon the relation of the individual to the community. To what extent does the individual have rights which no civic society can abrogate? To what degree is the individual the ultimate authority or judge in matters of morality and religion? When, if ever, can the individual delegate decision making in such spheres to others?

Although such questions have a decidedly modern ring, one would be wrong to think that analogues cannot be found in earlier ages. Cognate issues are indeed to be found in ancient and medieval times, both within the Jewish world and outside it. Plato and Aristotle, for example, address themselves to the worry of whether the human being is by nature a political animal or whether the human good is to be found outside the political arena. In Jewish thought this core issue is little different. Thinkers throughout the ages, from biblical through rabbinic and medieval to modern times, are preoccupied with the relation of the individual Jew to the community and to the world at large. One way the philosophers of Judaism characterized the issue was in asking whether knowledge of God, *ex hypothesi* the highest good and a cognitive attainment of a particular individual, is to be understood as a sort of contemplative activity which distances the thinker from the social and political realm or as an activity which motivates moral and political action; and if it is the latter, then how? Further, while premodern philosophers, Maimonides and Aquinas, for example, do not concern themselves with Kant's problem of whether morality and the moral law can be grounded in the nature of practical reason, they do worry about the general intelligibility of the law, about the linkage between reason and virtue, and about the capacity of human reason to secure, unaided, the good. They ask: What is the relationship between (divine) law and human reason? between law and morality? What is the ultimate source of obedience to the law?

This overview should at least make clear that philosophical reflection on the relation of the individual to the community is both perennial and universal. And as such, it is part of the tradition of Jewish philosophy. No one philosophizes in a vacuum, and as, I think, this volume makes amply clear, Jewish philosophy flourishes by engaging in lively dialogue with the entire Western philosophical tradition.

This dialogue presents itself both systematically and historically, and this volume consists of essays which emphasize one or the other aspect. Each of the essays in the first part sets out the general problem which confronts every modern Jew: How can the individual Jew retain a rich sense of self, while also remaining squarely within the historically covenanted community? Again, how can the individual Jew square a sense of autonomous selfhood with the ongoing reality of the tradition, however the latter is interpreted? In response to this problematic, the first two essays complement each other by virtue of their opposing philosophical affiliations. Eugene Borowitz, in "Autonomy and Community," takes up the issue of the individual and the community from the standpoint of an anti-Kantian religious existentialism. For Borowitz, arguing against both Hermann Cohen and Mordecai Kaplan, the crucial issue for the liberal, non-Orthodox Jew is how to develop a robust sense of a *Jewish* self, such that the (liberal) denial of the validity of the Sinaitic revelation does not undercut the individual's commitment to the Jewish people.

In response to Borowitz, Kenneth Seeskin, in "Autonomy and Jewish Thought," approaches the issue of individual freedom and autonomy and obedience to the Law from the side of a committed Kantianism. While fully cognizant of and sympathetic to the Maimonidean emphases on God's transcendence and surpassing wisdom, Seeskin wishes to defend a notion of Judaism which emphasizes a strong commitment to self-determination and autonomy. For Seeskin, insofar as the tradition is a tradition of laws directed to free individuals, it entails a notion of the self as a self-legislating, moral agent, an agent capable of assenting to the Law, of taking the Law upon oneself. But with this comes a problem: How can a free and autonomous individual, whose rationality requires obedience to universal law, rest content with a tradition in which he or she is commanded to obey a *particular* historical legislation? Seeskin faces the problem squarely, contextualizing it by reference to Platonic, Maimonidean and Kantian notions of autonomy and selfhood.

In the third and final essay of this part, Ze'ev Levy, in "Tradition, Heritage and Autonomy in Modern Jewish Thought," makes use of Hans-Georg Gadamer's theory of historical interpretation, his hermeneutical theory, in presenting his own view of the role that tradition should play in the life of the individual (Jew). Each human being is born into a tradition, but, lest one be crippled by it to the extent of forfeiting one's autonomy, one must 'stand back,' reflect upon, and then use the tradition for current purposes. With specific reference to Judaism, Levy, a secular Zionist, urges the modern non-Orthodox Jew, for whom Halakhah is not definitive of his or her being, to make every effort to invest those aspects of the tradition which are vital with new meaning. Levy's essay will profitably be read in connection with the earlier essay by Borowitz.

In turning from the general to the more particular, the second part presents, first, three historical studies. Each of these essays focuses on one or more historical periods and figures therein and attempts to tease out some normative implications for Jewish thinking about autonomy and the moral/political relationship of the individual to the community and to the world at large.

Lenn Goodman, in "The Individual and the Community in the Normative Traditions of Judaism," focuses on the biblical, prophetic and rabbinic periods and forcefully stresses that the modern tension between the individual and the community, a Hobbesian and Enlightenment development, is singularly absent in early Jewish literature. The early literature, the legal and moral code of the Torah and its rabbinic elaborations, presents a reciprocating relationship between the individual and the community, such that individual dignity is guaranteed only in the context of the community *and* that the community serves to foster individual well-being, materially, morally and intellectually. Fascism is thus precluded, but so too is the atomization of the individual which characterizes the modern industrial state. The reader will want to compare the view of human nature outlined by Goodman on behalf of the ancients with the modern view of the autonomous human being outlined in the essays of Borowitz, Seeskin and Levy.

In "The Elimination of Perplexity: Socrates and Maimonides as Guides of the Perplexed," I focus on the Rambam and, by comparison with Plato and the Platonic Socrates, try to show that the impetus which moves their respective attempts to force the would-be knower to confront and overcome his ignorance is moral and, even more importantly, political. Both Socrates and Maimonides hope that by eliminating and individual's perplexity and ignorance they shall thereby create better and more reflective citizens in their respective communities. For these two thinkers, the *summum bonum* is to be found not in other-worldly, apolitical contemplative activity, but rather in enlightened, metaphysically grounded, political leadership and legislation.

In turning to the modern era, Martin Yaffe, in "Autonomy, Community, Authority: Hermann Cohen, Carl Schmitt, Leo Strauss," constructs an historical dialogue, which, in microcosm, is *the* discussion of modernity, namely, the relation of the individual to the community. Cohen's late, Kantian-inspired, Jewish writings reveal (for Cohen) the Jewish sources as embodying an apolitical ideal for the human being (and Jew), an ideal of a cosmopolitan society commensurate with individual moral autonomy. In Yaffe's dialogue, such cosmopolitanism, such unconnectedness of the individual to political institutions, is strongly opposed by Schmitt, himself a former neo-Kantian like Cohen. Schmitt, for his part, wishes to 'politicize' human life again, and to find in the political community and the state the locus of morality and the human good. In responding directly to Schmitt, Leo Strauss accepts Schmitt's critique of Cohenian 'liberal' cosmopolitanism. But in reflecting upon Schmitt's statism, Strauss attempts to resuscitate a conception of the political which is at once attentive to the human need for community as well as to the abiding desire to transcend it, through philosophy. For Strauss, Plato and Maimonides, not Kant or Hobbes, are the paradigms for the modern Jew, indeed for every modern wishing to confront his or her tradition.

The volume concludes in a contemporary vein. The final two essays address themselves to contemporary Jewish perspectives on issues in communal responsibility and social justice. The reader will note in these last essays an emerging view of the individual as *by nature* a social being. This view, premodern in its orientation, may be understood as an alternative, indeed antidote, to the atomic, a(nti)social view of the individual which predominates in the modern period, and which motivates the very problem with which this entire volume is concerned. From this perspective, these final essays are of a piece with the prophetic and rabbinic conception of the human being outlined in Goodman's essay and in marked contrast to the modern conception outlined in the essays of Borowitz, Seeskin and Levy in the first part; put another way, these final essays present a view of human nature compatible with that of Strauss rather than that of Cohen.

Robert Gibbs, in "A Jewish Context for the Social Ethics of Marx and Levinas," illuminates the social theory of Marx and Levinas by comparing them with each other, and then fructifies the debate by injecting it with the messianic political ideal and the rejection of the state which one finds in normative (biblical and rabbinic) Judaism. Gibbs' essay is part of his own ongoing reflections about 'ethical sociality,' about the meaning and viability of such social institutions as enhance and preserve individual responsibility and freedom, but which are unencumbered by state sponsorship and control. The model for Gibbs is the sociality and sense of community fostered by *galut* Judaism in its creation of a society without a state.

In "Individual and Communal Forgiveness," Elliot Dorff turns his attention to the history of Jewish persecution by the Catholic Church and addresses himself to the meaningfulness, the philosophical intelligibility, of Jews forgiving Catholics for past wrongs, even though contemporary Catholics and Jews neither perpetrated nor directly suffered from those wrongs. In defending the intelligibility of such forgiving, Dorff develops a notion of forgiveness, "reconciliation," which he argues can meaningfully be extended by members of communities which are ontologically the same as those of the past, even though they are physically different from them. But meaningfulness and intelligibility do not, by themselves, carry prescriptive force, and thus in the final sections of the essay Dorff analyzes the arguments for and against extending such forgiveness to Catholics.

And now, let us begin.

Part One

Fundamentals and First Principles

Autonomy and Community

Eugene B. Borowitz

Where shall liberal Jews find a compelling sense of Jewish duty now that they deny that revelation comes to us in verbal form?

This question has always been at the heart of all forms of non-Orthodox Judaism and it has become increasingly troublesome as the early responses have proved inadequate, even as the press toward freedom has grown more anarchic. Few modern Jews will deny that self-determination is critical to our sense of personal dignity, though Vladimir Jabotinsky wanted the nation to act unquestioningly in support of its leader. And few believe that it will be possible to have any meaningful Jewish continuity without our people being able to make some demands upon us, though Alvin Reines teaches that Jews, like all human beings, ought rationally to do only what their personal free choice directs them to. For most of us, then, the issue is one of balance: what are the proper roles of the self and the group in determining what a Jew *ought* to do?

I stress "ought" because it is critical to this discussion to point to the problem of the urgency associated with the doing. There is a weak sense of "ought," that a given act would be pleasant or desirable if one would do it and, hence, commends itself to us. One often hears talk in the Jewish community about our traditions as resources or options available to enhance the individual's life. While there is value in this liberal approach to the Jewish heritage, certainly in apologetics, it has serious limits. For just as one may find this or that Jewish act valuable, one may or may not find another resource elsewhere that fulfilled the function as well or better. If Jewish survival involves more than preserving another group of possible behaviors, this weak sense of "ought" should not satisfy us. And that is precisely the problem: how might we understand Jewish duty as directing us with a strong sense of "ought," one urgent enough to give us an effective sense of obligation, though one not as stringent as God's own command to us?

This analysis already moves us to the philosophical heart of our problem. Ever since Kant's discussion of duty, though surely with roots going back to Descartes' arrogation of his right to judge all ideas faulty that did not commend themselves to his reason as clear and distinct, modern thought has located authority in the individual. It has no comparable, indeed remotely comparable, regard for the community. But surely that statement must be immediately nuanced. Philosophers seem always to have taken it for granted and Kant made it quite explicit that one of the signs of rational thought was its universality. That is, it could be understood by any rational thinker, if cogent it would compel assent, and if an ethical maxim it would apply to everyone. Thus, in the concept of universalism, Kant had a sense of the community of all rational beings and, in fact, a vital sense of the community of all human kind. His rationalism effectively integrated, and did not oppose, autonomy and community; as long as one is only concerned about community in this universal sense one need not despair of finding a philosophic way of linking the two.

The difficulties in dealing with community in contemporary philosophy arise precisely when we wish to provide a rational foundation for the authority of any lesser collective, for example, the state. Our preferred solution only proves the theoretical disparity between the self and the group. Following Rousseau, we believe that the most humane form of government will be one which expresses the will of its individual citizens. Democracy allows us to organize self-determining individuals into greater wholes and by their will to join the enterprise (knowing they will have some personal power in it), accepting its discipline over them. At its best, the democratic state will give wide latitude to individual conscience when it clashes with the will or needs of the majority. And, as we have seen so powerfully in our concern for Soviet Jews, we deem it to be a sign of decency in a government that it allows its people the right of emigration. In other words, if individuals feel that the state no longer expresses or might soon no longer express what they powerfully believe to be right, they should be allowed to leave and make a new social contract. In short, with the autonomy of the individual self-commending, the authority of the community is seen as essentially heteronomous and therefore problematic.

I do not mean by this example to deny the significance of social existence to individuals. Indeed, most of us gain our strong sense of the right to think for ourselves from our communities, whether the small one of the democratic family or the large one which teaches us civics. Our culture powerfully transmits and reinforces the validity of self-determination. It is a primary reason why we have made the idea so central to our existence. My interest has only been to point out the radical disparity between the cognitive status of duties arising from the self, whether directly or indirectly, and those coming from any community less than all humankind, understood as the universe of rational beings.

Hegel and Marx, of course, proposed ways around this difficulty. For Hegel, in an almost mystical way, the self at its philosophic best incarnates the Absolute Spirit which moves through reality and thus finds its fullest expression in the state that organizes and articulates the individual/Absolute will. Marx, calling the empowerment of individualism an idealogical excrescence of bourgeois capitalism, proposed thinking of persons as species-beings, as essentially instances of humankind. Neither solution commends itself to me, or to many others, largely because of the inordinate sense of rationality in Hegel and because of what we have seen happen in history when the state is made supreme and individuals utterly subordinated to it.

Jewish thinkers over the years have had some special difficulties to face in addressing this problem. For two reasons they have found it critical to defend a strong doctrine of individualism. First, Jewish rights in the modern world are dependent upon it. It is as persons, not as a community or nationality, that Jews have been welcomed as equals into their societies. Any effort on the Jewish part to insist that groups as such may legitimately put their group interests ahead of those of the various individuals in their midst would make discrimination or the ghetto reasonable. Second, the modernization of Judaism, that is the right to overthrow the classic authority of the traditional rabbinate and to determine new ways of being Jewish in the modern world, depends on the rights of conscience against tradition. Despite the paradoxicality of the assertion, Zionism, the movement to make nationhood the essence of one's Jewishness, finds its initial validity in the right of moderns to assert themselves against their inherited tradition and choose for themselves an alternative life style.

These reasons for the commitment to individualism remain so cogent that, despite all the difficulties the primacy of autonomy has brought into contemporary Jewish existence, most modern Jews make it primary in their lives, in varying degrees to be sure. This makes the problem of validating communal Jewish norms, traditional or contemporary, all the more perplexing.

Let us approach this issue by quickly surveying the first great response to this issue and the new difficulties it raised. I have in mind, of course, the neo-Kantian interpretation of Judaism as exemplified by its academic creator, Hermann Cohen. In his thought, the self orders its will in terms set by its rationality. In this system "autonomy" has the characteristic Kantian denotation. The self, *autos*, creates law, *nomos*, for itself which, because it is rational, commands one, since one is and ought to be a rational being.

As noted above, this version of autonomy will indeed relate one closely to the human community. It thereby also satisfies one of the two Jewish communal concerns in this area: it clarifies, through its universalism, why Jews should be equals in contemporary society. It also validates, by its emphasis on conscience and aesthetics, why modernizing Jews may and sometimes must break with Jewish community practice and teaching. This understanding of Judaism accomplished so much of modern Jewry's agenda that, particularly as a commitment to the primacy of universal ethics, it has remained basic to its ethos despite the inadequacies later generations have found in it.

The problem, of course, is that, like the common philosophic rationalisms, it validates the universal, making the particular secondary and, by virtue of always having to be justified in universal terms, inevitably problematic. For those modern generations whose Jewishness was deep and socially reinforced, this primacy of the universal came as a welcoming counterbalance (though its protagonists, of course, considered it not *part* of the truth but the *whole* of it). And it still does for many who, for whatever reason, are disturbed to discover that the Judaism they have been taught is grossly ethnocentric. But for all those modern Jews who for some time—in America since mid-century—have had little question about their general humanity but who want to know what properly drives their particular Jewish devotion, an essentially universal understanding of autonomy and community no longer answers their version of the question.

We can best appreciate the contribution of Mordecai Kaplan to contemporary Jewish thought in terms of this transition. He came to our problem not in our terms, those of Americans who, in Rosenzweig's terms, were making their way back to the center from the periphery. Rather he was part of that wave of immigrants who were determined that their Jewishness, in its rich ethnic particularity, must remain part of the modern life they had come seeking in North America. One may also describe this agenda negatively, that these immigrants found the older patterns of American accommodation to modernity too universal for them. Unlike most of this group, however, Kaplan thought it important to create and articulate a new theory of Judaism which would validate particularity while affirming universalism.

One measure of Kaplan's genius may be gauged from what he knew he had to accept from his liberal predecessors. With them he took it for granted that to be modern meant to be a rationalist and that rationalism meant a firm commitment to universal ethics. This meant that he had to face the problem of a framework in which particularism must be justified in universal terms. He undertook this burden because he agreed that for the many Jews still emerging from a cultural-spiritual ghetto, the fight for universalism had to be carried on. At the same time, for those who had become enamored of the equality that modernity offered, he wanted to make plain, in the same terms, the validity of the particular.

He solved this problem ingeniously by shifting the universe of discourse in which it was to be discussed from the idealistic to the naturalistic, specifically, to the level of observable human functioning in the world. He invoked the authority of science to define our human context, relying on sociology—and occasionally invoking psychology, though only in the most general terms—as his major hermeneutic for reading the Jewish experience and extrapolating the direction of its reconstruction. The ingenuity arises in selecting a science which not only deals rationally with particular groups but which makes the particular group the great creative force in human life. Thus, the universal, which was so threatening to specific Jewish continuity, could now be held in tension with the particular, validated as it now could be by a science.

Kaplan had no desire to undermine the individual by denying, in some rigid sociological fashion, that the single self had an internal authority of its own that was significantly independent of all that it gains from society. His commitments to autonomy were quite real. He affirmed that moral law was not socially determined but inherent in reality itself, and it always remained for him the one independent standard by which folk creativity should be judged. He was deeply devoted to democracy with its pluralism and right to dissent, insisting that it set the pattern by which the Jewish community ought to operate. And as one who exemplified the power of the single self over against the tradition, indeed even in opposition to the inherited liberalism, he could not deny autonomy without invalidating himself.

Such individualism he held in tension with the power and importance of the community. He let social science prove that individuals had a need to be in a social group and that, in almost every case, our supposed individuality is really a manifestation of our social situation. Thus, while we do have the dignity of autonomy, we will commonly express it in terms of our people's civilization. This is the natural thing to do, or in contemporary idiom, the healthy or mature thing to do. If for some reason that is not commonly taking place, as is true in modern Jewry, it is because the folk culture is not doing what sociology has taught us it ought to be doing, meeting the social needs of its individuals. In the Jewish case that arises from our coming to think of ourselves more as a church than as an ethnic group, as a religion rather than as a civilization, and from not resolutely reinterpreting our values and way of life in terms of the best of contemporary society. Thus, when Kaplan gives interpretations of Jewish ritual or belief, he regularly points out what the individual may gain from this in personal terms as well as in what its survival value is for the Jewish people. Kaplan does not see how, after the evidence of the social sciences, anyone can easily detach individuals from the community into which they were born. But he also gives their right to self-determination such sufficient weight that he believes the group must appeal to it to validate itself.

He also has a pragmatic argument for the social involvement of the individual. As a confirmed democrat, he wants all decisions about community norms to be made by the group as a whole. This is not only consonant with the way that we live in the greater society of which we also are a part, but, he notes, we will be more likely to do then what the group says, even when we are outvoted by others, because we were part of the decision-making process. I see in this not merely a social-psychological observation but a further recognition of the power inherent in the individual in this system which wishes, as an offset to excessive universalism, to stress the role of community.

With what urgency, we must now ask, would these democratically adopted community norms confront the individual Jew? I do not think that is an easy question to answer, though I think it is the critical one before us. Consider some versions of the question. Supposing the community's suggested action is an expression of the individual's highest moral standards, then in such a case individual and community are in full agreement and the potential issue before us disappears. Alternatively, if it had been the community, which by its action awakened the individual Jew's somnolent conscience, the individual would have been guided by the community and indeed should be grateful to it and to what it suggests. In both cases the authority behind the community's action is the concurrence of the individual. Something similar is true when the community norm, as in the case of many rituals or customs, is pleasant or enjoyable. I do what it says partially because it says so, but much more because I validate its suggested act. There is a good instance of this concurrence of interests in the Reform movement, generally recognized as fostering self-determination perhaps to a fault. With regard to Jewish education, most congregations have been able to institute and have their congregants abide by two community standards. In the one case, the confirmation ceremony, which took place originally when students were in the 8th grade, was twice raised until it is now standard in the 10th grade, with some congregations demanding an even higher standard. In the other case, almost all congregations will not allow for a full celebration of a Bar or Bat Mitzvah if the child has not been in training for two or more often three years. In both situations, the agreement of most Jewish parents that they wanted a reasonably adequate education for their child made the community norm possible and effective. I am certain that everyone can give other examples of harmony between autonomy and community whether in the Jewish community or elsewhere. In such experiences we can feel the truth of Kaplan's insistence that the community do what it can to meet the needs of individuals.

However, if the survival of Jewry and Judaism is our concern, the more interesting cases arise when I am indifferent to a norm or disagree with it. To some extent, we are all willing in such instances to do some things simply for the sake of the group. We will rouse ourselves to go to certain meetings or participate in certain activities. And we will do other things because we know people expect it of us, such as serving the socially acceptable repast after a family event. But in the usual case there is little urgency behind such folkway injunctions. Thus, for all that Kaplan makes of the Land of Israel as the center of Jewish civilization and Jewish culture, his social theory does not move many American Jews to perform the requisite acts they entail, make *aliyah* or, even make Hebrew our second language. We simply do not give the group that much independent sway over us.

That is true even in cases where community decisions have been democratically arrived at. But we have considerable cynicism these days about how 'democratic' such decisions really are, that is, the extent to which they truly express the consciences of those involved in making them. Besides, very much of the ordinary stuff of Jewish life is not seriously subject to significant democratic reconsideration: the solar-lunar calendar with its movable dates for the holidays and the mid-week occurrence of many of them; a Hebrew language that reads from right to left and has vowels above and below as well as in the middle of the consonant line; the ritual blessings for all sorts of events. These and others might be reworked in detail but hardly as institutions. We shall not be partners in determining the continuing validity of many such Jewish matters. They simply come down to us and, for all our reinterpretation, we need to face the issue that they may well be not what we want or would have devised but what, sociologically speaking, our people created. That gives them only a limited claim on our energy.

Kaplan knew this but thought that saying they were critical to our group continuity would make such honored practices an effective part of Jewish citizenship. Introducing the notion of what is 'critical' does shift the urgency inherent in group norms. If we feel that we stand at a special moment in our people's history, particularly if we believe our group existence is threatened, then many of us will be roused to action, perhaps even to sacrifice. But like the halakhic doctrine of *pikuach nefesh*, that is the exceptional case, not the stuff of long-range, everyday existence.

We have just been through a period when an effort was made—is still being made—to convert survival in this mode to the normal content of Jewish life. I refer, of course, to the institutionalization of "the survival of the Jewish people" in our community life, notably in our fund-raising and political activity, in the period from the Six Day War (1967) until now. It was in large measure phenomenally successful. In the amounts of money people gave, in the energies they devoted, in their willingness to make, against the Holocaust, the welfare of the state of Israel vital to their Jewish lives, loyalty to the group showed its great power. Even more impressive for the issue under consideration here was the way in which Jews disciplined themselves for the sake of what they saw as the communal good. With "the unity of the Jewish people" as a rallying cry, an unusually fractious and independent-minded community largely held back its occasional complaints about various Israeli actions and often refused to act on the promptings of its conscience. The truth in Kaplan's social vision of Judaism was never more concretely demonstrated. But so too was his one exception to the rule of group loyalty, ethics.

In three telling cases from the mid-seventies to the present we denied what our leaders told us was "good for the Jews" and insisted on defining it for ourselves until they came to agree with us, in some cases quickly, in some cases only with the greatest reluctance. Probably the earliest instance was the refusal of American Jewish leaders to accede to the Israeli requests that we adopt measures which would ensure a large flow of Russian Jewish emigres to Israel. Despite the high priority given to the needs of Israel and the obvious importance of immigration to its survival and well-being, our community refused to accede to the request. We believed that the right of individuals to decide where they wanted to go was more important than what seemed obviously good for the corporate welfare of the Jewish people.

The second instance was the Israeli response to the Palestinians and, by extension, to its incursion into Lebanon to destroy the P.L.O. From the massive community interdiction in the mid-seventies of Bereira, the first Jewishly reputable organization to challenge publicly Israel's approach to the Palestinians, a continual erosion took place in solid American Jewish community support for Israeli actions, no matter what. By the time of the foray into Lebanon and the penetration into Beirut, American Jews found they could no longer as easily repress their moral sense, applied here, as it had to be, to a realistic, political-military situation. And thus by the time of the *intifada*, American Jewish leaders and organizations were saying publicly what a decade before they had insisted was treason to the Jewish people as a whole.

And the final example is the response to the "Who is a Jew?" issue. Now "the unity of the Jewish people" suddenly reversed its meaning. Instead of requiring Jews to repress conscience to benefit Israel and thus the Jewish people, "unity" now was understood by most American Jews to imply pluralism, hence the right of individual, diverse opinion. The extraordinary urgency which was felt about this matter made itself felt precisely where it was most unexpected and where it counted most: in the American Jewish fund-raising apparatus. Over the years federations have carefully distanced themselves from anything having to do with controversy. They always insisted on remaining above all communal discord in the name of their higher functions, to unite all Jews for their common welfare and, as a result, to raise as much money as possible. The emotion behind the widespread American Jewish response to the possibility of changing the Israeli immigration law was so great—and, it must be noted, so disproportionate to the immediate substance of the issue—that federations nationwide broke with their established, well-founded practice of never getting involved in controversy and took a public stand on this issue.

I have not attempted by this analysis to invalidate Kaplan's teaching, only to point up the extraordinary disparity which even his thought sets up between the power of the individual and that of the community when it comes to commanding action. I have done so by giving my interpretation of the experience of the Jewish community in the past two decades because I believe, as Kaplan emphasizes, that is the level on which most Jews would directly sense it. But for those who are intellectually, perhaps philosophically, inclined, our experience relates intimately to the issue of appropriate authority. Consider how Kaplan sought to validate the claims of the group upon its members by having social science indicate what was true about human nature and human needs. Leaving aside the methodological question—whether any science should dictate the nature of a religious people—two immediate issues arise. First, much of the sociological data on which the theory of peoples and their civilizations is built rests on the observation of groups living in premodern fashion. How do we know that what was true of their social life continues to be true in the same way today? More specifically, is the character of a culture developed by an essentially secular, technological society essentially the same as that of a people living under substantially different circumstances? Second, assuming that the extrapolation is permissible, there is no basis for an easy move from what has been to what now ought to be. Such intellectual difficulties seriously undermine Kaplan's effort to make sociological force a compelling motive for significant Jewish action. I do not see any other secular intellectual resource which can validate the group with anything like the claims that conscience or the self is commonly understood to legitimately make upon us.

This line of reasoning has led me in a rather different direction, though not radically so. I think Kaplan was correct in recognizing it to be a major defect in the thought of his liberal predecessors that they did not give the Jewish people as such sufficient status in their thought. Indeed, I come to this point with special concern. I am part of that American generation whose troublesome question of Jewish identity was the transition from "How universal am I, the Jew?" to "What does it mean that someone as broadly human as I am is essentially a Jew?" Thus, agreeing with Kaplan and his Zionist mentor

Ahad Ha'am, I affirm that my Jewishness is as much continuity as present experience, as ethnic as it is personal.

With much of contemporary culture I disagree with Kaplan's view that modern thought is so well established and certain that it should set the terms in which Jews reinterpret their existence. I proceed one step further in denying that philosophic rationalism is the only tenable mode in which a sophisticated modern can discuss ultimate issues. Rather, I find the religious existentialism I have sought to develop and explicate over the years far truer to my own experience, most particularly to what I understand to be the truth of Jewish existence, than any alternative pattern of discourse.

My positive approach to this issue of providing a greater urgency to the Jewish community's claim upon me is to begin with the one source of authority which the contemporary intellect recognizes, the self. And my approach has been to insist that we can understand Judaism best in this period by interpreting it as a special form of selfhood. That is, if the most effective way of speaking of duty and obligation in the contemporary world is to do so in terms of selfhood, then we need to articulate a sense of Jewish selfhood. That should allow us to clarify how autonomy, normally so destructive of Jewishness by its universalism, could be the basis of a substantially identifiable Jewish life.

The negative move basic to this development may still proceed in rationalist terms, albeit critical ones. It involves the polemical question of the grounds for such confidence in the self that one is willing to make it, as against all inherited wisdom or institutions, the source of authority. I see no rational basis for such an assertion. The more we learn about the self, the more we are open to the full range of experiences which are part of its ongoing reality, the more we have reason to question its ultimate authority. I do not think it too much to say that when we ask the self to carry the load of all meaning and hope, it inevitably disappoints us. The self is more problem than answer.

I believe it necessary to carry out this polemical argument, not because I wish to deny that the self has any significance, but only to indicate that alone, in some Cartesian isolation, it is worthy of our trust. I reach this conclusion because the deepest truth I know is particularly Jewish. Any system which gives priority to the universal and relegates the particular to a secondary, inferior level is therefore unacceptable to me. I am therefore concerned to overcome any schizoid construction of the Jewish self, of the human being who is incidentally a Jew. My Jewishness is not incidental to anything, but primary to my existence. I understand Rosenweig to have discerned this in ways which it has taken some seventy years to clarify. In a postrationalist (and in that sense postmodern) era, Jewishness needs to be defined in terms of an absolute and foundational humanity, in terms of selfhood, not in terms of law, idea, nationality or ethnicity. The "reconstruction" of Jewish life that needs to go on must then proceed from the self that knows itself as a Jewish self.

This involves two affirmations which take us beyond contemporary rationalisms. The first explains the experience of the *benei noach* as well as our own. It is that the self is intimately grounded in covenant with God, thus giving it its inalienable dignity and its ground of responsible action. The second explains the fundamental reality of Jewish existence, that the individual Jew relates to God not simply as one of humankind but as part of the people of Israel's historic, ongoing covenant with God. I do not understand God to give us verbal revelation of what we ought to do as individuals/Jews. But knowing that my selfhood is indissolubly involved with God and the Jewish people means that my sense of Jewish duty now comes with God's presence behind it and as part of what I must do as part of the people covenanted to God, albeit interpreted through my specific individuality. In this way I can come to a new sense of "autonomy and community" which will recognize the power of thinking in terms of the self, yet so reinterpret it that "the community" now can make very significant demands upon me, though not with the ancient power of God's own words and institutions.

Autonomy and Jewish Thought

Kenneth Seeskin

1. Introduction

Autonomy is a notoriously ambiguous term.[1] In some instances it is a synonym for self-governing. Thus an action is autonomous if the agent is free of external constraints and does what he or she wants. In this sense, autonomy is morally neutral. A lustful or violent action can be as good an example of autonomous behavior as a merciful one. According to a second morally neutral sense of the term, autonomy is a synonym for spontaneity. Not all constraints on behavior are external. According to some thinkers, ordinary needs or desires can be impediments to free action if they are the result of causal factors beyond the agent's control. In this sense, an action is autonomous if it is initiated by the agent herself and has nothing to do with sensuous causes. A third view maintains that the crucial idea is not metaphysical but moral-psychological: a person acts autonomously if he can identify with the goals or desires that bring about the action, if he can view the action as his own. This view is motivated by the realization that while we often do what we want, sometimes, upon reflection, we do not approve of the fact that we want it.[2] Rather than spontaneity, the third view identifies autonomy with authenticity. And, finally, a fourth view holds that an action is autonomous if the maxim one imposes on oneself conforms to an objective, universal law. In short, autonomy is intimately connected with reason and means obedience to the moral law.

I take it as given that, according to Judaism, human beings are free agents who incur obligations. So while they are free to accept or reject the commandments (Deuteronomy 30:11–19), it is not enough to have the *capacity* for free behavior. We need an account of how or why a free agent decides to accept them. Can Judaism accommodate some notion of autonomy or does it require surrender to the will of God?

One of the most influential treatments of this topic is Eugene Borowitz's essay on the autonomous Jewish self.[3] In keeping with Buber's antinomianism, Borowitz rejects the suggestion that autonomy involves the imposition of an objective law or principle. Rather, the autonomous Jewish self is a tolerant and sensitive person able to respond to the conflicting needs of Jewish law and personal conscience. The autonomous self attempts to preserve his or her identity without abandoning the obligations incurred as a person living in covenant with God. In this way, Borowitz's conception of autonomy is based on a theory of religious authenticity. A person acts autonomously when she takes into account a range of choices, needs, or obligations and identifies with a responsible and Jewishly acceptable course of action.

Contrary to Borowitz, the sense of autonomy I wish to defend is the fourth or Kantian sense. There is, of course, a long debate on whether Kant introduced a morally neutral sense of autonomy (spontaneous self-legislation) in his later works or presupposed such a sense in the *Groundwork*. For the purposes of this discussion, however, I will assume that the Kantian understanding of autonomy cannot be completely neutral since apart from the moral law, there is no way to explain how the will can free itself of sensuous causes.[4] I hope to show that Kant's theory provides the best understanding of the claim that God's commands both issue from and are directed to a free will. In brief, this sense of autonomy is based on two claims: (1) that as moral agents, human beings are subject to law, (2) that every moral act is self-reflexive. But to put the matter this way is to call attention to a difficulty. Kant's idea of autonomy is part of his Copernican Revolution. Although there were a variety of people who anticipated the doctrine, it received its first explicit treatment in the *Groundwork to the Metaphysics of Morals*. How can a doctrine set forth by a gentile thinker in 1785 be part of Judaism's understanding of itself?

As an initial response, note that if Kant's ethics is revolutionary from a philosophic point of view, there is a respect in which, from an ordinary moral point of view, it is not. The last thing he wants to do is alter our basic sense of right and wrong. In the *Second Critique* he writes: "Who would want to introduce a new principle of morality and, as it were, be its inventor, as if the world had hitherto been ignorant of what duty is or had been thoroughly wrong about it."[5] Kant wants to clarify our sense of right and wrong, or to be more specific,

explain how it is possible. If, as Jewish law asserts, it is a duty to preserve life, tell the truth, honor father and mother, and refrain from
idolatrous worship, Kant thinks he is providing the philosophic foundation for these judgments. He does not think he is overturning them.

Thus it would not count against Kant to argue that the literature
of Judaism contains no explicit mention of the doctrine of autonomy.
There are passages such as Deuteronomy 11:26 and Psalms 19:8–11
that lend themselves to interpretation according to this doctrine, but
no passage that explicitly affirms it. Kant would reply that if the literature of Judaism conceives of human beings as moral agents, if it
understands human beings as incurring obligations, then it is committed to autonomy implicitly. To be sure, this is a controversial
claim, but we should not balk at the idea that a body of literature is
committed to a principle it does not actually express. A textbook on
arithmetic may contain no reference to set theory, but since set theory
is needed to explain why the foundations of arithmetic are valid, it
makes sense to say that the book is committed to set theory even
though its authors may be ignorant of it. So, when we find Hermann
Cohen arguing that the doctrine of autonomy is implied by Ezekiel's
injunction at 18:31 ("Cast away from you all your transgressions . . .
and make you a new heart and a new spirit"), we do not have to
argue that the prophet was himself a philosopher. The argument is
rather that this and other passages that suggest we have it within our
power to reject evil and choose righteousness are best understood as
saying that human beings are subject to a law whose validity they can
freely appropriate.

I emphasize the notion of law because given the ambiguity of
the word *autonomy*, it is easy for the prefix (*auto*) to overshadow the
root (*nomos*). According to Kant, autonomy is the imposing of law on
oneself, or better yet, the recognition that one is obliged to follow law.
But even these formulations can be misleading. What is the self? and
what is the law? For Kant, it is not the empirical self that makes this
determination but practical reason recognizing the demands of its
own rationality. For a modern-day Kantian like Rawls, it is the self
behind the veil of ignorance, which is to say the self stripped of any
aspect of particularity. And not any law will do. The only law reason
can impose on itself is a universal imperative. So autonomy is not
another name for personal conscience. A heinous criminal can follow
the dictates of his conscience if, as is clearly possible, his conscience is

perverse. In the sense in which I am using it, autonomy presupposes moral objectivity.[6]

It is also important to recognize that if a moral act is self-reflexive, it does not follow that morality is 'man made.' Morality involves the imposition of law on oneself. The ability to impose law rather than simply obey is what distinguishes human beings from inanimate objects and allows us to say that every human being possesses inherent dignity. Perhaps one could get away with saying that morality is rationally made or rationally imposed. But *reason* is a transcendental term whose application extends beyond the human race. If 'man made' means 'conventional,' Kant is as adamant as Plato that morality is not man made.

My plan is to present a thumbnail sketch of how the doctrine of autonomy came to be developed and what Kant thought it meant. I will then turn to the role of autonomy in Judaism. If my understanding is right, the doctrine of autonomy is and will always be controversial. But it is important to understand what the controversy is about. Although a person who accepts this doctrine can also accept a liberal interpretation of the law, there is no reason why the two have to go together. In principle, a person can accept the doctrine of autonomy and insist that all of the traditional laws of Jewish observance are binding. What is at issue is the deeper question of what we understand these laws to be. Are they ways of submitting to the will of another being or of recognizing the implications of one's own rationnality? How one answers this question will have an important bearing on how one conceives of God.

2. Development of the Concept of Autonomy

A. Plato

Although Plato does not defend the Kantian idea of autonomy either implicitly or explicitly, he is the first person to raise the question whether freedom should be understood in a positive or negative way. Does it involve doing what you want or doing what you *would* want if you possessed a clear understanding of the needs of your soul? The distinction is made in the *Gorgias* (468b). The context is this. Polus is defending a line in which a person can act at will doing whatever he or she wants. Socrates is defending a life devoted to lawfulness. At a critical spot, Socrates tries to make the point that all desires aim at a common end: the agent's well-being. If so, it is misleading to say that we want the immediate object of our action; rather, we want the object only in so far as it leads to or contributes to our good:

Socrates: It is in pursuit of the good that we walk when we walk, believing it to be the better course of action and, on the contrary, stand still when we do so, for the sake of the same thing: the good.

Polus: It is.

Soc.: And so in killing a man, if we kill someone, or exiling him, or seizing his property, we think it better for us to do what we are doing than not?

Pol.: Certainly.

Soc.: Therefore, it is for the sake of the good that all those who do these actions do them. . . . So if a person kills someone or exiles him from the city or confiscates his property, either as a tyrant or an orator, thinking it is better for him to do so, when in fact it is worse, I presume he does what seems best, does he not?

Pol.: Yes.

Soc.: But does he also do what he wishes—supposing it is really bad? Why do you not answer?

Pol.: No, I do not think he does what he wishes.

[*Gorgias* 468b–d]

In one respect, Socrates' position is paradoxical: the tyrant does what he thinks best but not what he wishes.[7]

What, then, does Socrates mean by wish (*boulesis*)? Cornford argued that wish is distinct from ordinary desire, the former being the desire of the true *self* for its own good.[8] Although there is no explicit reference to the "true self" in Plato, it is not difficult to see what Cornford had in mind. The tyrant does whatever he likes but still leaves his soul neglected; in that sense, he is always thwarting his own purpose. To build on Cornford's insight, we can say that the desire of the true self stands to ordinary desire as reality stands to appearance. This assumes that when it comes to one's own welfare, no one would be satisfied with appearance alone (*Republic* 505d3). This argument enables Plato to say, both in the *Gorgias* (467a) and the *Republic* (577e), that since the tyrant never does what he wishes, he has no power and is least of all people free. Plato is well aware that he is stretching the ordinary meaning of his terms. How can a tyrant not be free if he is at liberty to do whatever he wants?[9]

The answer is that for Plato, freedom is not value-neutral: it has as much to do with how a person acts as with what a person knows. In order to act freely, a person must have a correct assessment of the needs of the soul and the proper way of fulfilling them; ignorance can be as much a constraint as bonds or fetters. The proof is Plato's picture of the tyrant in the *Republic*: a man so enslaved by fear and passion that he is driven to the point of insanity. The gist of Plato's argument is that no one really wishes to be in this condition, even if it involves a large amount of what is usually referred to as personal liberty. If Plato is right, an individual may not be the best judge of what his freedom consists in. Polus, to take the most obvious example, is deeply confused.

We may conclude, with Dodds, that the *Gorgias* passage is the beginning of the "positive" conception of freedom: one is not free unless one acts in accord with reason.[10] The objection to positive freedom is well known. As Isaiah Berlin put it, positive freedom allows one to ignore the wishes of actual people, to bully, torture, or oppress individuals in the name of their 'real' selves.[11] The reply to Berlin is that he has an impoverished notion of reason and what sort of behavior it condones. But even if one is sympathetic with Berlin's criticism, one has to admit that the individual is not always the best judge of what he or she really wants. In Illinois for example, a girl of fourteen cannot agree to have sexual relations with a man no matter how much she insists she would like to. The law assumes that sexual relations at this age are so contrary to her well-being that she cannot give consent. Even if she asks the man to join her, he is guilty of statutory rape. For adults, similar problems arise with slavery, murder or suicide. In each case, the question of what an individual can consent to is more complicated than it first appears. The idea that we can simply *ask* the individual is mistaken because our understanding of consent is tied up with our understanding of ideas like human welfare and human dignity. So like the idea of freedom, that of consent is not value-neutral. It is assumed that one cannot consent to abandon one's dignity as a moral agent.

This view of behavior is not a theory of autonomy in the Kantian sense. Plato does not maintain that reason acts contrary to desire but, rather, that reason is itself a source of desire. Put otherwise, the Platonic ideal is not to overrule desire as much as to educate it. But Plato has shown that freedom is more complex than people might think. One cannot say whether a person is free without putting forward a whole theory of the self and the good life. Plato is convinced that when an adequate theory of the good life is put forward we will see that freedom involves access to truth. Without truth, the soul can get only a small portion of what it wants: it can satisfy some of the desires brought on by appetite, but few of those brought on by spirit, and none brought on by reason. In a word, freedom implies rationality.

B. Maimonides

Maimonides belongs in this discussion for two reasons: (1) divine volition plays a critical part in his understanding of creation, and (2) like Plato, he believes that human perfection involves access to truth. With respect to God, Maimonides fights a two-front war.[12] In book two of the *Guide*, he defends a theory of creation against those who believe that God and everything that emanates from Him are governed by an impersonal necessity. In several places, e.g., *Guide* 2.19 and 2.29, Maimonides explains that God can change the world order if it suits Him, even destroy it. In 2.19, he opposes the Aristotelians by arguing that the best explanation for the movement and diversity of the heavenly bodies is not that they emanate from an unchanging source but that they were created by a free agent according to a purpose. Why is Maimonides so anxious to reject the Aristotelian argument? He maintains (*Guide* 2.25) that the Aristotelian theory destroys the foundation of the law; in other words, if God is an impersonal force it is difficult to make sense of the imperative nature of the commandments. How can an impersonal force tell us what *ought* to be done?

But in other respects, Maimonides is sympathetic with Aristotle. He rejects the *kalam* view according to which causal regularities in the natural world are immediate consequences of the will of God (*Guide* 1.73). When it comes to the commandments themselves, he insists that God's will is never arbitrary. For example, he claims (*Guide* 3.25) that the world was not produced by will alone but by will acting in concert with wisdom. In 3.31 he considers the suggestion that the test of whether a commandment originates with God is lack of purpose. The idea is that God gives us laws that are so arbitrary that we could not possibly produce them on our own; in short, the commandments are a test of obedience. Maimonides rejects this idea on the ground that it would make God inferior to humans. If humans act with an end in view, is it not absurd to think that God acts without any direction at all? In reading this passage, we should keep in mind that Maimonides is committed to the principle of *imitatio Dei* (*Guide* 3.54). If divine activity is directionless, it would be impossible to argue that God is a moral exemplar. Maimonides therefore concludes that every commandment is given with the goal of human perfection in mind. I take this to mean that no commandments are purely revelatory in the sense that they bind without also educating (cf. Deuteronomy 4:6).

If I have interpreted it correctly, Maimonides' position has a Platonic ring: freedom requires rationality, not arbitrariness. Normally freedom implies ability to do otherwise, to will or not will (*Guide* 2.18). So while it may be the case that God could do otherwise, owing to His rationality and concern for human welfare (cf Psalms 19:7–9), He *will* not; God is a free but faithful and trustworthy leader. Yet, however comforting this conclusion may be from a religious perspective, it is problematic from a philosophic one. If God is a *perfect* leader, in what sense are the other possibilities before Him possibilities at all? In his introduction to the *Guide*, Pines argued that Maimonides' sympathy with volitionism is done "out of public spirit" in an attempt to "abet the faithful adherents of religion."[13] Maimonides' real sympathies, according to Pines, are with determinism. I think this reading is mistaken. The fact that a philosopher is involved with a problem—in this case, a problem that has been around for centuries—does not show that he is double-dealing. Notice, for example, that the same problem arose for Leibniz. God was free to create any number of possible worlds; but His goodness inclined Him to pick the best one. In what sense, then, are the uncreated worlds really possible?

Part of Maimonides' way of resolving the problem is to point out that since *will* is used homonymously with respect to us and God, we cannot assume that what is true of our will is also true of His (2.18). Our will changes as a result of external circumstances; but since God's will does not depend on external circumstances, change, if it occurred, would be self-caused or self-determined. In effect, the change would be "in" God's will from the beginning, so that it would still be true to say that God wills eternally. Does this solve the problem? Not entirely. The discussion of 2.18 could be taken to imply that self-determination is an essential condition of freedom. God is free because no force in the universe can act on His will except that will itself. We saw above that self-legislation is one meaning of autonomy. Still, Maimonides is far from providing a general theory of volition. Although he often speaks of intellect and will as two faculties, he is committed to the view that they must be one in God. How so? Maimonides has little choice but to fall back on negative theology: the nature of intellect and will in God are a mystery to us. In rejecting Aristotelianism, He is not claiming to *know* that God acts freely, but to provide plausible arguments for believing that He does.

With respect to humans, Maimonides argues that we should not view the commandments as arbitrary restrictions designed to push human endurance to its limits, but rather as ways of perfecting the soul. This does not mean that if one cannot find a plausible reason for a commandment, one is free to disregard it. Maimonides never doubts that all commandments are binding. Nor does he avoid an opportunity to point out that in ethics as well as metaphysics, human reason has limits. In *Guide* 1.2, for example, he rejects the Platonic view that ethical truths can be known with scientific rigor and adopts a position reminiscent of Aristotle: ethics involves "generally accepted things" or things established by convention. Sometimes, as with the dietary laws, the reasons Maimonides gives for obeying the commandments seem forced. It follows that, in one respect, Marvin Fox is right: reasons for commandments are given "after the fact"—after one has accepted the authority of the Torah.[14]

But in another respect Fox is wrong: revelation is not a "fact" but a process of rational understanding. As a rule, Maimonides plays down the miraculous quality of revelation and stresses the degree to which it involves superior understanding on behalf of the prophet (*Guide* 2.32–36). So Israel's acceptance of the commandments should not be understood as a leap of faith: it is a decision whose rationality can be defended at considerable length. Obviously it is better to follow a commandment in ignorance than not to follow it at all; yet this should not prevent us from seeing that obedience is not enough. For Maimonides, obedience is a means to a greater end: the love of God which, he insists, is equivalent to the knowledge of Him (*Guide* 3.52). In Platonic terms, Israel's acceptance of the commandments is based on a theory of the soul and the good life. Without entering the debate on whether Maimonides preferred the active life to the contemplative one, we can say that the commandments are designed to do more than provide for the bare necessities of human existence. Their purpose is to foster rationality, which, in Maimonides' opinion, means the acceptance of a full theological worldview.[15] So like Plato, Maimonides has a conception of the "true" or rational self, the self which seeks truth about God and the universe He created.

It follows that the process of supplying reasons is not an exercise undertaken after the fact, but part of the "fact" itself, part of the process of coming to love and thus to know God. Accordingly, Maimonides argues that it is not enough to accept religious doctrines on traditional authority (*Guide* 3.51). Those who enter the inner court of God are those who accept these doctrines on the basis of demonstration. Maimonides is not opposing talmudic learning and science.[16] Rather, he is claiming that philosophy and science complete the study of the Talmud so that human perfection requires both. According to Isadore Twersky: "[I]ntellectual achievement *raises* the level and motive of conduct."[17] Without reasons for the commandments, we can get a tolerable level of human existence, but by no means the ultimate level. It is clear that, like Plato, Maimonides does not accept a Kantian notion of autonomy. He does not conceive of human beings as self-legislating agents; on the contrary, he conceives of them as fallible agents placed in a universe too vast to understand. The commandments are a way of achieving as much rationality as possible. There is, however, nothing in Maimonides to suggest we have a faculty capable of knowing ethical truth *a priori*, nothing that implies we can achieve perfection by contemplating the implications of our own moral reason.

C. Kant

That brings us to Kant, who, to my understanding, was also fighting a two-front war. He begins by pointing out that a free action cannot be produced by natural forces or be part of a causal chain. What produces it? Kant replies that reason in its practical capacity can initiate causal sequences (*First Critique* A553=B581). In other words, reason, though independent of empirical conditions, can instigate changes in the empirical world. We would say that, in this capacity, reason is spontaneous. Unless it were so, we would have no grounds for imputing responsibility to agents. Their actions would be no different from the swinging of a pendulum or the ticking of a clock. The latter activities follow physical laws. What makes agents responsible is that they can determine their actions according to the *idea* of a law. In short, they can represent a moral rule to themselves and act on its behalf.

How do we make sense of a spontaneous cause? Kant insists that this idea has no empirical employment. Since all natural causes are determined by prior conditions, there is no natural explanation for how reason brings about action. The only 'proof' that can be given is moral: if everything were determined by natural causes, it would be meaningless to say that something *ought* to be done (A547=B575).

So even the most rudimentary moral theory requires us to think of human beings as the source of their own behavior.

If this is all Kant had said, his theory would not have created such a furor. He rejected determinism, but so did any number of his predecessors. He connected freedom with self-determination, but, again, this view was hardly revolutionary. The furor came in the *Groundwork*, when he tried to be more explicit about the moral conditions of free action. Granted that a free action must be independent of natural causes, the question raised in the *Groundwork* is this: Is independence enough?[18] Is it enough to say that the action is spontaneous, or must the agent act on the basis of a law that meets certain conditions? And if there is such a law, what is its origin? The crucial passage (431) is where Kant says that we can think of the will of every rational being as making universal law. Notice the qualification: *universal* law. Kant is not talking about a situation in which every agent decides what he or she wants to do, but one in which every agent recognizes the necessity of treating every other agent as an end in him- or herself. He goes on to say that the will is not only subject to this obligation, but subject in such a way that it can *regard itself as author*.[19] This principle enables Kant to say that freedom is not lawlessness (*Groundwork* 446). He opposes determinism by arguing that free acts are brought about by a part of us that is not bound up with natural causes. He opposes arbitrariness by arguing that this part of us is still governed by law; but the law it is governed by is self-imposed. Instead of coming from an external source, and requiring a system of rewards and punishments to insure obedience, it expresses the dictates of our own rationality.

We can understand Kant's position more clearly by looking at God. As a perfect agent, God cannot do otherwise than will the moral law. Kant insists, however, that this does not mean that God lacks freedom. On the contrary, it shows that God is completely free because He wills without interference from sensuous causes. Thus Kant rejects the suggestion that ability to do otherwise (will or not will) is an adequate definition of freedom. God is free because no passions or inclinations interfere with His moral reason. In one place, Kant claims God is free because He can will *a priori*.[20] In this sense, God is both the legislator and executor of morality. He is autonomous precisely because nothing gets in the way of His "true self."

Yet Kant's analysis does not end with God. If God cannot help but act autonomously, we can motivate ourselves to do so by acting on principle. If we succeed, we, too, become both legislator and executor: We both make the law and will that it be carried out. The question is whether the self-reflexive character of autonomous behavior obviates the need for a revealing God. Many have thought so. But in the terms in which this criticism is usually put, it is wide of the mark. To say that reason must be able to regard itself as the author of the law is not to say it is the author of the law in fact.[21] The Fifth Amendment to the Constitution says that a person cannot be forced to testify against him- or herself. Although I am not the author of this law, I have no trouble *regarding* myself as such. This means that I readily accept the Fifth Amendment as part of my obligation to respect the dignity of other rational agents. To use a familiar Kantian formula: I can look upon myself *as if* I were the author of the law; I can *appropriate* the law as my own even though it was written two hundred years ago. So there is no reason why Kant has to give up the idea of a revealing God. Remember that he is not claiming to be the inventor of morality. All he has to say is that *in principle* I can understand and therefore appropriate the obligations contained in the commandments.

Why the qualification "in principle"? The answer is that a person cannot relieve himself of a moral obligation by claiming he has difficulty appropriating it. Suppose a person should say that the prohibition against suicide is invalid because it makes no sense. It is my life. Why should I not be able to do with it as I please? Therefore, I cannot appropriate the law that prohibits it; I cannot regard myself as its author. Therefore, I am not bound by it.

Kant's reply would be that I am bound by the law whether I like it or not. Suicide involves the sacrifice of a human life, my own. If the moral law requires me to treat every human life as an end in itself, the fact that this life is mine is morally irrelevant. I am still obliged to treat it as an end in itself. In short, the person who refuses to accept the prohibition against suicide is analogous to the fourteen-year-old girl who wants to have sexual relations. No matter how much the person may think suicide is legitimate, he cannot look upon himself as the author of a law permitting it, and therefore cannot give consent. To the degree that the will is rational, or can be looked upon as rational in principle, suicide is always against one's will.

Why, then, do some think Kant has done away with a revealing God? The answer is that, for Kant, the historical origin of the law is not nearly as important as its moral validity. Imagine that I open a book and come across a geometrical theorem: Once I show that the theorem is true, the issue of its origin has no mathematical significance. By the same token, once I see that human life is an end in itself, it matters little whether I found this proposition in a sacred book, a secular book, or a comic book. The validity of the law is as necessary in the realm of morality as the Pythagorean theorem is in geometry. It is no surprise, therefore, that some think Kant has left God out of the picture. The fact of relevation, that God gave the Torah to Moses on Sinai, pales into insiginificance compared with the moral certitude of what was revealed.

Much of the existentialists' insistence on *commanding presence* is an attempt to remedy this problem. The existentialists want a situation in which a commandment is obeyed because it was revealed; Kant wants a situation in which it is obeyed because it is morally necessary. We can therefore understand Kierkegaard's objection that, if Kant is right, God becomes a vanishing point.[22] According to Kant, there is no such thing as *commanding presence* apart from reason's awareness that it is subject to a necessary law it makes for itself and for every other rational agent. Even if a voice spoke to us from heaven, we would not be justified in obeying it until we had assured ourselves of the moral perfection of its message. And the only way we can assure ourselves of the perfection of its message is to consult the demands reason places on itself. In Kant's universe, revelation has not disappeared, it has become abstract. Rather than a historical relation between God and Moses, it becomes an ideal relation between God and humanity. At bottom, it is the awakening of human moral consciousness.[23] If Kant is right, autonomy raises the level and motive of human behavior to the highest degree. For if the commandments are not derived from an external source, if they reflect the obligations *I myself* would impose on all humanity, there is no need to provide incentives for obeying them. They are in a literal sense what I myself regard as necessary.

3. Why Believe in Autonomy?

Having discussed autonomy, let us turn to its opposite, heteronomy. It should be clear that one can accept heteronomy and still maintain there are reasons for everything God commands. Such a person would point out that reasons have nothing to do with the binding force of what is commanded. By the same token, one can accept autonomy and maintain there are situations in which a person is obliged to do something he or she does not want to do. The issue raised by autonomy is whether *in principle* the obligatory force of the commandments are in accord with our deepest understanding of rationality. The objection to heteronomy comes in two parts.

The first part concerns the epistemological status of revelation. Can we accept the claim that a body of law is of divine origin without reflecting on the reasons for obeying it? Can we assure ourselves that it is God's voice we are hearing rather than a substitute, without asking ourselves what a perfect being is like? We can accept a body of law on the authority of tradition, but surely Maimonides is right in saying that this kind of acceptance is less than ideal. He argues (*Guide* 2.40) that in confronting a body of law, we must ask whether the opinions it instills are true and whether the behavior it enjoins is conducive to human perfection. In other words, acceptance is not a simple procedure. Unless we take care to insure that the law is in accord with our idea of perfection, we run the risk of taking something less than perfect and making it an object of ultimate concern.

The usual reply is that human reason is fallible. How can we be sure that our idea of perfection is valid? The answer is that we cannot be completely sure until we arrive at a fully developed, completely articulated moral theory. Until then, we have no choice but to admit that our idea of perfection is subject to revision. But if reason is fallible, so is "faith." If there are risks in trying to formulate an adequate understanding of perfection, there are greater risks in thinking we can get along without one. Clearly we cannot assure ourselves that we are listening to God by citing lightning, thunder or voices in the air. Nor can we follow Judah Halevi by citing the "evidence" of 600,000 witnesses. If Kant is right, we have no choice but to consider the content of what is revealed. Does it ask us to turn away from evil and devote ourselves to goodness? If so, we must have some idea what goodness and evil are, some way of determining that the message we hear is not an arbitrary injunction, but a commandment worthy of a divine being.[24]

The second part of the objection concerns the fact that heteronomy is *in*compatible with our idea of a perfect or holy will. People often believe that by following God blindly we are paying homage to His authority, surrendering our will to accommodate His. But if Kant is right, such people have things backwards. The problem with heteronomy is not that it puts God on too high a plane, but that it puts Him on too low a plane. It depicts God as an agent who seeks the degradation of another agent. Instead of trying to educate His worshippers by asking them to reflect on the reasons for their behavior, the heteronomous conception depicts Him as a leader who wants obedience above all else; in effect, it depicts Him as a tyrant. We can think of heteronomy along the lines of Hegel's master/slave dialectic. At first it seems the master has the upper hand. But once we realize that the master does not recognize the dignity of the slave, and thus cannot have his or her own dignity recognized by another agent, we see that it is really the slave who comes out on top. If God were to command in a heteronomous fashion, then, from a moral perspective, we, the victims of heteronomy, would be superior to the perpetrator. This is analogous to Maimonides' claim that those who think that God commands without a reason make humans seem more perfect than their creator (*Guide* 3.31). The only description worthy of God is to say that He commands with full knowledge of and respect for the dignity of His worshippers. This does not mean everyone must agree with the commandments or that obeying them is easy. Perhaps no one will understand all the reasons until the end of days; but at least we can say that understanding is the goal to which they point.

Another way to see this point is to recognize that in Judaism revelation is not a simple matter of issuing orders; it is a pact or covenant. This does not mean that God and humans are copartners in devising the terms. It means, rather, that revelation carries with it the all-important notion of *consent*. Whether we view God as asking for consent or holding a mountain over the Jewish people to insure that He gets it, the point is still that revelation and therefore covenant involves mutual respect. As Hartman put it, the covenantal relationship "should never ask the relational partner to give up that which is essential to his or her sense of dignity and worth."[25] If Kant has taught us anything at all, it is that dignity and worth are impossible without rational reflection and obedience to law.

On the other hand, we have seen there is a difference between a medieval rationalist like Maimonides and an Enlightenment rationalist like Kant. For Maimonides, there is only one legislator: God. For Kant, *every* rational agent is a legislator in the sense that he, she, or it is a potential member of the kingdom of ends; every rational will is a law unto itself. In the last analysis, what the opponents of autonomy object to is the possibility that God and humans might confront each other as equals. In his attempt to preserve human dignity, it is as if Kant has deified human beings. In other words, the problem is not that he opens the floodgates to anarchy, but that he conceives of morality along monadological lines: as a system of rules imposed by individual agents on themselves.[26] To understand my obligations toward God or other people, I must first reflect on *my own* idea of morality. By affirming rationality in myself, I affirm it everywhere else in the universe. In biblical terms (Deuteronomy 30:14), morality is not in heaven but inscribed in our hearts. We are, as some have put it, an inner citadel. But if this is so, what happens to the idea that morality involves reaching *out*, if not to God, then at least to other people?

The answer is that turning within is not a psychological process. The self that looks within is the self stripped of all aspects of particularity, the thing in me that apprehends universal truths. If the Kantian metaphysic of reason and nature is objectionable, one can reach the same insight by thinking of the self as an anonymous contractor behind the veil of ignorance. This is another way of saying that the self that legislates morality is not me personally, not the fallible creature writing this paper, but me ideally, the creature who sees every rational agent as a being of infinite and inestimable worth, a being made in the image of the Creator. The doctrine of autonomy assumes that if I *could* look at the world from this perspective, seeing an image of the divine in every person, I would be looking at the world as God sees it. In short, the doctrine of autonomy assumes that the difference between God's respect for humanity and mine is the result of my finitude; it arises from the fact that my vision of humanity is limited and colored by hatreds, attractions and jealousies. So God and humans do not confront each other as equals; the assumption is that God's respect for humanity is consistant with mine to the degree that I have a clear idea of humanity in myself. Does this mean God cannot shroud Himself in mystery? In one respect, no. Kant would be the first to admit that we have no knowledge of the origin of the universe, of the way that God works within it, and of its future direction; what is more, we have no hope of obtaining any. But God cannot shroud Himself in mystery if that means acting in an arbitrary or humiliating fashion. If He did, He would cease to be an object of worship and become instead an object of pity.

Why should I obey God? Again the Kantian answer is that obedience to God is, at the same time, obedience to my true self. To the degree that I can regard myself as the author of the commandments, there is no need to provide an incentive for obeying. The need for an incentive arises only if I cannot regard myself as the author, if the commandments are and will always remain a mystery. Perhaps there are aspects of religious experience Kant has misunderstood; certainly there are aspects of Judaism he did not understand. But there is one point on which he is certainly right: The moment one asks for an incentive to obey the commandments, the moment one needs to weigh rewards against punishments, one cheapens religion and puts oneself at a considerable distance from the inner court of God.

Notes

1. For a review of the recent literature on autonomy as well as a discussion of the various senses of the form, see Christman 1988.

2. The classical discussion of this problem is Frankfurt 1971.

3. Borowitz 1984.

4. For further discussion of this issue, see Allison 1990, pp. 94–99.

5. *Critique of Practical Reason*, p. 8.

6. For further discussion, see Rawls 1971, pp. 516–18.

7. Socrates' distinction between wish and what a person thinks best does not necessarily follow ordinary usage. Note what Polus says at 467b: "What you say is shocking and outrageous." For further discussion see Seeskin 1987, pp. 136–39, 151–52. For other references to this distinction in classical Greek sources, see Aristotle, *Nicomachean Ethics*, 1113a15ff. and the *Definitions* of the later Academy, 413c.

8. Cornford 1927, p. 306.

9. One answer is to say that two conceptions of freedom are at work in these passages: one value-neutral, one not. For further discussion, see Dodds 1959, p. 236.

10. Dodds, ibid.

11. Berlin 1969, p. 133.

12. Cf. Fox 1990, pp. 270–84.

13. Pines 1963, pp. cxxviii–cxxiv. Cf. Harvey 1981. Harvey thinks Maimonides is actually committed to an Aristotelian position, but that this position need not imply determinism.

14. Fox 1990, p. 138. For criticism of Fox, see Hartman 1976, p. 260 and Novak 1983, pp. 275–304.

15. See Novak 1983, p. 279.

16. On this point, see Kellner 1990, pp. 86–89. Cf. Frank 1985.

17. Twersky 1980, p. 511. Cf Hartman 1976, p. 205 as well as Frank 1985, pp. 494–95.

18. Unfortunately, Kant's theory is not as clear as we might like. According to the received interpretation, he speaks as if there are two aspects to the will: one that imposes the moral law (*Wille*), one that accepts it (*Willkür*). The problem of how the two are related, or if they are two at all, is still being debated. The problem of their division is analogous to the medieval problem of how intellect and will are one in God. For further discussion, see Beck 1960, pp. 196–202. For a more recent discussion, see Allison 1990, pp. 129–36.

19. Cf. Rousseau, *The Social Contract*, p. 27: "Obedience to a law which one has described to himself is freedom."

20. Kant, *Lectures on Philosophical Theology*, p. 104.

21. One critic of Kant who sees this point is Fackenheim 1973, pp. 41–42.

22. Kierkegaard, *Fear and Trembling*, p. 68.

23. Cohen, *Religion of Reason*, p. 79.

24. Kant, *Groundwork*, p. 76.

25. Hartman 1987, p. 122.

26. For further discussion of this criticism, see Schrader 1963, pp. 65–77.

References

Allison, H. 1990. *Kant's Theory of Freedom*. Cambridge: Cambridge University Press.

Beck, L.W. 1960. *A Commentary on Kant's Critique of Practical Reason*. Chicago: University of Chicago Press.

Berlin, I. 1969. "Two Concepts of Liberty." In *Four Essays on Liberty*. Oxford: Oxford University Press, pp. 118–72.

Borowitz, E. 1984. "The Autonomus Jewish Self." *Modern Judaism* 4: 39–55.

Christman, J. 1988. "Constructing the Inner Citadel: Recent Work on the Concept of Autonomy." *Ethics* 99: 109–24.

Cohen, H. 1919. *Religion of Reason out of the Sources of Judaism*. Translated by S. Kaplan. New York: Frederick Ungar.

Cornford, F.M. 1927. *Cambridge Ancient History*, Vol. 6. Cambridge: Cambridge University Press.

Dodds, E.R. 1959. *Plato: Gorgias.* Oxford: Oxford University Press.

Fackenheim, E. 1973. "Abraham and the Kantians." In *Encounters Between Judaism and Modern Philosophy.* New York: Schocken Books, pp. 31–77.

Fox, M. 1990. *Interpreting Maimonides.* Chicago: University of Chicago Press.

Frank, D.H. 1985. "The End of the *Guide*: Maimonides on the Best Life for Man." *Judaism* 34: 485–495.

Frankfurt, H. 1971. "Freedom of the Will and The Concept of a Person." *Journal of Philosophy* 58: 5–20.

Hartman, D. 1976. *Maimonides: Torah and Philosophic Quest.* Philadelphia: Jewish Publication Society.

Hartman, D. 1987. "Human Autonomy and Divine Providence." *Tikkun* 2, no. 1: 121–124.

Harvey, W.Z. 1981. "A Third Approach to Maimonides' Cosmogony-Prophetology Puzzle." *Harvard Theological Review* 74: 287–301.

Kant, I. *Foundations of the Metaphysics of Morals.* Translated by L.W. Beck. New York: Liberal Arts Press [=*Groundwork to the Metaphysics of Morals*].

Kant, I. *Critique of Practical Reason.* Translated by L.W. Beck. New York: Liberal Arts Press.

Kant, I. *Lectures on Philosophical Theology.* Translated by A.W. Wood and G.M. Clark. Ithaca: Cornell University Press.

Kellner, M. 1990. *Maimonides on Human Perfection.* Atlanta: Scholars Press.

Kierkegaard, S. *Fear and Trembling.* Translated by H.V. Hong and E.H. Hong. Princeton: Princeton University Press.

Novak, D. 1983. *The Image of the Non-Jew in Judaism.* New York and Toronto: Edwin Mellen Press.

Pines, S. 1963. "The Philosophic Sources of *The Guide of the Perplexed*." In *The Guide of the Perplexed.* Translated by S. Pines. Chicago: University of Chicago Press.

Rawls, J. 1971. *A Theory of Justice.* Cambridge: Harvard University Press.

Rousseau, J.-J. *The Social Contract.* Translated by W. Kendall. Chicago: Regnery Co.

Schrader, G. 1963. "Autonomy, Heteronomy, and Moral Imperatives." *Journal of Philosophy* 60: 65–77.

Seeskin, K. 1987. *Dialogue and Discovery.* Albany: SUNY Press.

Twersky I. 1980. *Introduction to the Code of Maimonides (Mishneh Torah).* New Haven: Yale University Press.

Tradition, Heritage, and Autonomy in Modern Jewish Thought

Ze'ev Levy

1. Tradition and Reality

Nobody begins everything anew; each generation relies on what has been accumulated, in theory as well as in practice, by former generations. This is what lies at the bottom of the concept of 'culture' or 'civilization'.[1] Cultural acquisitions are preserved by 'tradition' which forwards them from one generation to the next. Through it, cultural treasures of the past are kept alive and maintain their relevance for the present. Hegel's famous concept of "objective spirit" also referred to tradition as a reality which is more or less independent of man's will and decisions. It is a kind of independent element which obeys its own rules and imposes at the same time certain claims and constraints. If, for example, a religious Jew fasts on Yom Kippur, this is not his personal or spontaneous decision to do so; he fasts because religious tradition commanded him to do so. He is, of course, free to decide whether to fast or not, whether to keep this traditional religious commandment or not, but fasting on Yom Kippur is fixed in tradition; it is tradition which prescribes his behavior in this regard. Through it, man subscribes, in his thoughts, feelings and practices, to what has been transmitted to him. He is not engaged in any creative or autonomous activity. The individual thus turns into a member or link of an all-encompassing objective spiritual framework. The more his society is conservative and traditionalist, the more it endeavors to conserve established customs and mores as faithfully and strictly as possible, and to prevent any deviation from them. Digressions then occur in spite of peoples' intent and mostly without their being aware of them. Mindful nonconformity, however, requires initiative and spontaneity. In order not to be subjected unquestioningly to the age-old and the sacrosanct, in order to open up new vistas of creative and reinvigorating activity, one needs audaciousness of thought. Kant, addressing his contemporaries on the subject of enlightenment, called out: *Sapere audi!* ("Dare to be wise!").[2] As against that, one common counterargument proclaims: What power has individual originality in comparison with a rich tradition which has crystallized in the course of many ages? What power has one man, or even one single generation, as against a tradition of thousands of years? This argument can be interpreted in a twofold way:

1. Tradition reflects the storing up of spiritual and cultural values which do not represent mediocre or average achievements; it preserves the contributions of intellectual geniuses, of mental giants. It transmits to us spiritual treasures which we could not have acquired by ourselves. We enjoy what our forefathers provided for us; we sit down to a "prepared table." This was what Joseph Karo, the famous kabbalist and halakhist of the sixteenth century, had in mind when he composed his *Shulchan Arukh.*

2. Since we cannot acquire by ourselves everything that has been accumulated in the past, objectivity prevails over subjectivity: personal initiative disappears. In Hegel's terms, "objective spirit" overshadows "subjective spirit."

This may entail negative as well as positive results. On the one hand, man turns into a slave of antiquated institutions and customs whose meanings and significations he very often no longer understands. On the other hand, tradition, as one of the manifestations of "objective spirit," points to "man's preeminence over the beast." An animal adjusts to nature by instinctive inclinations, while man relies on gathering experience and knowledge. Cultural traditions replace the biologically hereditary instinct by which animals adapt to their environment. As a cultural being, man is necessarily a traditional being.[3] At first sight it looks as if the principle of autonomous creativity and self-perfection of man clashes with the fact that every individual is born into a given cultural tradition which has already done part of the work for him. But this need not be a detrimental loss at all; on the contrary, it can and ought to be a gain. It frees man from the necessity to repeat what has already been achieved by his ancestors, and so affords him more time to create something new. Heritage is not the same as heredity. (In Hebrew there also are two closely related but different words to express this distinction—*torasha* and *morasha*.) But, the linguistic proximity, and sometimes analogy, in most European languages, and in Hebrew as well, is prone to engender confusion. It might strengthen, inadvertently, those tendencies that seek to stress the obligatory and absolute authority of tradition. But once again, tradition, *ex definitio*, when ridden of some of the religious connotations of the term which still prevail, means to conserve and transmit the cultural, and in particular spiritual, achievements of man from the past to the present and to the future. From this point of view, the aforementioned distinction between hereditary instinct and cultural heritage entails another significant consequence. Since one's relation to tradition is not instinctive but acquired, conservation of tradition implies *education*. It is therefore no surprise that divergent modes of education towards the values of tradition have become a most controversial issue in Israel; they are liable to provoke a 'cultural war.' Religious, and in particular orthodox and fundamentalist groups aim at inculcating those values which they believe not only to be most important but absolutely compulsory, while nonorthodox and secular Jews wish to preserve those values of the Jewish heritage which they consider to be meaningful in modern times and of lasting significance. This is a portentous quandary, involving also the issue of tolerance versus nontolerance. The orthodox protagonists of tradition believe their values to be sanctified by divine origin; they consider themselves to represent its only genuine spokesmen, and therefore to act as the legitimate interpreters of Jewish tradition. In passing, one ought to note that this demonstrates that traditions grow in a social framework. If man were a solitary being, relying only on instincts and improvisations, would he be able to cope with all the challenges and assignments which he faces in the course of his life? It seems unlikely. Tradition puts at his disposition, in multiple domains, necessary foundations for life and existence which it is then up to him to adapt to ever new situations. From this point of view tradition is some kind of requisite for elaborating and continuing the original culture of a given society. So one of the tasks of tradition is to facilitate man's coming to grips with his surroundings, and not just to impose on him additional bonds. Unfortunately, this constructive aspect escapes attention and is almost completely ignored. The "traditionalists" also disregard another important aspect, namely that tradition (or traditions) provide(s) only partial answers. The historical reality in which man lives differs from the historical reality in which the tradition(s) grew. A modern look at tradition must therefore include also some *critical* dimension; contemporary man should adjust it to new situations as well as to his personal capacities and inclinations. This was Franz Rosenzweig's approach to tradition when he recommended that every individual should observe traditional religious norms of Judaism in line with his personal capability. Tradition should never delete human autonomy and individuality or come in their stead. Michael Landmann also stresses these points:

> Life again and again poses unforeseen situations for which no predesignated traditional answer exists. We can thus rely on tradition to alleviate our burden of decision only to a limited extent; otherwise we must establish what must be done on our own—carried by tradition and within its framework. As we need not constantly be creative, so we cannot live exclusively on our traditional heritage.[4]

Here, hermeneutics comes to our help. To accept a tradition, whatever it be, means to interpret, judge and select values by contemporary standards. Martin Buber considered this to be the paramount task in relating to tradition. The crucial question, of course, will be how to decide on the criteria for justifying such a selection. After all, the fact that something is handed down to us does not entail that it should be accepted unquestioningly.

By analogy to Spinoza who characterized Substance (God) as *natura naturans* and *natura naturata* at one and the same time,[5] one could designate man as creator of tradition and created by it: Tradition is engraved on him, but he also engraves new patterns on it, in conformity to changing times. Contrary to some views, when the accumulating cultural treasure, our spiritual-cultural heritage, grows richer, man's creative power increases too. Though man's intellectual capacities in antiquity were not inferior to those of modern man,[6] his intellectual vision certainly was more limited then. But when man knows less, he is usually more reluctant to engage in initiatives of his own; he is then more inclined to accept what the elders and ancients bequeath to him. Relationship to tradition is therefore influenced by some almost instinctive feeling that everything old and venerable must be endowed with authority. One encounters this frequently in the Bible and the Talmud, sometimes with the explicit intention to convince the present-day congregation that it is intellectually and spiritually inferior to the first generations: "If the earlier [scholars] were sons of angels, we are sons of men; and if the earlier were sons of men, we are like asses."[7] We are therefore enjoined to accept the authority of the ancient and earlier sages. The Bible itself already referred to "the elders of the congregation" (Leviticus 4:15). In talmudic times the elders were regarded as the truly wise: "The elders of the Court delivered him to the elders of the priesthood."[8] One could supply many more examples; in the Talmud we find: "There is no old man but that he is wise."[9] In societies where such views prevailed, every violation of tradition was considered to be sacrilegious and blasphemous. This is what some critics of traditionality have labeled "the dead hand of the past." Schematically it is possible to discern between traditional societies that lay emphasis upon the past, modern societies that lay emphasis on the present, and antitraditional societies (usually in times of revolutions, but this also holds for the beginnings of the Chalutzic settlement in Eretz Israel) which look towards the future. According to the religious tradition of Judaism, "Moses received the Law from Sinai and committed it to Joshua, and Joshua to the Elders, and the Elders to the Prophets, and the Prophets committed it to the men of the Great synagogue."[10] All those who received and transmitted the Torah introduced some changes, but these amendments were intended to assure its eternal and changeless essence because Moses received the Torah from God in a whole and perfect form.

2. Tradition and Philosophical Hermeneutics

This inquiry into the function of tradition is mainly concerned with the relation of modern man to religious tradition, to the authority of ancient religious sources, and of (sacred) texts. The paper will not deal with religious ways of life in Judaism, although the latter are evidently derived from those texts. Likewise the paper will not dwell on the important linkage between tradition and the belief in revelation, always a prime subject in Jewish and Christian thought, in the middle ages as well as in modern times. Religion considers revelation to represent the main origin of tradition and to endow it with its compelling, authoritative character. This point was overlooked by those who claimed that humanism and enlightenment simply exchanged one kind of tradition by another; their spokesmen replaced the authority of the religious tradition by the authority of Greek tradition. (Although this was mainly characteristic of Christian thought, Yehuda Abarbanel's [Leone Ebreo's] *Dialoghi d'Amore* can also be cited in this connection.) The fundamental change consisted in the founding of authority in man. Authority no longer eluded judgment by intellect and reason. Of course, human authority is not the same as divine authority. Religious tradition is based on the authority of a divine revelation which occurred in the distant past and was then recorded in sacred texts. Therefore, it is presented dogmatically, commanding unquestioning acceptance; that, in itself, was considered to be a characteristic feature of tradition. But this is no longer the case with the rise of the 'humanist tradition.'

One cardinal problem has already been hinted at above: When the cultural level of man rises, his fear of the novel and the unprecedented diminishes. His self-confidence grows. One might say that tradition gives us back, at least *in potentia*, what it has taken away. It puts at our disposal cultural treasures and spares us the effort of having to recreate them. At the same time, it not only gives us a free hand for new creative work, but it also provides many of the prerequisites which enable us to build additional layers, in order to reinvigorate the whole (cultural) edifice and 'improve' it. What matters most is that the new edifice which we exert ourselves to construct will rest on a solid base. These are no mere metaphors; they are the crux of the issue. By being capable of 'improvement,' cultural and spiritual traditions empower their beneficiaries to *amend* them. Those parts of the cultural legacy which have become obsolete can be replaced by more relevant and significant ones through fresh creative activity. Tradition is not one and the same for the whole of mankind; its contents and forms differ from one people to another, from one age to another. No tradition can pretend to absoluteness.

There remains, however, an antimony of grave ethical implications. Man, whose very essence is embodied in his faculty of free choice and decision, needs tradition which, for its part, predetermines many of his decisions. Tradition, thus, is one aspect of the philosophical antinomy of freedom and determinism. However, this antinomy does not restrict man's freedom. Tradition indeed predetermined certain patterns of man's behavior and decisions, and therefore puts certain constraints on him; religious tradition wants beliefs to be believed because they have been believed before, to observe forms of behavior and worship because they have been observed previously, etc. Nevertheless, this ought not to prevent man from making new or even contrary decisions, instead of the traditional ones. To be sure, tradition makes it more difficult for him to change former behavior patterns and to make new decisions; indeed, this is one of its declared aims. It is important, however, to stress that the coercive element of tradition—what Durkheim called "contrainte sociale"—decreases with the ascent of culture and spiritual life. The individual gradually feels himself less restricted by tradition, and more at liberty to develop his creative capabilities. Philosophy, the free and conscious exercise of man's reason, is from this point of view antagonistic to all that tradition stands for. The battle between tradition, in its rigid and coercive form, and philosophy is still being waged, although the gulf between them certainly can and ought to be bridged. But we should not go too far. A philosopher is never completely dissociated from earlier normative consensuses and traditions, though he may contest them. Philosophy depends, at least to a degree, on certain thought traditions, even if it rebels against them or alters them, while tradition, contrarily, is not dependent on philosophy, but requires obedience. Only when philosophy becomes a challenge to tradition, because the latter cannot be reconciled with the dictates of reason, does tradition attempt to defend itself by philosophical arguments too. Philosophers then take upon themselves the assignment to serve as "guides of the perplexed," in order to rescue (intelligent) believers from their confusion; that was Maimonides' well-known aim stated in his preface to the *Guide.* As Katz has well noted the crisis itself between philosophy and tradition is inevitable.[11]

   In opposition to philosophy, there emerged in France, in the beginning of the nineteenth century, various ideologies whose common denominator was 'traditionalism.' They aimed at conserving traditional social, political and, in particular, religious beliefs and modes of life. Although unjustifiable by reason, the latter were taken to represent an adequate expression of social reality, and especially of a society whose religious beliefs were taken to be anchored in revelation. These beliefs, transmitted from one generation to another, ought to be, it was said, accepted unquestioningly. According to 'traditionalism,' no truth can be known save through traditional beliefs. Traditionalism thus runs counter to rationalism on the philosophical level and to revolutionary or reformative tendencies on the social-political plane. It also cannot be squared with the agnosticism of Kant's transcendental philosophy, notwithstanding Kant's own famous dictum (in the second preface to the *Critique of Pure Reason*) that he had to replace knowledge by belief. Kant's notion of "belief" was an epistemological category and had no religious connotation. It was no accident that the term 'traditionalism' began to spread during the French Revolution and its aftermath. Traditionalism turned into a philosophy of history and political program of the enemies of the revolution.

It was conservative in politics, anti-individualistic in epistemology and ethics, and fundamentalist in religion. Its spokesmen railed against *les philosophes* and accused them of having prepared the soil for the revolution They especially denounced Voltaire and Rousseau, the alleged destroyers of tradition and corrupters of youth. Of course, not all of the French traditionalists were of the same brand. Joseph de Maistre and Louis de Bonald endeavored to bridge traditionalism and rationalism; they denounced the individualism which seemed to them the principal danger to the authority of the Church; on the other hand, F.R. de Lamennais urged the view that the Pope represents the highest authority, and from him emanates truth to all mankind. One encounters, more or less, the same conflict between philosophy and tradition in modern Jewish thought too, as we shall see. Our main question will therefore be: How does a (religiously) liberal or secular Jew comprehend his relationship to the spiritual sources of his past?

3. Tradition and Alienation

A religious man, an orthodox Jew, assumes the sources of his beliefs to be sanctified and obligatory. Therefore, they entail fixed forms of religious behavior and a life-style that safeguards their binding nature. One might discern a certain difference between Judaism and Christianity on this matter. Tradition is usually held to guarantee certain religious principles, transmitted to the believer from Holy Scripture by presumably competent interpreters. Christianity says so expressly, according to Leo Baeck:

> The tradition which the church guarantees and through which the church itself is guaranteed is therefore the tradition of dogmas, tradition of the right belief. Only what is dogma or can become dogma is true tradition.[12]

In Judaism, on the other hand, there has been, from medieval Jewish philosophy to Mendelssohn and to the present, controversy as regards articles of faith (dogmas). According to the regnant Jewish view, tradition guarantees a proper religious life-style. No more was considered necessary. Until the Enlightenment and the subsequent rise of a national conception of Jewishness, "Jewish tradition" and "Rabbinic tradition" were conceived as synonymous. Only with the decline of Rabbinic authority, does one encounter for the first time attempts to elucidate the meaning of tradition for a modern Jew. One of the most fundamental elements of the (Rabbinic) Jewish tradition gradually disappeared, namely the assumption that the Jewish people must stick to distinct traditions of daily behavior which separate them from other peoples. With modernity, however, these particular religious ways of life looked more and more archaic to modern Jews. Therefore, their reservations and criticisms of traditional patterns of life very often involved, inadvertently perhaps, an exaggeratedly pejorative and derisive approach to tradition as such. They did not pay sufficient attention to the important role which tradition had performed in Jewish life throughout the ages.

Some resentful assessment of the value and validity of certain Jewish traditional norms thus became part of the modern critical attitude towards tradition. One might even say that the attitude of the modern secular individual to tradition creates a double *alienation*—one, substantially existential, and another, historical. Both manifest the ambivalence of the modern approach to tradition. When one judges tradition critically, one runs the risk of estrangement from the spiritual treasures, ethical values, etc. which have been handed down by tradition from one generation to another. One is cast adrift. Our reservations as to the orthodox *forms* of tradition which look outworn and sometimes even repugnant (e.g. the status of women according to Halakhah, the definition of "Who is a Jew?", etc.) are liable to lead to an unjustifiable belittlement of all its ideational *contents.* Yet, the latter also comprise many vital elements of much relevance. They assure the linkage to his spiritual, national, and social heritage. On the other hand, when one judges tradition uncritically, the result is often estrangement from decisive, contemporary, existential, and social problems. One then undermines one's own basic autonomy as a human being. This last point is extremely important when dealing with the Jewish tradition, the normative foundations of which differ considerably from the political, cultural, and religious traditions of general, contemporary society.

Nathan Rotenstreich[13] has distinguished between three spheres, relevant to the issue of tradition in Judaism:

1. Tradition—in Hebrew *massoreth* or *massorah*—as a textual discipline whose task is to assure an accurate literal transmission of the Bible. The emphasis is on the *formal* aspect.

2. The whole of the writings and commentaries that make up the "Holy Scriptures" of Judaism. Here the main emphasis is put on *content.* There is, however, no clear-cut separation between these two

spheres. It is hermeneutics that mediates between them. Textual interpretation indeed fulfills a preponderant role in consolidating Jewish
religious tradition. Unlike other religions, Judaism is founded on the
Book, and for the guardians of its tradition it was more or less self-evident that no text, *a fortiori* no ancient sacred text, is accessible to
understanding without interpretation. The question then became
which hermeneutical line to follow—rabbinic, philosophical or mystical.[14]

3. The entirety of the Jewish religious ways of life, as they have
been shaped throughout the ages. This sphere is associated to the two
former ones, because it gets its chief inspiration from the Bible. But in
this case, priority is given to the *historical* aspect. According to Rotenstreich, this third sphere exhibits a unique aspect of Jewish tradition
which has no counterpart in the tradition of other religions. He
describes the reciprocal relationship between these three spheres as
follows: "Tradition in its theoretical sense is the content of consciousness, consolidated by generations, and the causal force that constitutes the reality of the generations. The domain of history converges
into the sphere of meaningfulness."[15] Rotenstreich thus points out a
unique all-embracing and converging dimension of Jewish tradition
which cannot be found elsewhere.

Whereas Rotenstreich wishes to underline the distinctive features of Jewish tradition, its uncritical champions, however, believe it
to incarnate something much more global and exhaustive than the
traditions of other peoples and religions. They conceive of tradition
not merely as the linkage between a contemporary Jew and his spiritual heritage, but as the sole guarantee of Jewish existence throughout
the ages. According to them, a critical stance toward tradition constitutes not only a danger to the religious values of Judaism, but an
attack on its national-historical essence. This outlook aggravates the
emotional tension which accompanies every debate on the quiddity
of tradition inside Israel. It is expressed in statements such as the following by Charles Liebman:

> Jewish tradition has already been defined and interpreted
> by terms of certain Halakhic rules, that is to say norms of the
> Law. The only legitimate participants in the debate are those
> who accept these norms as binding. Those who accept the bind-
> ing nature of the tradition, even if they interpret it in various
> ways, cannot respect the views of those who are not committed
> to it. Somebody who does not keep the dietary laws or the Sha-

bath as prescribed by the Halakhah (the traditional rules of which are not subject to discussion) cannot voice his opinion in the debate as to what Halakhah advises. . . . There exists a greater danger that these people will find in the Halakhah everything they search for. Therefore, for better or worse, only orthodox Jews, they alone, may decide on this matter which is of prime importance to non-orthodox Jews too.[16]

According to Liebman, since modern life is by and large based on nontraditional ways of life, a Jew whose association to religious tradition has diminished must feel himself alienated from tradition. He has not yet exchanged an old tradition for something else but has been thrown into a world which seems to him empty, lacking all the characteristic and familiar features of tradition. Science and technology that dictate the rhythm of modernity are completely estranged from such traditional activities as religious ceremonies, observance of religious holidays, prayer, etc. Prayer, by its very essence, symbolizes affections and expectations that a rational and scientific conception of reality has dismissed. This does not mean that science is inimical to prayer. It is simply indifferent to it. Science is in no need of traditional religious beliefs. The latter are very often an obstacle to scientific progress. (Copernicus, Galileo, and Darwin come to mind). However, the passage from tradition to absence of tradition often engenders uneasy feelings of alienation and discomfiture.

In this connection, another problem deserves to be pointed out. Various Jewish thinkers of the nineteenth century—religious as well as non-religious—emphasized the universality of ethical values in the Bible. One encounters this tendency, among others, in Moritz Lazarus's *Die Ethik des Judentums*[17] and in Hermann Cohen's *Religion of Reason out of the Sources of Judaism*.[18] Such 'universalization' is likely to nurture, and indeed did, the paradoxical supposition that if the 'eternal' traditional values of Judaism have become an integral part of western culture, there is no longer any need to link them to the particular tradition which had been their cradle. The paradox thus revealed is that the universal significance of these values, many of which were formulated for the first time in the ancient sources of Judaism and cherished by *its* religious tradition, can now be dissociated from that tradition.[19] A Jew must thus come to grips with the following dilemma: Either to dissociate himself from the Jewish tradition and to link his whole destiny with the general culture which has absorbed many of the values of that tradition, *or* to estrange himself from general cul-

ture, notwithstanding the many values *it* has drawn from the Jewish
sources, in order to cleave to the Jewish religion with all its particular-
istic, traditional features, fixed by Halakhah. Neither horn of this
dilemma seems acceptable or desirable for a Jew wishing to maintain
his ties to Judaism and his Jewish heritage, and at the same time to
participate in the cultural and social life of modern society.

Moreover, the strong emotional attachment to tradition which
has always been a distinctive feature of many generations of Jews is
nowadays likely to nurture alienation from man's spiritual and creative autonomy. This is not limited only to the practical-ceremonial
aspects of religious worship. Every extreme traditionalist view tends
to encourage the argument that all the great ideas of mankind were
already pronounced in the ancient sources. These sources embody the
highest and most powerful spiritual authority. Every deviation from
tradition is then denounced as heresy. One then becomes entangled in
a net of prejudices that predetermine his modes of behavior and
thought. Spinoza already criticized, in his *Theologico-Political Treatise*,
these undesirable manifestations of religious tradition. A century
later it became an axiom for the Enlighteners that to succumb to any
spiritual authority whatsoever, including that of tradition, meant to
neglect autonomous reason which is man's supreme faculty.[20] This
rationalist view became in its turn subject to severe criticism by the
aforementioned spokesmen of 'traditionalism' (de Maistre, de Bonald,
de Lamennais) in the aftermath of the French Revolution and by
many thinkers of the Romantic movement, especially in its later reactionary trends. They wished to defend one paramount form of
authority, namely tradition. According to them, everything sanctified
by tradition conserves its educational authoritativeness for contemporary man too. From this viewpoint, the world-view of Romanticism
was no less conservative than that of 'traditionalism,' and represented
a clear retrogression from the liberal world-view of the Enlightenment. Romanticism tried to disguise these aspects by presenting tradition as a natural-historical phenomenon of returning to the erstwhile literary and poetical sources of the nation. Most Jewish thinkers
in the nineteenth century were torn between these two diametrically
opposed positions. The Enlightenment position was taken over mainly by the advocates of the Reform movement; the Romantic movement, for its part, inspired, among others, the neo-orthodox thought

of S.R. Hirsch, but traces of it can also be found in the liberal philosophy of religion of Steinheim.

4. Tradition and Historical Retrospection

A philosophical analysis of the notion of tradition makes it clear that the two aforementioned forms of alienation do not exhaust the problem. There exists also a third way which combines deliberate participation in the intellectual life of the *present* with a balanced, unbiased, and sympathetic view of the important task that traditional values, including even those that are no longer viable, have fulfilled in the *past*. As noted, modern man, in his relationship to tradition, is threatened by two forms of alienation: alienation from the sources which tradition incarnates, and alienation, conscious or unconscious, from one's self as an autonomous, thinking, and creative being. Does this mean, as Gadamer suggests, that one encounters tradition mostly in distorted forms?[21] He is certainly right that a reactionary conception of tradition may lead to the most abominable ideological perversions;[22] but he also asserts that tradition embodies elements of freedom and historical consciousness. It is man who makes the final decision as to which aspects of the heritage of the past to preserve for the present. There need not be an inevitable opposition between tradition and reason. Even in times of revolution man does not jettison all the cultural and spiritual achievements of the past.[23] A proper understanding of the *Geisteswissenschaften* entails an appropriate appreciation of the role of tradition. Traditional texts, usages, and customs have applicability to the age of their appearance, creation, and formulation. But we who belong to another age are alienated from this original world. One cannot inhabit an age in which one no longer belongs. The question therefore is whether a hermeneutical effort is capable of 'restoring' the original world that was the birthplace of the tradition. Can hermeneutics keep alive values which stem from a distant age, and if so, then how? "The great productive achievements of scholarship always preserve something of the splendid magic of immediately mirroring the present in the past and the past in the present."[24] Gadamer has introduced into his hermeneutic philosophy an important idea which contributes to a constructive and balanced understanding of the role of tradition—the concept of "fusion of horizons" (*Horizontverschmelzung*).[25] Without entering into all its diverse connotations and implications, I want to show some of those aspects relevant to our inquiry.

Contemporary man can no longer inhabit bygone ages where traditions were born and consolidated. A proper understanding of tradition must take the present as the starting point of its historical retrospective. Yet at the same time one also must take into account the cultural horizons of those who produced and shaped tradition(s) throughout the ages. This will widen and enrich one's own intellectual horizons. But one must never forget that our horizons and those of the past are not the same. There exists, however, an affinity or association between them which makes possible a "fusion" of the two separate horizons. Tradition expresses a relationship between man as he lives and thinks today and man as he lived and thought in the past. The issue, therefore, is not simply the identity or nonidentity, or the likeness or unlikeness of present and past values, but the possibility of transacting some merger of the distinct spiritual, cultural, and intellectual horizons that formed and form the framework of those values.

Hence, one must distinguish between historical memory and tradition. In the first case, a barrier of remoteness in time separates us from the past, a barrier of which we are very well aware. The distinctive feature of tradition, however, consists in the past's 'penetrating' into the present. Tradition fulfills an active factor in present life. Nonetheless, this distinction between historical memory and tradition is not so clear cut in Judaism as this dichotomy might have suggested. Judaism frequently blurs the line between historical memory and tradition. To wit: "Everybody must regard himself as if he departed from Egypt" (at *Pesach*), "in those days at this time" (at *Hanukkah*), eating leavened bread during *Pesach*, building a *sukkah*, lighting candles during the week of *Hanukkah*, etc.—all of these bear witness to the blurring of the dicotomy. Perhaps it would be more correct to say that the more historical memory refers to an earlier or archaic age in Jewish history, the more it is sustained by tradition.

Another concept of Gadamer fits this inquiry well, a concept which usually carries a negative connotation: *Vorurteil*. Gadamer, however, wishes to retrieve the original literal meaning of this word, "pre-judgment" (not "prejudice"). Certain opinions are, according to Gadamer, *legitime Vorurteile*.[26] They took shape in the past, but still influence, inadvertently, our modes of thought (and behavior) in the present. Nobody starts from a *tabula rasa*. Thought patterns that have evolved in the past are transmitted from one generation to the next.

Interestingly, in German as well as in Hebrew the same words are used for "tradition" and "transmittance": *"Überlieferung"* in German, *"massoreth"-"messira"* in Hebrew. Tradition cannot be separated from history. The very activity of transmitting and receiving implies a hiatus between different generations—one that transmits and another that receives. Tradition is one of the mediating limbs that bridge this gulf. It is only at a later stage that we who belong to the receiving generation are entitled, or even impelled, to scrutinize our traditional beliefs critically. We then attempt to ascertain whether our *Vorurteile,* our "pre-judgments," i.e. our initial beliefs, are still meaningful, relevant, and valid. Again, "pre-judgment" reveals ideas, beliefs, and customs of the past which have been handed down by tradition. It enables us now to view in retrospect those texts of the past that formed the foundations of our traditions. The prefix "pre-" in "pre-judgment" reminds us that our judgment was not yet final; it is still liable to undergo critical reexamination.

Traditional outlooks, as reflected by 'sacred' texts, are not limited to the relations between the authors, promoters, and interpreters of those texts and their audience in a certain historical age. Their meaning is also determined, and very much so, by the new historical situation. A rationalist approach to tradition entails an historical awareness and sensitivity that perceives the tension between texts of the past and their meaningfulness for the present. In this regard, another concept of Gadamer is also helpful, namely *wirkungs-geschichtliches Bewusstsein,* "consciousness of the influences (or effects) of history."[27] The tension between past and present is attenuated when we achieve a better comprehension of the two distinct historical horizons whose very distinctiveness tradition tries to overcome. For modern man (and Jew) "fusion of horizons" means an unbiased appreciation of past traditions for present needs. For Jews in particular, that had been the program of the 'liberals' in the nineteenth and twentieth centuries. They proposed to eliminate outdated forms of religious worship, in order to conserve substantial contents. They believed that this would make Judaism acceptable to modern enlightened Jews.

5. Tradition and Interpretation

Notwithstanding all these distinctions and tensions between past and present, contemporary man has no difficulty in understanding the meaning of traditions which were shaped in the past. This understanding derives from the fact that we—as readers, researchers, interpreters, and most importantly, as possessors of certain values—can *apprehend*, intellectually and emotionally, texts and creations of the past. This paper deals with religious traditions but it applies *pari passu* to literary, artistic, social, and political traditions. Clearly, we cannot identify ourselves with everything implied or prescribed by tradition in regard to belief or practice, but we are certainly aware of the bond which links us to our national and spiritual heritage, and to what it stands for. Such openness towards the values of tradition, without adopting every part of it unquestioningly, enables us to reach a genuine understanding of it without giving up our intellectual autonomy. The context of interpreting tradition is determined to a great extent by an interpreter who himself is conditioned by the spiritual horizons of his time. This does not entail that his interpretation is arbitrary or subjective. After all, the contemporary context on which the interpreter of religious traditions depends is itself conditioned by that very tradition of which the Bible was the first and principal base. (In Israel we sense the firm bonds with the distant past of our people in its homeland very strongly.) Everybody is connected intellectually—in philosophy, history, literature—to a certain tradition, whether he himself is aware of the fact or not. Of course, not every tradition is of the same kind. Religious traditions are usually more conservative than artistic or literary traditions. The latter adapt themselves more easily to change and innovation. Moreover, great achievements in art or science are very often the outcome of a radical rupture with tradition.[28] For a liberal or secular Jew, there is this lesson to be drawn: He ought never to imitate intolerance against other views, a distressing feature of most orthodox and fundamentalist groups. He must combine criticism with tolerance.

Tradition, transmitted from one generation to another, borrows much of its authority from the authoritativeness or prestige of (supposed) eyewitnesses in the distant past.[29] But modern man may have doubts as to the validity or the authenticity of such testimonies. This, in turn, gives rise to various attempts to understand the contents of tradition by philological, psychological, and historical interpretation. Modern historical consciousness exacerbates that which romanticist hermeneutics had been extremely sensitive of, namely misunderstanding and misapprehension. Spinoza had already said that only what is not self-evident needs understanding.

It follows from all this that the constructive role of tradition consists in the very act of transmitting, of handing over. It is destined to mediate between past and present, to blend two distinct spiritual horizons which would have remained estranged to each other without its intervention. Tradition in itself is therefore not to be considered as something obsolete or passé, but as something quite relevant. This comes vividly to the fore in the important role which tradition plays in recent hermeneutic thought.

I have already referred several times to Gadamer. It is not incidental that in his reflections on the role of tradition he stresses the *dialogical* quiddity of hermeneutics. His meditations on the relationship between text and interpreter bring to mind Buber's philosophy. "Tradition is no simple *Geschehen* which is known by experience and can be appropriated but it is mainly a *language* (*Sprache*), i.e. it addresses us as a *Du*."[30] This hermeneutical understanding of tradition as an I-Thou relationship endows it with an additional important dimension: One does not relate to the other, in this case to tradition, as to a mere object or means; one also does not disavow that tradition transmits meaning. On the contrary, a dialogical attitude reinforces openness and willingness to listen to it. As Gadamer put it: "*Zueinandergehören* = *Auf-einander-hören-können*." By this word-play Gadamer makes it clear that belonging together ought to imply the capability of listening to each other.[31] Understanding hermeneutics as a dialogical activity is important. In interpreting traditional texts, hermeneutics inaugurates a dialogue and a reciprocal relationship not only with different historical horizons, but with earlier cultural (and religious) traditions as well. However, let us not forget that such "dialogue" is mere metaphor; a tradition or a text can never become a "real" partner in a dialogue; therefore, the dialogue with tradition (especially written tradition) is ultimately no more than a dialogue between the person who reflects on tradition and himself. The important question, however, is not whether the rapport with tradition displays a dialogical or monological relationship, but rather the conclusion that such a (religious) relationship involves openmindedness towards divergent views. Therefore, a dialogical approach can bridge the gap between a modern (secular) Jew and the Jewish tradition of the past, without subtracting either from the individual's autonomy and self-respect or from the inherent values of the tradition.

6. The Predicament of the Modern Jew

Several critics of Gadamer are annoyed by certain conservative implications of his philosophical hermeneutics. They accuse him of wishing to preserve truths by tradition. This was the accusation raised by Habermas under the slogan of "*Ideologiekritik*." While Gadamer is concerned with *interpreting* tradition in order to comprehend its meaning, Habermas criticizes its meaning in order to *change* the tradition. As noted above, every linkage to tradition, even if guided by progressive and liberal motives, inevitably comprises some element of conservatism, or even submissiveness to authority. Tradition endeavors to conserve something from the past for the present, and at the same time it is reluctant to be questioned about it. Although he probably had no such intention, Gadamer's view of tradition resuscitated attempts to rehabilitate some notion of authority and tradition in their religious sense. The Christian theologian B.J. Hilberath attempted to modify Gadamer's philosophical hermeneutics in order to adapt it to this purpose.[32] However, one ought not to confuse the idea of "authority" and "obedience," as Hilberath interpreted them. Gadamer had in mind normative and methodological deliberations, functioning as some kind of authoritative paradigm. His notion of reality was not "absolute" (in the original, literal sense of the word, "absolved," i.e. "free"); it was not without any tie to the fundamental mediating paradigms of the past. Such "thought paradigms" are one form of "tradition" in the modern sense. (One might even discern a certain affinity between Gadamer's conception and Kuhn's concept of a "paradigm" governing "normal science."[33]) According to Gadamer, however, what matters is the *historical* impact of the *changes* that have taken place and still take place in paradigms. It makes sense to speak about conditions and criteria of existing paradigms only in the framework of a historical perspective, i.e. in the framework of the continuity of tradition.[34]

Hilberath reproached Gadamer for not mentioning any explicit traditions, and in particular the Christian religious tradition. A concrete tradition must be corroborated by a concrete paradigm that belongs to a concrete historical situation. For Christianity, this paradigm is God revealing himself through Jesus, while in Judaism it is God's revelatory act of conferring the Torah at Sinai. But given this, one is ensnared in a vicious circle: Religious tradition depends upon a crucial paradigm, but that paradigm can be confirmed only by belief in the tradition. This is no mere "hermeneutic circle," but a *petitio*; it is of no help to one who does not *already* accept the tradition as indisputable truth.

When Gadamer speaks about tradition, his conservatism, deplorable as it may be, does not cleave to ideas (and ways of life) on account of their presumed authoritative status, acquired in a distant past and transmitted by tradition. He underscores their *intrinsic* substantial value. This is precisely the predicament of the modern Jew. Ought he to cherish tradition as an ancient and venerable sacred creation, to espouse a conservative and pietistic attitude? Or ought he to respect tradition for those spiritual and ethical values that are still valid and relevant today? There may be divergent views as to which values to maintain and which ones to drop. What ought to be kept in mind, however, is the following: Understanding the constructive role of tradition in history is not identical with accepting unquestioningly all its contents. This is crucial when one speaks about the place of tradition in contemporary Judaism. To evaluate it from the perspective of the hermeneutic "fusion of horizons" is likely to widen one's intellectual conceptions and vistas. Anyone who perceives only proximate matters has narrow-minded horizons; his comprehension is limited. A broad-minded person, however, enjoys wide and open intellectual horizons, and, what is more important, is tolerant of the intellectual visions of his fellowmen. This is the connecting link between understanding tradition and the "fusion of horizons," because to embrace tradition without viewing it from a contemporary vantage point entails narrow-mindedness. One remains captive to his *Vorurteile* in the negative sense of the word. This is one of the crucial issues confronting the modern secular Jew. As a result, "heritage" seems to me preferable now to "tradition." As noted, "tradition" means "what has been 'handed over' to us." "Heritage," on the other hand, indicates that we are "inheritors," that is active subjects, free to decide what to do with the inheritance. Perhaps this distinction is a bit artificial, but linguistically, especially in Hebrew, it is not arbitrary at all. There are numerous instances in the Bible and the Talmud which testify to this.[35] In the Talmud "tradition" comprises everything which belongs ("traditionally") to the Bible: habits, laws, historical events, values etc. So "tradition" (*massoreth*) became "heritage" (*morashah*). One, however, ought to keep in mind that if the spiritual heritage is the creative product of man's activity in the past, this creative faculty of man never stops. It continues to the present, and beyond. What man has created, he is also capable of changing by new creative acts. Unlike religious tradition, drawing its authority from belief in an act of divine revelation, his spiritual heritage is not forced upon him. It is not absolute and does not pretend to be so. One can freely deviate from it when some of its components cease to be viable. It is reconcilable with his autonomy. From this standpoint, autonomy is not adverse to tradition, but functions inside it, and even more so when "tradition" is conceived of as "heritage."

This was Buber's view when he founded his philosophical anthropology on religious tradition. Although he considered the philosophy of Plato to represent the paradigm of all philosophical reasoning, he did not believe it was as efficacious in creating an influential tradition as was Isaiah's prophecy. Isaiah represents the source or paradigm of an *authentic* religious tradition, according to Buber. Religious tradition of this kind ought to bring about, in Jewish life, an interior change equal to what Zionism tried to accomplish on the exterior plane. According to Buber, Zionism fulfills only a part of its task, unless it draws its inspiration also from the Jewish religious heritage. Tradition, as interpreted by Buber, assigns every Jew the task of "returning to the sources of his being," as manifested in the Bible and especially in the books of the prophets. One ought to take advantage of the spiritual power of the ancient Jewish sources in order to shape Jewish life at present. However, what Buber considered to be the most important point brings us back to the core of our inquiry, namely, that the continuity of Jewish tradition and adherence to it do not abolish spontaneity, autonomy, and change. Every religious tradition is (or ought to be) subject to constant re-examination and renewal because its absorption concerns contemporary needs.[36] Religious traditions which have become obsolete fail in this regard. They fall short of the goal for which they were designed. Furthermore, according to Buber, religious tradition also serves as a kind of collective memory of the people. This has always been an important and characteristic feature of Judaism.

In his famous letter to Gandhi, Buber asserted that living religious tradition is an outcome of the interplay between the people and its physical surroundings; it is not a consequence of metaphysical speculations by lonely thinkers.[37] This last remark may give the (erroneous) impression that Buber allotted priority to religious tradition over philosophy. This is not the case. For him, tradition and philosophy are intertwined. He explicated tradition by philosophical arguments. His assumption that there are no traditional patterns "once and for all" but that tradition ought to be reassessed and revived in every generation according to the needs of the new age, is eloquent evidence of his positive impression of philosophy. Further, the assumption exhibits an inevitable tension between Jewish religious tradition as conceived by Buber and Jewish tradition in its conventional forms. Buber believed that Jewish life, impregnated with authentic religiosity, is possible only on one condition: Religious tradition must lead man back to the true origins of religious experience, namely, revelation, encounter, and dialogue between God and man. It should not be subordinated to institutionalized patterns of religious tradition. As noted, these origins are the Bible, in particular the prophets, but not the Halakhah. Although Buber was a religious thinker, there exists an abyss between his approach to tradition and the attitude towards tradition espoused by those who consider (and nominate) themselves to be its authorized interpreters and official spokesmen. So Buber's religious view of tradition shows much affinity to the nonreligious view of the modern secular Jew, despite their divergent conceptions of religion and religiosity.

This gives rise to a final problem. No one denies that the religious tradition of Judaism is above all embodied by Halakhah. There clearly exists a strong rapport between the Bible and the Talmud, but Buber seems to disregard the latter, one of the chief factors that engendered problems for the modern Jew with regard to the Jewish tradition. The modern Jew has few difficulties with his relationship to the Bible. For him, it is no longer the Holy Scripture. One of the characteristic features of the Zionist movement in Palestine, and afterwards in the state of Israel, was the renewed preference of the Bible, which had been a subsidiary element of Jewish tradition and education in the Diaspora. For the Chalutzim and the young Israelis, the bond to the Bible was emotional. It symbolized the negation of the *Galut* and the affirmation of Eretz Israel. Eretz Israel ceased to be the "Holy Land" and became the "homeland." Hebrew ceased to be the "holy language" and became the colloquial and literary language of Israel. However, the Bible was conceived not only as the literary expression of the historical bond to our forefathers; rather, the Bible is based, from a strictly religious viewpoint, on the cardinal presupposition that man has been created in "God's image," i.e. that he is a rational being, responsible for his acts. Such a view presents a wide range to man's autonomous and free deliberations; it can even be accommodated with the (liberal) viewpoint of modern ethics, whether in its religious or secular versions. Yet it still remains true that every tradition, by the very essence of tradition, obstructs, to a greater or lesser degree, man's free and autonomous thought. Unlike philosophy or science, which views man as above all a thinking, *questioning*, and inquiring being, religion pretends to provide him with all the *answers*. However, as long as tradition is conceived as *Vorurteil* in the sense of "pre-judgment" and not of "prejudice," as long as it is not considered to be binding absolutely, but to be subject to critical reassessment and open to change, it can serve as an unbiased and constructive challenge for modern thought. Then and only then does it deserve respect and appreciation. Autonomy does not mean negation of tradition, but rather choice as to what to adopt from it and what not. The principal question is not whether tradition is binding, but what kind and which parts of tradition to preserve. Selection is an inseparable part of *every* society. What has been rejected by orthodoxy in one age may become acceptable again in later generations, and vice versa. The Chasidic movement which was fiercely denounced by Rabbi Elijah, the "Gaon of Wilna," has become, on the one hand, the very symbol of Jewish religious and orthodox myth, while, on the other hand, it was depicted by Buber as a paradigm of a rebellious religious "underground" tradition.[38]

Halakhah, however, does not restrict itself to interpreting the Torah as it was given, according to traditional belief, to Moses at Sinai. It formulates and fixes all the particular and specific norms and rules of behavior that obligate a Jew and determine every detail of his daily life. Only by their meticulous observance is his Jewishness fully realized. This view underlies the uncompromising and intransigent demands of Jewish orthodoxy, especially in Israel, and its hostility to all other varieties of Judaism. This entails a threefold predicament: (1) Halakhah imposes such exacting and stringent obligations that a nonorthodox Jew has not only great difficulty in observing them, but most of them do not even make any sense to him. (2) Halakhah imposes upon him outdated and archaic beliefs against which his intellect revolts and of which he is morally bewildered. (3) Orthodoxy, especially in Israel, endeavors to usurp, by every possible means, including, not least, political pressure, ever more domains of public life, in order to restrict civil rights which belong to the sphere of personal convictions and conscience.

As noted, the Jewish tradition is usually identified with the Rabbinic tradition, with Halakhah. This became one of the mainsprings of the nonorthodox Jew's predicament and discontent, *a fortiori* of the secular Jew who attempted to define his relationship to tradition. The secular Jew who wants to clarify to himself and to others the nature of his spiritual-national legacy which was transmitted in the past by a religiously normative tradition must now make a deliberate choice between tradition as the totality of Jewish life or tradition as historical consciousness. The first alternative is precluded because it entails ways of life and beliefs which no longer are acceptable to his intellectual outlook and to his conscience. The second alternative, however, allows for an appropriate understanding of a continuous tradition, with which he can give assent intellectually and emotionally. Of course, it still remains debatable whether and to what extent one can distinguish in Judaism between tradition and religion. The same problem exists on the general plane, but in Judaism there emerge many very troubling and difficult questions. Due to the extraordinary extraterritorial history of the Jewish people, the particular religious norms of Judaism operated for a long time as distinctive traits of national identity.

However, with all respect to these historically unique circumstances, the modern Jew who conceives of tradition as an expression of his spiritual heritage still cannot escape the unavoidable obligation of making some free choices of his own. Some modern scholars liken tradition to a quarry. Just as Michelangelo selected from the quarries of Carrara such marble as served his sculptural designs, so we ought to choose those precious stones of our tradition that comply with our modern consciousness. There is, however, a slight flaw in this metaphor. As regards tradition, selection alone does not suffice. It is not enough to dismiss those elements that are no longer acceptable to us and to keep those that are. It is at the same time incumbent upon us to endow the latter with new meanings and values that conform to our contemporary intellectual horizons. The latter are now common to modern Jews and all modern men. In other words, it is not sufficient to recognize certain values of tradition in a passive way; what matters is to shape them into something new and independent. How to do this is certainly a difficult question. This paper has only attempted to highlight some of the urgent problems and to venture a few suggestions with regard to the complex issue of tradition and autonomy.

Notes

1. Some of these problems formed the topic of several recent international congresses: The fourteenth Congress of the International Association for the History of Religions, Winnipeg, Canada, 1980 ("Traditions in Contact and Change"); The seventeenth World Congress of Philosophy, Montreal, Canada, 1983 ("Philosophy and Culture"); the sixth East-West Philosophers' Conference, Honolulu, Hawaii, 1989 ("Culture and Modernity").

2. See, among others, Kant's famous essay on the quiddity of Enlightenment: Kant 1921, pp. 161–71.

3. "As a cultural being he is, by the same token, necessarily a traditional being." Landmann 1985, p. 50.

4. ibid., p. 171.

5. *Ethics*, prop. 29, scholium.

6. See, among others, Levi-Strauss 1966.

7. Tractate *Shabbat* 112b, The Babylonian Talmud, *Moed*, vol. I, p. 549.

8. *Yoma* I, ch. 5, The Mishnah. London: Oxford University Press, 1938, p. 163.

9. *Kiddushim* 32b, The Babylonian Talmud, *Nashim*, vol. IV, p. 159.

10. *Aboth* 1:1, The Mishnah, op. cit., p. 35.

11. Katz 1958.

12. Baeck 1981, p. 49.

13. Rotenstreich 1972a, pp. 11–23.

14. Rotenstreich 1984, p. 7.

15. Rotenstreich 1972a, p. 22.

16. Liebman 1984, pp. 17–18, my emphasis.

17. Lazarus 1901.

18. Cohen 1972.

19. See also Rotenstreich 1972b, p. 128.

20. This had been Kant's stance in his essay on the Enlightenment; Kant 1921.

21. Gadamer 1980, p. 129.

22. Gadamer 1975, pp. 261–69.

23. ibid., pp. 265–69.

24. Gadamer 1980, p. 131.

25. Gadamer 1975, pp. 289ff.

26. ibid., p. 261.

27. "Das Prinzip der Wirkungsgeschichte," ibid., pp. 284–90; "Analyse des wirkungsgeschichtlichen Bewusstseins," ibid., pp. 324–60.

28. See Kuhn 1970.

29. In Jewish philosophy such views became famous, e.g., in the wake of Yehuda Halevi's *Kuzari* and M. Mendelssohn's *Jerusalem.*

30. Gadamer 1975, p. 340.

31. ibid., p. 343.

32. Hilberath 1978, p. 38.

33. Kuhn 1970, especially chapters II–V.

34. Wuchterl 1982, p. 167.

35. "And I will cause you to pass under the rod, and I will bring you into the tradition of the covenant." (Ezekiel 20:37); most English translations write "bond" instead of "tradition" in this verse, but that is less correct.

36. "[A]bsorb and transform . . . in response to the demands of the hour"; Kaplan 1967, p. 264; see also p. 261.

37. Buber 1939.

38. Buber 1920, p. 51.

References

Baeck, Leo. 1981. "Does Traditional Judaism Possess Dogmas?" In *Studies in Jewish Thought: An Anthology of German Jewish Scholarship,* ed. Alfred Jospe. Detroit: Wayne State University Press, pp. 41–53.

Buber, Martin, 1920. *Drei Reden über das Judentum.* Frankfurt a. M.: Literarische Anstalt/Rütten & Löning.

Buber, Martin (with Judah Magnes). 1939. "Two Letters to Gandhi." In *Pamphlets of the Bond.* Jerusalem: Rubin Mass, pp. 1–22.

Cohen, Hermann. 1972. *Religion of Reason out of the Sources of Judaism.* Translated by Simon Kaplan. New York: Frederick Ungar.

Gadamer, Hans-Georg. 1975. *Wahrheit und Methode: Grundzüge einer Philosophischen Hermeneutik.* Tübingen: J.C.B. Mohr (Paul Siebeck).

Gadamer, Hans-Georg. 1980. "The Universality of the Hermeneutical Problem." In *Josef Bleicher: Contemporary Hermeneutics.* London: Routledge & Kegan Paul, pp. 128–40.

Hilberath, B.J. 1978. *Theologie zwischen Tradition und Kritik: Die philosophische Hermeneutik H.-G. Gadamers als Herausforderung des theologischen Selbstverständnisses.* Duesseldorf.

Kant, Immanuel. 1921. "Beantwortung der Frage: Was ist Aufklärung?" In *Sämtliche Werke*, 1. Band. Leipzig: Inselverlag, pp. 161–71.

Kaplan, Mordecai M. 1967. "Buber's Evaluation of Philosophic Thought and Religious Tradition." In *The Philosophy of Martin Buber* (*The Library of Living Philosophers*), ed. P. A. Schilpp and M. Friedman. La Salle: Open Court, pp. 249–72.

Katz, Jacob. 1958. *Massoreth Umashber* (*Tradition and Crisis*). Jerusalem: Bialik Institute.

Kuhn, Thomas S. 1970. *The Structure of Scientific Revolutions*. Chicago: University of Chicago Press.

Landmann, Michael. 1985. *Fundamental Anthropology*. Washington D.C.: Center for Advanced Research in Phenomenology & University Press of America.

Lazarus, Moritz. 1901. *Die Ethik des Judentums*. Frankfurt a.M.: J. Kauffmann.

Levi-Strauss, Claude. 1966. *The Savage Mind*. Chicago: University of Chicago Press.

Levy, Ze'ev. 1985. "Hugo Bergmann on Philosophy and Religion." *Grazer Philosophische Studien* 24: 115–34.

Levy, Ze'ev. 1989. *Baruch or Benedict: On Some Jewish Aspects of Spinoza's Philosophy*. Bern/New York: Peter Lang.

Liebman, Charles S. 1984. "Approaches to the Relations between Jews and Gentiles in Jewish History and in Israel Today" (Hebrew). *Quivunnim: A Journal for Judaism and Zionism* 25: 7–18.

Rotenstreich, Nathan. 1972a. "On the Concept of Tradition in Israel" (Hebrew). In *Jewish Existence in the Present Age*. Tel-Aviv: Sifriat-Poalim, pp. 11–23.

Rotenstreich, Nathan. 1972b. *Tradition and Reality: The Impact of History on Modern Jewish Thought*. New York: Random House.

Rotenstreich, Nathan. 1984. "Jewish Tradition in a Modern World" (Hebrew). *Gesher*, vol. 30, 1/110, pp. 7–12.

Spinoza, Baruch. 1962. *Hebrew Grammar* (*Compendium Grammatices Linguae Hebreae*). Translated by Rabbi M. Bloom. New York: Philosophical Library.

Spinoza, Baruch. 1982. *The Ethics and Selected Letters*. Translated by Samuel Shirley. Indianapolis: Hackett Publishing Company.

Wuchterl, Kurt. 1982. *Philosophie und Religion*. Bern and Stuttgart: Hauptverlag.

Part Two

Historical and Contemporary Perspectives

The Individual and the Community in the Normative Traditions of Judaism

Lenn E. Goodman

1. Introduction

In 1980 the Knesset of Israel severed the last formal ties between Israeli and British law and instructed judges who could find no grounds for a decision in statute, case law or analogy to form their decisions "in the light of the principles of freedom, justice, equity and peace of Israel's heritage." A large body of British precedent and principle had already been taken up as statute during the years 1922–1980, when British Mandatory law was the system of normative recourse in default of more direct legislative instruction. But now, when the historic step was taken of severing the connection to the colonial past, the Knesset was careful to specify that recourse to the traditional canon should be to its humane and justice preserving principles.[1] No parochial traditionalism was to be erected on the basis of this law, which reestablished a formal, governmental status for the ancient legal canon. Rather the intention was to reopen the Israeli legislative/juridical process to a source of inspiration from which it had been too long cut off and to reenliven in a modern context the most universal human values that find articulation in the context of Judaic Law. What are those values and how are they to be disentangled from the particularities which body them forth concretely in specific epochs? How are the timeless principles to be teased out of their historic settings and reintegrated into new contexts, where the social circumstances may vary widely from those of the original formulations? This question is the fundamental constitutional question for all societies which hope culturally to preserve and juridically to build upon the legal achievements of the past without the mortmain of accepting norms determinatively because they express the values of the past.

The question has been asked repeatedly throughout Jewish history. Indeed, the fact that it has been addressed so often and in such widely different social and historical contexts provides us with a material basis for addressing it ourselves. For it is characteristic of religions based on the concept of a transcendently revealed scriptural document as constitutional foundation—thus of Judaism, Christianity and Islam—that they regard that document not as a fixed archaeological record but as a timeless, ever new touchstone of inspiration, whose very ambiguities are the keys of new and always relevant meanings. Fundamentalist or revivalist movements of reform are characteristic of the monotheistic scriptural communities precisely because the mere positivity of a doctrine, a document, a practice, can never be accepted as an adequate expression of the profundity of meaning in symbols whose function as signifiers is to point beyond particularity, towards a Source of absolute and transcendent perfection. New effort is constantly required to reopen what are construed as the true and original intentions of the revelation and its law. But the locus of those intentions is only fictively and projectively discovered in the past. The actual locus is in a realm of normative virtuality which the individual aspirant or community strives for, atavistically or creatively, by radical departures from the normative center of gravity in pursuit of particular themes (thus generating heresy), or by closely reasoned steps of argument or almost imperceptible shifts of emphasis which work from intuitive sensitivity to the continuity of those themes, generating evolution. The process is always selective and interpretive. Its practical outcomes may be inspired or misguided, thoughtless or inspiring.

In the case of Judaism we find an immense variety of form and content in the historically variegated efforts to articulate the fundamental norms, but three underlying, related and interactive, idioms—the Mosaic, the prophetic, and the rabbinic. Strictly historical studies of the emergence of each of these forms from its antecedents and alternatives, while widely undertaken, rarely address the questions we have asked. Often such studies degenerate into an historic noting of differences, suggesting that the values and themes of an epoch or text have been understood once its mode of discourse has been analyzed and its idiom and terms of reference labeled—"Wisdom Literature," "Priestly Document," "Elohist Tract," and so forth. While such historical analysis can be valuable, it is of limited use for our more philosophic and interpretive purpose. When the end product of historical stratification is no more than a series of strata, or the outcome of textual analysis is the snipping of a textual tradition into tiny slips of paper or parchment whose scattered array belies thematic unities which were self-evident to the individual and diverse authors of a collective literary and cultural achievement (despite their diversities of language, social background, even cosmology), then it may be useful to complement the familiar methods of critical historiography as applied to our canonical sources with some measure of the ahistorical method which the biblical and rabbinic authors themselves adopted in responding to one another's thoughts—not by way of denying historicity, but by way of seeing our way clear of history and thus perhaps in some measure transcending it.

The Torah, as Maimonides explains in the second chapter of his *Guide to the Perplexed*, is not a work of history or poetry (although it uses the techniques of history and poetry) but a book of laws. And if such a book is to be critically appropriated as a possession for all times then it cannot be read purely as an expression of its times (that is, of the language and limitations of its original audience, whose understanding it accommodates), but must be read also and simultaneously as a contribution to an ever-living discussion, taken up in diverse terms by different generations but still pursuing the same issues and still resting its case on the same values, the same underlying appeal to a particular conception of what is absolute and what is compromisable. Our purpose in the present essay is less to note the shifts of language and of scene then to uncover underlying and perennially normative unities. The task is necessarily creative, active and collaborative, for the aim is not to reach a point at which we no longer notice whether we are reading Hebrew or Aramaic, Arabic or English, but rather to raise our own consciousness, through what we elicit from old texts, to the level that it is themes, indeed appropriable themes, that we encounter. The continuities of theme through the historic overlay of their variegated expressions provide us with the clue we need to the underlying unities—in this case, as to the relationship of the individual and the community. What we find in the sources is that the familiar dichotomy, the cliche of a zero sum game between the interests of the community and the deserts of the individual, rests on assumptions which the normative tradition of Judaism, like most traditional normative systems, does not share. Rather than a competition, the Torah and the works that elaborate and explicate its principles set forth a complementarity of interests between the individual and the community. Autonomy is seen not as the antithesis but as the aim of the norms of the community; and the fulfillment of the individual is both the means and the end of the fulfillment of the law—although, of course, for this to be true, individual fulfillment cannot be defined arbitrarily, situationally or subjectively, but must be understood so as to comprehend within it both the moral and the spiritual dimensions of our being.

2. The Biblical Norms

The people of Israel, who are the cultural bearers of the Jewish religion and law and whose ethnic unity is forged by their historic past and future relation to that religion and law, originated as a people in a crisis. The crisis of Israel's experience as an identified minority, persecuted and enslaved in Egypt,[2] precipitates the Judaic idea of the individual and of the dignity of the individual in particular as one of Israel's central values. The marks of that experience are visible in the norms of the Mosaic law and form a basis of selection for the materials which that Law preserves in its cosmological, historical and even protohistorical (mythic) preambles. The same circumstances that form the nation form that nation's conception of the individual and of the rights of the individual. Let us survey some of these. They are formative of much that comes after, both within Israel and throughout the West. For it is these ideals that give normative content to the identity of Israel and form the normative basis of all Christian claims to be the true or new Israel, all Muslim claims upon the parentage of Abraham and heritage of the prophets, and all modern secular revisions, openly acknowledged as in Locke, the Deists, Republicans and Philosophes, or structurally transformed, as in Spinoza, Freud, Marx, Weber, Durkheim or Levi-Strauss.[3] Even where the specificities of application are superseded, transcended, sublimited or sublated within Judaism or outside it, the original thematic is crucial to the elaboration of the tradition.

What then is the legacy of Egypt? There is to be no permanent slavery, except at the express demand of the individual enslaved.[4] Correspondingly, the system of debt slavery from which Joseph profited in Egypt (Genesis 47:20) is abolished: There is no permanent alienation of land but only what is in effect a forty-nine-year lease.[5] Hence there is no permanently dispossessed class or caste. Correspondingly, there is no regular tenure of land for priests or Levites.[6] No interest is to be taken on loans from fellow Israelites,[7] and their debts are to be remitted in the seventh year, when the land is given its 'sabbath'—left to lie fallow.[8] Thus, in principle, Israelites will always return to their familial estates. The cycle or debt slavery and dispossession, with its correlative amassing of lands in the institutional priesthood, is to be broken permanently.[9] From the Book of Ruth we learn that the system did not function perfectly. But the ideas it enunciates become a permanent heritage.

The Torah plans for the elimination of poverty and states that its laws of land tenure, debt release and redemption, if fulfilled, will end the condition of destitution (Deuteronomy 15:4–5). Yet it allows for the persistence of poverty even as it plans the means of its elimination. The rationale for the provision of surplus 'gleanings' as the patrimony of the poor is the same as that for the prohibition of injustice to the stranger, retention of a dayworker's wages overnight, or taking in pawn a widow's clothing, a poor man's cloak beyond sundown, or any person's millstone—the same as that for the prohibition against selling one's kidnapped brethren or entering a debtor's house to claim collateral: "Remember that you were a slave in the land of Egypt" (Deuteronomy 24:6–7, 10–15, 17–22). Unlike Francis Galton or Garrett Hardin, the Torah does not plan for the elimination of need by the elimination of the needy. Galton, the modern-day founder of eugenics, hoped for a humane elimination of human misery by social programs of state aid to the advantaged and organized discrimination against the destitute, which would gradually but inexorably breed out inferiority and promote superiority within the human population. Hardin, our own contemporary, advocates a new ethic for "spaceship earth" which would apply the methods of "triage" to entire races and peoples, withholding food aid from the starving, so as to suppress their numbers and prevent their "swamping the lifeboat" or laying waste the "commons."

The Torah, although the expression of a far less prosperous and secure age than our own, does not read the human condition as requiring or even permitting such desperate and self-defeating measures. It expresses confidence that the well-being of humanity and life at large will not fail if creatures are fruitful and multiply and fill the earth. And, legislating for the destiny of Israel, it seeks to ensure, through the active participation of all Israelites, that the poor not be allowed to die out and vanish from the land by becoming dispossessed: To keep them alive, restore them to their property and see them well established is a blessing for the entire nation (Deuteronomy 15:7–11; cf. Leviticus 25:35). The value guiding the scheme is that of human self-sufficiency—every man under his own vine or fig tree.[10] Thus, even when the prohibition against interest taking is overturned by a legal fiction, in the interest of commerce,[11] even when the extra-Judaic growth of the Judaic idea of freedom leads to the abolition of slavery, or when the intra-Judaic growth of exogamy (already underway in Biblical times) leads to weakening and dissolution of the norms of levirate marriage once designed to protect matrilineal rights within a patrilineal social structure,[12] the ideal of the economically autonomous individual remains—not merely as an ideal, but as a foundation of concrete legal obligations, such that the poor can sue at law for their just maintenance,[13] and the true fulfillment of charity can be defined not as self-sacrifice nor as condescension but as the imparting to another of the means of self-sufficiency.[14]

Crucial among the Mosaic institutions which reflect the Egyptian experience and its aftermath is the Sabbath. The petition for a holiday from construction and related duties was the original demand with which Moses approached Pharaoh (Exodus 5:1). The request was rejected on the grounds that a cessation of labors would represent a breaking free of the Israelites from their subordination to and functional identification with their work (Pharaoh says, "Why, Moses and Aaron, do you sunder the people from their work? Go back to your toils"—Exodus 5:4). Pharaoh refused to accept the differentiation of the Israelites from their assigned labors, just as he refused to accept the differentiation of Moses and Aaron from the rest of the laborers. In the cosmological myth that expresses the Mosaic conception of the universe at large, the Sabbath has become a symbol of the absolute autonomy of the individual, the existential irreducibility of the individual to his work. It is for this reason that God Himself is represented (Genesis 2:2-3) as ceasing from work. God is the Creator, but His identity is not confined by His function; and man, who is created in God's image—all who come under the sway of the Law—are obliged to rest and thus dissociate themselves from a merely functional role. Even animals are not to be worked on the Sabbath, lest servants be excluded from equal enjoyment of the Sabbath rest (Deuteronomy 5:14–15).

The Sabbath is said to be a symbol of the divine act of creation (Exodus 31:17). But the symbol reenacts not the work but the cessation. Its placement on the seventh day is established in one of those wonderful plays on words (which can be duplicated in English), of which the Bible is so fond, between seven and septum in the sense of stoppage (Genesis 2:1–2). The Sabbath symbolizes creation because it teaches us that God does not create by constraint: thus not eternally, not in a uniquely predetermined pattern, not even in a fixed and immutable pattern. Freedom is the condition of existence, and creativity is the condition of freedom. The metaphysical freedom of creativity of which Bergson spoke is the foundation of political freedom. Its first and logically most primitive case—thus its symbol and paradigm—is the freedom not to act. Here the seemingly inexorable nexus of custom and the determination of the future by the past are broken. We emerge from a closed to an open society when the enslavement of the gods to genealogy and passion or to the mere undisrupted flow of seasons and moments is broken and the idea of the Sabbath discovers for us in the cosmos the possibility of an open universe.[15]

Ethically, again from the experience in Egypt, we have the commandment: Thou shalt not abhor the Egyptian[16]—a remarkable structural transformation upon the ethos of vindictiveness, which directly gives the lie to Nietzsche's professed discovery of the workshops of morality in the spirit of vengeance (See *Genealogy of Morals* 1:7). On the contrary, ethics as such takes its rise dialectically in the moral transcendence of merely reactive responses. In the Mosaic Bible the schematic type of the commandment not to despise the Egyptian is characteristically generalized and expanded in a variety of ways: There are commandments not to hate one's brother in one's heart,[17] not to oppress or vex a stranger,[18] to love the stranger,[19] to love one's fellow as oneself.[20] The very concept of universal sympathy finds articulation *pari passu* with the elaboration of the dialectical significances of the commandment "do not despise the Egyptian." Even the idea of one law for the stranger and the home born alike[21] can be seen as a dialectical counterpart of the ethical response to Egypt, and the process is still going on when Jesus admonishes: Love thine enemies. The Torah does not utter that command, but it does command us, paradigmatically, to assist our enemy in righting and reloading his fallen beast of burden (Exodus 23:45). The admonition is interpreted as serving to moderate the passion of enmity and to release its hold upon our character—and the hold of enmity in general upon the communal ethos.[22]

A crucial corollary of the Biblical injunction to love the stranger as ourselves was the idea of equality before the law. The conception is as formative of the idea of law as it is of the idea of humanity. It rests on and thus indirectly voices the idea of the existential dignity of the human individual. The social articulation of the law and the institutional articulation of the community exist to serve and promote that dignity, not as an alternative to the service of God but as the principal means by which God desires and intends to be served.[23]

The *mise-en-scène* of Biblical revelation was a society in which vengeance or the threat of vengeance, mitigated by blood payment, was the familiar vehicle of the exaction of justice in cases of death or even injury. The Torah reflects on the resultant loss of human dignity when it pictures primitive times—Lamech boasting to his wives in the days of eponymous myth and praeternatural longevity, "I have slain a man for wounding me, and a boy for bruising me. If Cain's vengeance is seven-fold, then Lamech's is seventy-seven fold" (Genesis 4:23–4). In the rhetoric of machismo, a man's vengeance was the measure of his worth; and, in the days before the imparting of the Law, every man did what was right in his own eyes.[24] But in the eyes of God and therefore in the eyes of the Law, all men are of equal existential worth. It is forbidden to judges to show favor to wealth, stature, poverty, or even merit.[25] The Torah is not embarrassed to admit (Exodus 18) that the idea of deciding cases on the basis of uniform rules came to Moses from a foreign source, his Midianite father-in-law, Jethro. But uniformity alone does not imply equality of treatment. It only tends in that direction. A law might hold that individuals should be treated uniformly according to their station or their stature.[26] The idea of a level of uniformity such that social standing—dominance or prominence—has no revelance whether with regard to the crucial issues of justice rests on the conception of the equal and positive existential desert of persons. Yet the idea of uniformity of laws fosters the recognition of such categorical deserts, just because recognition of a minimal level of such deserts is a moral requirement of the functioning of any law: Minimally, for example, there is a uniform desert of access and applicability of laws. More positively, there is a need for definition and exclusion of partiality.[27] The requirement that each king of Israel write out the Torah in his own hand (Deuteronomy 17:18–20) points in the direction of constitutionality and underscores the idea that all are subject to the law. There is fuller recognition of positive existential desert in the law which allows passersby to take from a field fruit sufficient for their needs without being considered thieves, or the laws which exempt the betrothed from military service (Deuteronomy 20:7; cf. 20:5–6) and the newly married from both military conscription and public civil obligation (Deuteronomy 24:5).

In a practical sense the very principle of the rule of law presses for the realization that justice involves equality, that is, equal treatment of equal cases.[28] Thus, the provisions for a permanent, public, written law.[29] Fused with the idea of the inviolable positive worth or dignity of the individual, existentially as a creature of God and a being beyond price,[30] the idea of the invariance of rules with persons became the most powerful ethico-legislative tool ever devised. It meant, to begin with, that recompense for deaths or injuries must be equal, proportioned only to the injury and not to the stature or grandeur of the party offended against.[31] Worth was a matter of dignity, but the dignity of all human beings (being existential, a concomitant of what we are) was alike and positive for free or slave, man or woman, young or old.

It would take centuries to single out—and the task is by no means completed—those dimensions of human dignity that are truly existential from those claims of the ego or of custom that are merely encrustations of the universal desire for dignity—at one's own or others' expense. But an immediate requirement, when the idea of equality of human dignities was first enunciated in the context of a vengeance culture, was the distinction between murder, manslaughter and accident and the elaboration of an institution (the Cities of Refuge) to protect homicides who were non-murderers from the exaction of blood vengeance.[32] Correspondingly, there was capital punishment (not vengeance) to protect society from acceptance of blood payment or exaction of corporate accountability in cases of murder.[33] The demand that every person bear accountability for his own offense[34] articulates the identity of the moral individual and renders vivid the status of that individual (qua moral agent) as the determinative actor in history, upon whose choices and omissions, virtues and weaknesses the fate of the community at large will rest.[35]

God Himself is seen to oversee the uniformity of the law, and the principle becomes so powerful that Abraham, the founder of the peoplehood and mission of Israel (to be a blessing to the nations of the world), is represented as arguing and bargaining with God for the application of the rules of uniform justice to the people of Sodom and Gomorrah: "Wilt Thou sweep away the innocent with the guilty? Perhaps there are fifty who are innocent in the city as a whole. Wilt Thou sweep them away and not bear with the place for the sake of the fifty who are innocent in its midst? Far be it from Thee to do such a thing, to slay the innocent with the guilty, so that the righteous and the wicked fare alike. Far be it from Thee! Will not the Judge of all the earth do justice?"[36]

The procedural guarantees: presumption of innocence, protection against self-incrimination, rules of evidence and testimony, which together form the glory of the legal system of the modern West, are by and large reflections and developments of the Biblical placement of equal and positive valuation on individual human dignity.[37] Even habeas corpus and the right to a jury trial, which are not historically biblical institutions, are assimilated to the absoluteness and sanctity of the other protections, which God Himself is expected to respect. Job, in the midst of his persecutions, can expect a trial.[38] And the visions of apocalypse called forth by the conception of God's cosmic justice take on a juridical, procedurally safeguarded form. God formalizes His covenant with Israel by calling heaven and earth to witness;[39] no default of the covenant will be determined merely on one party's say so. The procedural guarantees that operate on the human level (between one human and another, as it will be expressed) safeguard personal liberty, life and property, to be sure; but, most crucially, they defend human dignity, biblically defined so as to engulf and transcend all of these.

Ritual royal incest was a feature of the Egyptian absorption in death and afterworldliness;[40] and the Mosaic laws of incest, responding to that feature, impart a special moral relevance to the abhorrence of incest—a moral revelance of particular significance to the constitution of individual dignity. The Mosaic laws situate themselves as 'laws of life' between the death-oriented customs and institutions of Egypt and the orgiastic blood rituals of Canaan, both of which are to be eschewed—the laws of the society departed from, and the customs of the society to be displaced, which are said morally to have polluted the land, made it unfit for habitation by the Canaanites.[41] The genealogies of both Egypt and Canaan are traced to Ham, whose sin in violating the dignity of his father is said to be the basis of the curse he bears.[42] The curse is not a racial stigma on the Cushites but a cultural blot on the ancient Canaanites and ancient Egyptians, the stigma of an impure ethos. The laws of life, which represent the blessing counterpoised against such curses, phrase the prohibition of incest in the language of the violation of privacy.[43] They find their mythic grounding in the story of Eve's creation out of Adam's flesh. The conclusion, biblically drawn: "Therefore shall a man leave his father and his mother and cleave unto his wife, and they shall be one flesh" (Genesis 2:24).

The family as biblically constructed by the myth provides a matrix for the emergence of individuality. Personal identity is preserved and nurtured by the protection of sexual privacy. It is not to be submerged within the supervenient identities of the parental household. As a result it matures and emerges sound, whole, and independent, capable of entering a mature relationship with another autonomous person and adequate to the construction of a new household. The preservation of privacy nurtures the construction of personal individuality, and the individuality thus preserved constructs the family and community in which individuality is nurtured. This cycle affords the biblical rationale, paradigmatically, for the prohibition of incest, but also, on another level, for the functioning of all communal and social institutions, as matrices for the emergence of the individual.[44] The prohibition against incest applies not to Israel alone but to all humanity. The conception and articulation of its meaning are distinctively Mosaic.

It is noteworthy that the paradigm of the marital relationship is dyadic in the cosmological myth: his father's and his mother's house, cleave unto his wife. Despite the social accretion (and long tolerance) of polygamy, the dyadic paradigm persists: the way of a man with a maid (Proverbs 30:19), thy neighbor's wife (Exodus 20:14)—or Job's.[45] Marital exclusivity even becomes the model of the exclusivity of intimacy in the relation between God and Israel.[46] Ultimately, under new social conditions, polygamy will be spewed out, not as a result simply of 'cultural influences' (for one must always ask what leads a given cultural pattern to be appropriated and another to be neglected or rejected), but as a result of the powerful dynamics of the idea of monogamy itself. The same process has been going on in modern times among thoughtful leaders of Islam. The dialectic is characteristic of one way in which scriptural ideals operate, not always in a revolutionary fashion but sometimes over a long period of time, transforming what is tolerated into something that is intolerable, through the dialectic of social, cultural and intellectual considerations with the primary givens of scripture itself. The outcome is reaffirmation of the primary values and the spitting out of what is gradually, dialectically revealed to be incompatible with them, whether anthropomorphism, slavery, or polygamy.

Biblical legislation, explicated by way of biblical mythology does much to formulate individuality as we know it. But the state in biblical times is not the principal threat to individuality. The modern sovereign state, which fosters and threatens individuality, the totalitarian state which seeks to exploit and submerge the individual, even the omnicompetent welfare state do not yet exist. Such institutions as are created biblically are construed as ancillary to the interests of the individual and the community rather than antithetical to them. The biblical absence of a sharp dichtomy between the interests of the individual and those of the community—a common feature of traditional societies—either expresses naivete or marks a happier epoch than our own in the integration of groups, and of individual desires. I sense both naivete and wisdom in the failure/refusal of the biblical (or traditional) Weltanschauung to perceive a conflict between individual and communal goals: naivete, in that certain freedoms of the individual simply have not been entertained and certain powers of the group and potentials for abuse simply have not been confronted; wisdom, in that the individual has not been isolated radically from a larger social body which extends across the bounds of personal atomicity not only over space but over time.[47]

The fundamental social commandment of the Mosaic corpus, the commandment of Leviticus 19:18, "Thou shalt love thy neighbor as thyself," is paradigmatic both of the Mosaic method of legislation and of its goals *vis-à-vis* the integration of the individual in the community. In terms of goals, this commandment both rests upon and fosters individuality: for it is addressed to the individual moral agent and seeks the good of other individuals. Yet in so doing, it establishes bonds of fellowship and fellow feeling (*re'ut, fraternité*, a sense of community)—not only a sense of common interests but an articulation of shared concerns, an identification of the good of another as one's own concern, a sense of identification such that one regards oneself as benefited when one's fellow profits and injured when he or she is harmed.[48] And the commandment is not left an isolated abstraction but interpreted in its context biblically by a variety of concrete material actions that fulfill it in the sense of giving it operational meaning. These range from the immediate concern with banning vengeance and grudges (loc. cit.) to the prohibition of talebearing on the one hand and diffidence on the other (v. 16.). Indeed, the commandments associated biblically with the Golden Rule form, as Maimonides showed, a tight nexus or system, arising from the primal commandment to pattern ourselves on God's ways (whence our concern for the deserts of our fellow humans is to be derived) and expressing itself, for example, in a delicately balanced pair of obligations to rebuke our fellows when they do wrong, but not to shame them.[49]

The tight bond of the individual to the community is a familiar feature of ancient and traditional societies. Socrates is unable to accept life beyond the polis that he knows and in which (however partially and unfairly) he is known.[50] Plato, in the *Republic*, cannot address the question of justice without dealing congruently with the private politics of the soul and the public foundations of legitimacy. Aristotle argues that a person who would live alone is either above or below the level of humanity—a beast or a god; for man himself is by nature a creature of the polis (*zoon politikon*). Somewhat provincially, even chauvinistically, Aristotle argues that the fully human life—the humane life, we might say, is possible only for a free man in a (Greek) polis. As a reflecton of social realities the claim is not as far off the mark as its ethnocentrism might lead us to expect: Slaves cannot be said to enjoy humanely fulfilled lives or we could not pronounce categorically, as we do, that slavery is wrong. Greek women rarely had the access to the intellectual pursuits of public participation that would have made them fully free. And non-Greeks seemed to Aristotle to be submerged in nonparticipatory autocracies, debarred of the institutions of the agora, palaestra, baths, theaters, schools and public places that allowed the articulation of individuality within and through the structures of the community. It was through such institutions as these that Greek individuality came to be what it was. Greek literature, Greek science and mathematics, Greek philosophy and art are its testimonies, each unique and irreplaceable. Biblical morality, with its kindred institutions of biblical law, universal and objective history, the theology implicit in biblical mythology (which followed more doggedly than Aristotle the unitive promptings of naturalism, mysticism and morality but did not slight, as Aristotle did, the idea that understanding is to be sought and found by way of history and tales of early beginnings) is a comparable and complementary achievement, capable of synthesis with the best intellectual or institutional achievements that the Greeks or others could offer.[51] Just as one story can absorb another as its subplot, the Israelite ideas of universal history, objective truth and justice, subsume what they find valid in all cultures and spew out what they find incoherent with the structuring values of their overarching vision, rejecting or reinterpreting not only what is foreign to their spirit externally, but even what is internally unsound, before the uncompromising tribunal of truth. It was not for nothing that God chose a stiff-necked nation, a nation inured to the practice of criticism. For the fruits of Israelite criticism may be intellectual or social, but its roots are moral.

Surveying the biblical canon, Maimonides, a philosopher imbued with the teaching of Aristotle as well as the wisdom of the Torah, finds explicitly that the institutions of the community serve to foster the articulation of the individual. Maimonides defines the underlying purpose of law Platonically as the integration of disparate human interests and characters. He differentiates divine from human laws on the basis of their goals. Human laws seek only to regulate our material interactions—to adjudicate our conflicts, restrain aggression and overreachng, allocate impartially the goods and ills which our shared situation as members of a community opens up to us. A divine law pursues two higher goals: the improvement of our character (Plato's 'education') and provision of the possibility for our intellectual/spiritual fulfillment (Plato's vision of the sun, Aristotle's intellectual life).[52] Both higher goals are approached by way of symbols, not merely by the familiar legal means of prescription and sanction. Moral improvement is attained by practice of paradigmatic actions. Their symbolic significances attach us on the level of habit and loyalty to standards of reasonableness whose abstract formulations we may be wholly unable to articulate. But mere verbal articulation is largely irrelevant to their moral appropriation as facets of our character. In general terms these virtues are spontaneous, reliable, effectual dispositions toward thoughtfulness and contextually sensitive appropriateness of act and expression.[53] The terms are Aristotelian, but the goals are biblical. Intellectual/spiritual perfection is not imposed but invited by way of the symbolisms of myth,[54] the Bible's oblique discourse about God. The problematics built into that discourse, in which prophets boldly speak of the Creator in the terms applicable to His creation, awaken us to the literal inapplicability of all predications to the Divine, while at the same time directing the understanding towards the idea of a Being of absolute perfection, a Being whose likeness with ourselves we may develop only by perfecting ourselves as human beings and whose glory consists in His creation of each thing for its own sake, not for its sensuous gratification or aggrandizement, nor for His own, but for its perfection as an emblem of the perfection which is divine.[55] No biblical injunction escapes classification under one of these three headings: cooperation (civil and penal integration in pursuit of the common good and avoidance of the most basic ills), moral improvement (the establishment or even institution of kindness, generosity, human dignity, and other strengths of character as the basis of our ethos),[56] and intellectual perfection (the invitation to holiness, critical apprehension of the Transcendent, and the concomitant ability to interpret the divine law to others, morally and intellectually, allowing them too to become morally autonomous and, insofar as humanly possible, intellectually self-sufficient.)[57]

Just as Aristotle founded his understanding of politics on empirical study of some 158 constitutions, Maimonides did not draw his interpretation of the biblical legislation from the air but founded it on the catalogue he made of the 613 commandments of the Mosaic law, on his systematic explication of the Mishnaic code, and on his own recodification of the entire halakhic corpus, the body of rabbinic law, in his fourteen volume *Mishneh Torah.*[58] No law was found whose aim was subordination of the interests of the individual to the group. Although Maimonides did believe that the community is more important than the individual,[59] he grounded the importance of the community biblically in the dignity of its members. He argued that it is part of the legal method to make general rules whose application in exceptional cases might disaccommodate individuals. But even that application was seen to be in the interest of those individuals, which animal short-sightedness (appetite and passion) might lead them to misperceive. Maimonides did not share the modern idea that the individual is always or necessarily the best judge of his own interests, but rather shared the biblical idea that lawlessness is the social resultant of each person judging his own case.[60] Similarly, Maimonides did not share the modern idea of each individual working out his own destiny, but rather shared the biblical idea that the destiny of individuals is wrapped up in the destiny of their fellows and their forbears and descendants. Here Abraham finds fulfillment not merely in his personal discovery of God (still less in his personal wealth), but rather in the promise that through his descendants all the peoples of the world will be blessed. Moses finds fulfillment not in his personal fortunes or even solely in personal experience of God, but in his responsibility for the people—seeking to know God's ways for the sake of learning how to govern (Exodus 33:13), wishing to God that every one of his people were a prophet (Numbers 11:29), and praying to God (Exodus 32:32) that he be blotted from God's book before God allow the destruction of the people for their lapse. Moses is unable to accept life apart from the nation (and unable to accept a substitute nation) in just the way that Socrates is unable to accept life apart from Athens.

3. The Prophetic Reformulation

The writing stemming from the times of the Judges, Kings and Prophets of Israel express a major revision, in which the biblical ideals are reconstituted and the conception of human individuality reformulated, redefined and at the same time reinstated in a reenlivened conception of the nisus of the Mosaic message. Our analysis of the Mosaic themes shows that the construction of human individuality was a central concern among them. Yet no 'definition' of the human individual emerges. The reason is twofold. First, the Mosaic idiom is not conceptual but concrete. So regardless of the conceptual nature of its themes, no expression like *zoon politikon* can be expected to emerge. Second, to speak of individuality is to speak of freedom, and to define individuality is to delimit freedom. The Torah bears enough of a prescriptive load without seeking to define the normative personality. This was done in later ages, reading the role of saint into the patriarchs, or making rabbinic sages of David, Boaz, even Shem and Eber. But the biblical law, in addressing all ages, defines no normative type. Rather it opens the space for human individuality to construct itself. In opening up rather than defining that space it uses the same method of silence and negativity that it employs to allow our minds to construct the idea of God: Man is created in God's image, and God is to be assigned no delimiting shape. Every title of perfection belongs to God, and every imperfection is to be denied of Him, even the imperfections implicit in the limitations of our positive predications. The same, in ethical terms, is to be true of man: No vice is to restrain him. The very word for sin is 'stumble.' No wrong is to be construed to be in our interest as individuals or as members of our people or community or of the whole human race. Just as God's sovereignty is founded in righteousness, man's fulfillment is founded in righteousness, and righteousness does not undermine itself.[61] Tragedy is not inevitable.

No stereotypic role is to delimit human scope. The character we are taught by practice and example bears fruit in any human context: Kindness, thoughtfulness, self-respect, purity and holiness are always relevant virtues. The intelligence we are invited by symbol and indirection to develop as the growing core of our identity is an open-ended potentiality for understanding, not limited by a preconception of what it is normative to say or think, but enticed toward the pursuit of an understanding of God, who is infinite, and of His creation, whose wonders, subtleties, complexities and nuances are illimitable.

The egotistical I does not appear in the Mosaic canon except in passages of self-betrayal like Lamech's boasts to his wives or Cain's demand, "Am I my brother's keeper?" There is no celebration of the heroic ego in the Pentateuch for the same reason that there is no portrayal of the personality, lineaments, ancestry or ultimate motives of the Creator. The Torah is not a saga but a law with its accompanying cosmology, history and ethical tableaux. God is absolute, not to be confined to human terms or explained by way of reduction to the terms of the phenomena which His act is taken to explain.[62] Man is not absolute, but his dignity, hence his freedom, is a kind of finite absolute. Like God he is an end in himself, sufficiently so that all of the prescriptions made to him can be predicated upon two: the love of God and the love of self, which is not a sin but an axiom, without which the commandment to love one's fellow as oneself would be an empty formalism. Yet the biblical love of self is not self-exaltation, but the pursuit of self-perfection, which includes the perfection of the moral and social self, as we might express it in Platonic or Aristotelian terms. In the biblical idiom: "Circumcise, then, they heart" (Deuteronomy 10:16, further defined at Deuteronomy 30:6, Leviticus 26:41). Polytheism is the ethos of Lamech elevated to level of cult. The epic celebrates human vices and virtues as reflections of divine counterparts, themselves projected from the vividness of the human drama. The hero of the epic idiom is the human boaster, reflected (with the help of a bard or professional celebrator of heroic deeds) back down from the heights on a superhuman scale, and thus still bearing (at least fictively) some of the aura of divinity. It is for this reason that there will be heroism but no epic heroes in the Torah.

With the emergence of the history whose meanings the Torah defines, the emergence of the people whose mission (Exodus 19:6) it elaborates as the project of becoming a holy people, and the emergence of the individuals whose autonomous personalities the biblical laws make way for, we do see the emergence of personal individualities: a David whose lyric spirituality articulates a unique identity, a Jephtha whose desperate isolation bespeaks a hunger for social integration, an Amos or Hosea who can articulate the phenomenology of prophetic experience in the categories of familial or even visceral intimacy. Each personality incises the moral values of the original revelation with a clarity heightened by new experience, but given depth by the shared experience of the common past.

It might be imagined that the notions of individuality and personality do not emerge from the communal matrix until, say, the Renaissance or the Enlightenment, with the new literary form of the familiar essay of Montaigne. But this notion is an illusion, founded in part on the romantic anthropology of the type canonized by Levy-Bruhl and others who imagine that in traditional societies culture is somehow undifferentiated from nature, categories are unreflective and undifferentiably compact, so that individuals *cannot* differentiate themselves from the mass, from one another, from the group and its norms, from natural objects and natural kinds fixed in the iconography of totem and taboo. Such anthropological views have long been discredited by the work of Levi-Strauss, and of Malinowski before him, on the structure and functioning of laws, the categories of thought and the shape of ritual and myth in tribal societies. Yet the ideas persist because of the romantic, emotive appeal and projective usefulness of their invidious characterizations of the 'other' as belonging elsewhere than the we in the nature-culture polarity.

As for the literary expression of personality, the essay, a more intimate and less formal mode of expression than the public oratorical mode associated with the treatise, emerges from the ancient epistolary art exemplified in the letters of Seneca and is well developed in the medieval Arabic *risâla*, which preserves the intimacy of tone by preserving the epistolary fiction that a single close friend or confidant is addressed. We have fine examples of the form in full flower in Maimonides' *Guide*, Ibn Ṭufayl's *Hayy Ibn Yaqzân* and the *rasâ'il* of the Ikhwân al-Ṣafâ. Authors like Umberto Eco fail to capture the liveliness and directness of medieval thought in large measure because they fail to enter into the vivacious and candid direct address of such works, and so encounter not an author's mind but an alien and dead, almost runic object that they are pleased to call a text.

But epistolary prose is not the only avenue to the intimacy that allows the expressive emergence of personal individuality. The same poet warrior who danced naked before the ark of the Lord and created that still livid spiritual intimacy by which *we* bless our Creator—David, the shepherd slingsman who sang his troubled king to sleep, who married that king's daughter and was loved by that king's son, even as he displaced him, is also the founding figure of an intimate genre not of prose but of poetry. The genre of the psalms is not the work of a single pair of hands, any more than the genre of the essay is. But it is the vehicle of a personality whose failings we feel we know as intimately and profoundly as we know the spiritual heights of his ambitions. It is no accident that David's is the name, despite his failings, so often and so consistently chosen as a namesake, for his personality does emerge as few do from antiquity. David does emerge as a hero and epitome of many of the humanistic values of the Torah, although his individuality is in no way predictable as their outcome or made a paradigm of their subsequent fulfillment.

Yet it is no accident that sexuality is present everywhere in the personality of David, in his beauty, his appeal to the maidens as a warrior, his flawed relations with Michal, his displacement of Uriah, even in the last flickerings of his bodily warmth on his deathbed. Biblical personhood finds its center in the sexuality which is the first strong focus of the natural emergence of individuality in all of us. It is because all of us have inward sexual aspirations, desires, vulnerabilities, and deserts that the Law legislates as it does, not because the Torah seeks invasively 'to regulate every aspect of life,' but because the Torah seeks to define and protect that individuality of which our common sexuality is the paradigm and in many ways the core. Even the modern (and ultimately incoherent) notion that there are areas too intimate for law to enter is a product of the privacy and dignity that the Torah seeks to demarcate and defend.

Against the intractable problem of rape the Mosaic canon addresses both a civil and a penal remedy. There is no notion that the offense is a mere larceny against paternity. Rather, the heart of the offense is captured in the idea of the humbling of the victim, a degrading of her dignity. The Mosaic remedies are clearly an attempt to mitigate the excesses of the prebibilcal honor-shame culture (Genesis 34). But the remedies proposed, death for the rape of a betrothed or married woman, or marriage without possibility of divorce for the rape of a single woman (Deuteronomy 22:22–28), rest on the assumption of an established civil society in which criminal penalties will be exacted and in which communal relations are such that marriage is conceivable between a woman and a suitor who has forced her, so that the law need only enforce both parties' earnestness in their relations. The idea of premarital intimacy without courtship is not considered (cf. Genesis 34:4, 6, 8–12), and the possibility of rape as a form of social aggression rather than as a form of libidinal excess within a civil society is not prescriptively addressed. Even in the story of Dinah, where the roots of violence might have been detected in the ambiguity of Shechem's behavior, the narrative assimilates Shechem's motives to those of an overzealous suitor. With the decline of civil standards, excesses of the type only dimly suggested in the story of Dinah became extreme (Judges 19–21), and without a central government to enforce principles of proportion there were not only the violence and atrocities of anarchy but also the reemergence, in place of civil or criminal accountability, of collective blood liability of the sort condemned by Jacob in his sons (Genesis 34:30, 49:5–7) and vigorously combated by the later prophets (Ezekiel 18:4). It was in such a context, a context of lawlessness, that the prophet and judge Deborah emerged as a military and political figure answering to the needs that would create the biblical monarchy. The song of Deborah is an expression of her people's sense of triumphant vindication at the overcoming of their terrorized vassalage to a brigand state whose pillage had cleared the roads of travelers (Judges 5:6). Deborah pictures the mother of the brigand general Sisera waiting at a latticed window for her son's return, and her well-protected ladies answering her doubts with images of the booty that has delayed the chariots: "a cunt, two cunts for every man-head." The women, whose fantasies goad their sons's search for heroic self-aggrandizement, picture even the delicate finery of the female captives: embroidered cloth in many colors around every neck as spoil (Judges 5:28–30). The day is not Sisera's, however, but Deborah's and Jael's, and the voice lifted up in triumph, more articulately than that of Miriam at the sea, is that of an individual who differentiates herself proudly from the community and its leaders, who ride on white asses: the precincts of Israel were vacant, the people could not draw water without terror of the whirr of arrows—"until I arose, Deborah, until I arose, a mother in Israel." No words spoken for or about or against women since—not the long tradition of petulent misogyny or timid fastidiousness, not even the sickly sweet uxoritudes which seek to circumscribe a woman's 'place' with platitudinous praises—could take away from all women afterwards the sense of pride and vindicated right that accrues from Deborah's triumphant singing in the first person, not arrogant or spiteful but finding triumph in the restoration of civility: And the land had peace for forty years.

The tradition of misogyny that grows from Hellenistic folk attitudes and attaches itself to the _obiter dicta_ of many later authorities is well entrenched in medieval Judaism, where woman in the abstract is often the projective repository of social ambivalences about the emotions, the passions, the senses and the body, and where the articulation of institutions is often deflected from its theme of imparting ethical dignity, through the assignment of deferential, disadvantaged and sometimes disparaging postures to women in the concrete. Yet the accretion cannot completely cover over the normative themes. When the biblical law sought to make provision for the survival of every Israelite house, Moses could ascertain from God Himself that the daughters of Zelophehad spoke rightly in laying claim to their father's inheritance (Numbers 27:7). The ruling did not become a basis for equal inheritance of daughters with sons in rabbinic law. Rather, daughters and their descendents took second place to any surviving sons and their descendants. But daughters came ahead of any other claimants including fathers, brothers, sisters, grandfathers, and the rest of the relations of the deceased. And male heirs were obligated to support their unmarried sisters, even if the provision of support reduced the men to beggary. Commenting on the biblical provision, *Sifre* remarks, "Man prefers men to women, but the Creator shows equal consideration to all."[63]

Our ideas of equality may differ from those of Moses or the Rabbis. Such alterations are inevitable with the change of social and economic circumstances. Where we look for recognitions of autonomy, earlier sources may seek equality in the provision of maintenance. Not every age or situation makes possible the economic role of the strong woman pictured and celebrated in Proverbs 31, who invests in foreign trade and agricultural real estate while carrying on a flourishing textile and garment industry under her own roof. Such a woman is a fitting examplar of the biblical ideal of economic self-sufficiency and is textually regarded as the just recipient not only of her children's praises but of the profits of her enterprise. Her activities are not found in every epoch and are not possible in every social circumstance. What is constant is the ideal of dignity that emerges from her portrayal even more clearly than the tableaux of the enterprises on which her particular realization of that dignity depends. Edith Hamilton writes:

The Bible . . . looks at women as human beings, no better and no worse than men. . . . The Old Testament writers, writing of a general's great victory, Barak's over "Sisera with his chariots and his multitude," would set down how he cried out to a woman when she bade him go fight, "If thou wilt go with me, then will I go: but if thou wilt not go with me, then will I not go." And Deborah answered, "I will surely go with thee." Bad women and faulty women are plainly dealt with. . . . "A continual dropping on a very rainy day and a contentious woman are alike," but the criticisms are always reasonable and well founded. So too is the praise. After a long acquaintance with the remarkable ladies of the romancers and poets of other lands, it is refreshing to stand on firm ground with the author of the last chapter of *Proverbs*, whose mother, we are told, had taught him, and who had never an idea that woman was the lesser man or some bright angelic visitant.[64]

In the prophetic idiom the Mosaic themes are not discarded but taken up, sublated and sublimated, reinterpreted and redefined: where the biblical law had provided ritual means for the purging of unexpiated guilt, the prophets demand spiritual cleanliness and moral purity, drawing more explicitly from the Mosaic repertoire of themes the underlying premise that there is more to man than what lives and works and dies, not an afterlife, necessarily, but a dimension of our being that is not exhausted by our overt acts but lives on a level of the unseen, the level of prayer and intention, social act and omission as well as social presence in the Temple throng or fighting force. The idea is not absent in the Mosaic canon. Indeed it is implicit there throughout, in the ritual concern with unaccounted blood, which might pollute the land (Deuteronomy 21:7), in the institution of the Sabbath, and even in the self-revealing words of Cain, the splendid dramatic irony of his intended sarcasm before God: "Am I my brother's keeper?" But in the Prophets, the Mosaic theme of an unseen dimension becomes more than an explicit thesis—"man does not live by bread alone, but by everything that issues from the mouth of the Lord does man live" (Deuteronomy 8:3). It becomes an organizing, structuring principle: Social and spiritual obligations are linked with moral responsibilities, and their onus rests on the same unitary individual who, as the Mosaic law insisted, must be held accountable for his own actions.

The prophetic recasting of the Mosaic message is a simplification of that message, not in the sense of detraction from any of its elements—for all remain present and accessible in the Law as a public document—but as an underscoring of its principles and a synthesis of their themes. Thus an Amos can mention a particular prohibition, the keeping of men's garments in pledge (2:8), and reenliven the outrage of its violation into a symbol indicative of the full range of social neglect. He can castigate luxury or present the Temple cult as an obscenity, in view of the hypocrisy implicit in the moral standing of those who rely upon it for their sanctimonious spiritual exercises (Amos 5:12–24; cf. Malachi 1:7–8). Isaiah likewise: "Hear God's word, ye Lords of Sodom"—so, the prophet addresses the great ones of Judah and Jerusalem, fearless of the Kings whose names are prefaced to his message, including the one (Menassah) who put him to death—

> Give ear to the Torah of our God, you people of Gomorrah: "What need have I of your many sacrifices," saith the Lord, "I am surfeited with burnt offerings of rams. . . . When you come before me, who sought this of you, to trample My courts? Bring Me no more false oblations. Incense is loathsome. . . . I shall not bear iniquity in assembly. . . . When you pray at length, I do not hear; your hands are full of blood. Wash and cleanse, remove the evil of your doings. . . . Seek justice, aid the oppressed, defend the fatherless and take the part of the widow. Come now, let us reason together," saith the Lord, "though your sins be red as scarlet, they shall be as wool." (Isaiah 1:11–18).

A Micah (6:8) can sum up the full requirement of God from man as presented in the Torah: "only this—to do justice, to love kindness, and humbly to walk with your God." The reduction is a synthesis, not a winnowing.[65] Like the words of Hillel (*Shabbat* 31a), which it antici-pates, Micah's summation could well be accompanied by the rider, "The rest is commentary. Go and learn it." For the entire Torah can be construed as interpretive commentary, giving concrete definition and material content to the ideals of justice, kindness and humility. The prophets do not merely comment on the Mosaic norms. They voice the principles on which those norms and the accompanying narra-tives are commentary. The prophets synthesize, but their act of syn-thesis is analytic. It joins together the threads of abstraction to reform a living fabric, and the apprehension of the pattern in that fabric demands scrutiny of their own lives by all who critically confront it. The individual who emerges from wrestling with a Micah or an Amos—*a fortiori* with Isaiah or the Book of Job—will not be one who can complacently assume that the world was made for his amuse-ment or for his family's prosperity. The acid cynicism of Ecclesiastes dissolves shallow worldliness, just as the Israelite irony ("Weren't there any graves in Egypt?") dissolves all complacent afterworldli-ness.

The idea of universal human brotherhood and the idea of the consent of the governed are two of the social corollaries of the related biblical ideas of men's universal existential equality and dignity before their Creator. In Mosaic terms the relationship between God and creation is construed contractually, as a covenant entered freely by God and by His creatures: Israel has a covenant with God, and the people are seen publicly and unanimously accepting its responsibilities upon themselves, clearly recognizing and accepting their responsibility for the misfortunes that will follow any failure of theirs to abide by its terms—that is, to uphold the morally and symbolically freighted precepts of the divine law.[66] It is perhaps necessary in this context, where so much of our familiar and wishful thinking about covenants and promises centers on the ideas of rights and privileges, to emphasize a more elementary dimension of the idea that the covenant between God and Israel is a contract: The consent of the governed is a consent to be governed. It involves the assumption of duties, and that assumption is construed to be corporate and for all time, not individual and not contingent, but existential. When Israelites undertake to observe God's laws and customs, to keep the Sabbath as an eternal sign between themselves and God, to tell their children of the exodus from Egypt, they are making commitments as a people, not only to the preservation of their peoplehood, but to the preservation of a specific reading of the significance of that peoplehood. They are bringing to bear the full resources of culture and familial tradition to ensure that the core values which locate and lock that significance in place will not be lost.

The duties and the dignities which the tradition embeds and embodies will be sacred to the community. The community itself becomes an object of concern insofar as it bears the values and ideas that impart its identity. But the community as such will not become sacred. It will not become an end in itself. Even the idea of a king or ruler other than God, ultimately even the idea of a human messiah, will become morally and therefore intellectually problematic. The individual must not 'break away' from the community. But he is not the creature of the community. Rather, the community exists to foster the growth of the individual, whose adequate development is definitionally assumed to feed and foster the growth, perpetuation and advancement of the community.

The biblical figure for the covenantal relationship between Israel and God is that of a marriage relationship or a relationship between parent and child. A marital relationship is not simply an agreement for the exchange of goods or services but a commitment of one's being. A parent-child relationship is not simply abrogated for "nonperformance of specified duties" or nonrecognition of due obligations. God, the prophets say, reflecting on the vicissitudes of history, may chastise His people, but will not forsake them. The people, for their part, in committing themselves to God and God's law for all generations, are recognizing an existential bond with one another, a bond that goes beyond the literally contractual and extends into their conception of their identities as individuals, in reference to the common history they have experienced, the common situation they now confront, and the common destiny they pursue, as fellow Israelites, as sharers in a particular transpersonal, intergenerational confrontation with God.

In the post-Mosaic prophets the implicit Mosaic imagery of a marriage compact is more fully developed: the relationship freely accepted in the course of its duration has established bonds that neither God nor man can abrogate arbitrarily. God will not forsake His children nor the wife He has espoused—or, placing God in the maternal role, God will give suck to Her children at Jerusalem and not forsake them.[67] The existential recognition of God for humanity extends not only to Israel but to all nations: this too is a covenant, with all the children of Noah, requiring of them humane observances, the rejection of murder, blasphemy and the like. Primordially there is a covenant (whose sign is the rainbow) with nature at large, by which God guarantees the world against another, future cataclysm. God's promise of stability to nature is one foundation of the rootedness of biblical naturalism in biblical monotheism. For God's grace, operative in nature, is the fundament of the stability of natural law, and natural law in turn is the foundation of the belief in a universal and objective Goodness, the concept by which monotheism purifies the idea of God itself.[68]

That Israel's relationship with God and with God's law is corporate and cultural goes hand in hand with the expectation that this relationship is existential and unique. Uniqueness follows from the fact that every nation's cultural history, in its depth and complexity, progressively determines a distinctive path—in literature, in art, in law—as individual determination and decisions demarcate the finer scale of our personal paths and odysseys. It is by reason of the uniqueness of the determinations that transform general values into concrete decisions that no two literary classics or artistic masterpieces are identical. Israel's historic commitment of its corporate culture in a determinate way to the intepretation of the commands of the Transcendent God forever sets the terms of reference of the norms of Jewish tradition and defines the large categories to which reference will be made: Truth and goodness, for example, will always be construed here as inseparable. Since the values are universal, the principle, stated at such a level of generality, may appear to be vacuous or commonplace. But even at this level, subtle determinations have been made—truth, not relativity or emptiness; goodness, not power or cunning. And as the elaboration unfolds in detail, historically, the uniqueness becomes pronounced. The theme is not exclusivity, for the values enunciated invite emulation, but there is a distinctiveness in the mode of articulation sufficient that commitments are made to symbolic modes which will appear arbitrary if viewed externally to their own logic. We are to have no other God; and, while the God of the Universe cannot be conceived to have no other people, He will know no other people in quite the way that He has known Israel. This fact, arising from Israel's unique civilizational consciousness, as we have seen, confers obligations, interpreting Israel's mission as a nation set apart, a nation of priests. Israel must be a light to the nations of the world, and a blessing to them—construed by the rabbis to mean that those who observe the behavior of individual Israelites and witness the ethos of the Torah should be moved to say: Blessed is the man whose God is that man's God.

The rabbis record that in the Temple of Jerusalem sacrifice was offered for atonement of all nations' sins (*Sukkah* 55b). In the Prophets the universality of God's goverance as Creator, Ruler and Judge generates a universalism with regard to the nations that is deeply rooted in the Abrahamic idea of God's universal justice. The prophets cannot conceive of the exclusion of all humanity and all nature from the ultimate consummation that the projection of God's plan is clearly understood to intend: All nations worship God, wittingly or unwittingly. All will participate in the universal peace brought about by knowledge of the Lord, which will well up and cover the earth like water. None will be excluded from the prosperity and dignity of that peace; when they shall beat their swords into ploughshares and their spears into pruning hooks, nation shall not wage war against nation and men shall no longer study warfare.[69] When the prophetic ideals are more conceptually spelled out by the rabbis, the most powerful yearning for freedom and national self-determination coexists (with seeming paradox in world historical terms, but with the utmost moral naturalness) alongside an explicit renunciation of all desire for worldly domination: The nations whom hardship or custom have rendered wolfish or lionish in their ethos will lie peacefully with their more pastoral fellow peoples, as a direct result of the ideas of the divine law going forth from Jerusalem. Israel shall be the little child that leads them, not by power of coercion or threat of violence, but by example. Living by her laws, Israel will demonstrate the strength and wealth of human goodness, and other nations, whether peaceable or turbulent in their past histories, will willingly follow and build upon Israel's example.[70]

The identity articulated by the prophets is that of the moral person, the social critic, visionary of the virtualities of defeat or triumph that lie implicit in each course of action, demystifier of God's intent. Boldness, as the rabbis tell us, is a requisite of prophets, and Maimonides argues that prophecy will not be restored until Israel has regained autonomy in her land, for in exile and subjection, Israel's spiritually inclined and insightful men and women, who have the philosophic and poetic gifts of prophets, lack the confidence to voice their visions publicly—or even to experience them clearly and articulately.[71] The moral courage of a Moses to confront a Pharaoh, or of a Nathan to use parable to bring the passionate King David to pass sentence on his own act (2 Samuel 12), or of an Elijah (1 Kings 18:18) to answer King Ahab: "It is not I that have troubled Israel, but you and your father's house, by abandoning the commandments of the Lord"—such courage in all its instances is the product of the prophetic sense of mission, a commitment which defines a personality and sets its alienation from its times into an articulate vision and prescription. The outcome is not merely an eremitic wailing or withdrawal, but a vivid analysis of the source and remedy of grievance, a historical conspectus that refuses to submerge itself in mere chronicling of national or royal glories, and a spiritual consciousness that is above isolating itself in mystic *ascesis* or sacerdotal complacency. As Amos expresses the compelling urgency which individuates the prophet: "The lion hath roared, who will not fear? The Lord God hath spoken, who can but prophesy?" This too—the compelling urgency of moral truth—is never lost to the successors and heirs of the prophets. It becomes the existential basis of a civil right, the right of free thought and free expression (cf. Job 4:2, 7:11), but it retains a broader base than that, voicing the sense of urgency that lies behind the quest for truth at large and the desire to impart it once discovered. Maimonides articulates this sense of urgency in the idiom of his emanative metaphysics (*Guide* 2.11, 12), generalizing his conception of the highest phase of charity: It is the desire to explain, to write books, to make others capable in thought much as God does not withhold but imparts being and truth, to make all things, as it were, self-sufficient, in their being, in their actions, and in their understanding, for only God is self-sufficient absolutely.

4. The Rabbinic Idiom

The achievements of the rabbinic literature relative to our theme are again to recast, reformulate and reconstruct. The new idiom is studious, dialectical, respectful of sources and deferential to precedents, punctilious with distinctions. Superficially the rabbis seem prone to view the biblical revelations more as oracular words—springboards and pegs of doctrine—than as great moral laws. Yet beneath the apparent manhandling of language and texts, they are profoundly sensitive to the conceptual issues, the moral and spiritual thematics of the authentic tradition. The rabbis save the world of biblical norms in a context alien, hostile and in a practical sense overwhelming, by intellectualizing the life of Torah, transforming Torah in large measure from the pragmatic rule of society to a realm of ritual and intellectual virtuality, where the Temple cult is not practiced but studied, where prayer replaces sacrifice as the principal vehicle of spiritual expression, where talmudic *haverim*, fellows or associates of the rabbinic collegiality, seek to observe the laws of Levitical purity as a kind of reenactment of the old priestly function, laying claim to a spiritualized and intellectualized successorship to the priests, and making every family table a ritual surrogate of the altar of the Temple in Jerusalem.[72]

The initial task of the Rabbis and their predecessors who laid down the case law that is constitutive in the Mishnah was to delineate the applicability of the biblical legislation in concrete cases. It was in this sense that the rabbinical authorities (like the Justices of the American Supreme Court) were interpreters, not legislators. None of them was a Moses or even a Hosea. As the discussions of their decisions eddied and swirled to form the body of material that makes up the Mishnaic code and its extensive and digressive commentary, the Gemara, much was swept into the discourse of common sense, allegory, ritual fastidiousness, legend, logic, homily, rhetoric, hyperbole, superstition, word play, philosophy, anecdote, science and lore. The engulfed material was of all degrees of relevance and of all qualities. Narrowness and cosmopolitanism, cynicism, despair, sophistication, piety, and skepticism came together with optimism, idealism, hope, credulity and critical analysis.

Looking back on the priestly heritage with some ambivalence, the rabbis could mourn sincerely for the loss of the Temple cult, with its clearcut therapy of atonement "for all your sins," while at the same time striking a melancholy ironic note, reflecting on the possibility that the high priest who conducted the rites of atonement might well be an illiterate. To be not of the *sons* of Aaron but of the *disciples* of Aaron was the rabbis' ideal.[73] They looked back on the destruction of the microcosm centered spiritually in the Temple cult with a mixture of nostalgia, grief and hope for something new, which they would help to build—a way of life whose expressive values were as skewed to those of the priests as were those of the Prophetic age to the age of the Patriarchs. Much that would unfold of the rabbinic way of life and system of values would be self-stultifying or even self-euthanatizing. The narrowness and superstition of some of the rabbinic attitudes and beliefs would place a mark on Judaism from which it would take centuries to recover. The process of sifting sense from nonsense in the rabbinic corpus is not yet completed, and in some quarters has not yet begun. Yet for the critical and watchful miner, these veins yield gold.

Commenting on a particularly astute affirmation of divine transcedence by the sages, Maimonides remarks, "Would that all their words were like it!"[74] The miasmic character of much that is found in the rabbinic sources renders all the more brilliant and beaconlike the important thematic insights of the greatest of the rabbis. Many are pertinent to our theme: rabbinic bookishness bespeaks an intellectualism that is not an unworthy reflex of the spiritual purity and earnestness of the prophetic books and that blossoms as a reverence for the intrinsic value of learning; Torah for its own sake becomes a motto in the rabbinic canon. And the meaning of 'Torah' shifts from nominal, practical norm to intellectual, active study. Study of Torah, i.e., study of the rabbinic apprehensions of God's Law, becomes a value held worthy to be weighed against the entire prescriptive content of the Law itself.[75] Talmudic study is recognized to be an open-ended quest without the sense of defeat that prior generations had felt at the thought of an unending exploration,[76] and the subject active in such study is the individual, abetted by a catena of study partners who link each scholar, mind to mind, with the lively community of fellow scholars in all lands and ages. The goal of the inquiry is the perfecting of the understanding of the individual. Paradoxically, but perhaps predictably, the maturation of talmudic study as a way of life led to a hardening which limited independent explorations for those who lived and worked within the prescribed tradition. Yet it called forth, almost demanded, the most independent and creative intellectual and artistic explorations for those who ventured forth from it, in or even near its penumbra, to test its categories, claims and values in the larger world that was their proper sphere.

Practical fulfillment of the Torah as a way of life was, of course, not discarded; but it too underwent a sea change. The Tannaim (the Mishnaically cited authorities of the 1st century B.C.E. to the 2nd century C.E.) and Amoraim (the Talmudic elaborators of the written Mishnah after its compilation by Judah the Prince in the 2nd century) saw their task as one of concretizing the biblical norms, defining their boundaries and marshalling or corralling them into a system. Some brittleness in the new complex was perhaps an inevitable byproduct of the process. Precautionary extension and delimitation were natural as well, all based on the distinctively rabbinic sensitivity to biblical thematics. But hardening was not inevitable, and limits were consciously set to the growth of rigorism and the overgrowth of legalism. The rabbinic maxim was that biblical commandments and the rabbinic ordinances regarded as their interpretations (e.g., the daily strapping on of phylacteries for prayer by way of fulfilling God's commandment to keep the divine imperatives constantly before our eyes and to "bind them for a sign upon thy hand"—Deuteronomy 11:18) were to be performed not slavishly for the sake of a reward but "for the sake of heaven"[77]—for their own sake as intrinsic goods, because they were the will of God, and thus, as symbolic acts of worship and spiritual expression.

The idea of infusing every moment of life (waking, and even sleeping, if the ritual codes are heeded fully) with the awareness of God's presence was not unworthy of the prophetic spirituality and the Mosaic goal of imparting holiness to all creaturely acts. Even when history and the circumstances of exile and persecution had robbed the biblical commandments of their full robustness as a military, political, economic, and social code, the surviving community, conceiving itself as the providential remnant spoken of by the prophets (e.g., Zaphaniah 3:13), could still infuse the entirety of internal communal and personal life with the mission of holiness prescribed in the Torah of Moses and kept alive at the familial and communal levels in marriage and family law, in the commercial dealings among Israelites that external powers allowed to be regulated internally, in spiritual and intellectual exercises and acts of worship, and

in ritual expressions such as those embedded in the dietary laws of
kashrut, the clothing regulations which the Law prescribed and custom elaborated, the regulations of Sabbath observance, and the rituals
and proprieties of the festivals and fasts which the calendar appointed.[78]

Again, the ultimate subject of all these dimensions of what came
to be identified as Jewish life was the ultimate moral agent, the individual, articulated in the community and assigned a role and a goal
by the norms of the community, but regarded in those norms as a
freely choosing agent whose life could be imbued with holiness and
made as a whole an act of worship, by the suitable inclination of
moral choice. The perfection of the life of the individual remained the
goal. And again the outcome was twofold: the notion that fulfillment
of the divine commandments was an end in itself rather than a means
to an end (a notion vigorously rejected by Maimonides in *Guide* 3:31;
he argued, as we have observed, that the commandments serve to
promote the good life materially, morally, and intellectually) fed
upon rabbinic legalism to generate a kind of legal positivism which
no longer had regard for the moral, spiritual and intellectual thematics of the Law.[79] Or alternatively (and in widely varying degrees and
types of combination), the same rabbinic idea, the idea of the intrinsic
value of the *mitzvot* as divine commandments, allowed the moral,
intellectual and spiritual values that had inspired the articulation and
interpretation of those commandments to percolate through them to
every aspect of daily life, throughout each workday, Sabbath or festi-
val, imparting the intentionality of holiness to each human act or ges-
ture and creating a realm for the expression of true piety even in
seemingly trivial human choices and experiences.

The moral problematic of sifting legalism (and its accompanying
obscurantism, authoritarianism, dogmatism, patriarchalism, and the
rest) from piety (and its accompanying adventure of the intellect and
spirit and challenge to the will, patience and personal character) rested, of course, upon the individual, the same who was the subject and
the victim or beneficiary of the system at large. As Elijah, the Gaon of
Wilna, remarked (the tradition in my family is that both of my mother's parents were descendants of his): Torah, like rain, nourishes both
beneficial plants and noxious weeds (*ad* Proverbs 24:31, 25:4), It was
the modulation of inner human choice that determined whether beautiful or ugly characters emerged from engagement with the Law.

Both the Bible and the Talmud are the products of many hands
and many centuries. If we include within the literature of the rabbinic

mode of expression the Responsa, Codes, Midrashic elaborations of the legal (halakhic) and narrative (aggadic) aspects of the tradition, we can say that rabbinic literature continues in the talmudic mode down to the present day. The biblical idiom, by contrast, speaks in so commanding a voice that only commentaries remain possible: imitations would be parodies, and even the commentaries often fall victim to their material, submerged in the authority of its nexus and unable to do more than follow and elaborate its themes or stories, expatiate on its words, elaborate on its laws, compare interpretations of its sense, dissociate or reassociate its parts and strands and elements, or otherwise catch hold of its beauties or lose themselves in its forests. Some resynthesize a way of life or thought congruent with those that scripture projects; others fail to rise to a synthetic grasp of the scriptural values and ideas. The Talmud can be a window on the scriptural world, but only when scripture itself is not submerged, reduced to the handmaid of rabbinics.

Talmudic discourse, with all its Aramaic jargon and technical shorthand has one great advantage over biblical discourse, related to that of being a living if at present rather arid stream—perhaps a *wadi*, parched at times, but in season alive with torrents and freshets like the flood channels, the *afiqim* of the Negev, which are made the simile of our life by the psalmist (Psalms 126:4). The advantage lies in the dialectical character of rabbinic discourse. Glossing God's use of the first person plural in the Genesis cosmology ("Let us make . . ."), the rabbis remark that even God does not set about His undertaking without consultation.[80] With rare exceptions (like the Book of Job, the heart of which is a sustained and concerted dialogue, and perhaps Ecclesiastes and the Song of Songs, which seem to me to be rooted in an internal or even fantasy dialogic structure) the biblical voice is not dialogic. Prophecy speaks with the authority of God Himself. Rarely does it expect its sentences to be answered. Rabbinically there is constant conversation and cross-talk, with voices raising and addressing problems about the Torah or about one another's proposals and their implications, sometimes in a dialectic that extends across centuries, as opposing or potentially opposing views are juxtaposed from the full range of the rabbinic canon and with reference to the full range of the biblical canon. No possibly relevant corner of experience, science or lore is excluded from view. That the resultant discourse should emerge as anything more than noise is a tribute to the thematic coherence of the rabbinic problematic and to the discipline of the redactors and students of the rabbinic materials. The exposition was anything but conceptual in its structuring and idiom. Yet to the scholars whose familiarity with the written and 'oral' canon was intimate, a remark in any sector could instantly illuminate almost any other, with never a fear that the insight afforded would be less than germane. The establishment of dialogue as the basis of the talmudic discourse ensures that the rabbinic literature becomes and remains conscious and critical—far more self-conscious and far more self-critical than the authoritative biblical idiom ever could become.

Rabbinic humanism is the fairest achievement of the two thousand years of rabbinic discourse elaborating upon the biblical themes in this dialectical mode. The rabbis apply the full rigor of the legalism and proceduralism which they derive from the Torah and the Prophets to mitigate the severities and asperities of the Torah and Prophets themselves. Thus the laws of evidence and testimony are forged into a powerful obstacle to capital punishment: not only must two witnesses concur independently and in circumstantial detail before the presumption of innocence gives way in capital cases, but there must also have been explicit warning to the criminal immediately prior to his act for an offense to count as capital.[81] No self-incriminating testimony is even admissible as evidence. For, it is argued, a person may have a desire to die.[82] Duress is out of the question. Ancient survivals like the "bitter waters" are quickly hedged about with restrictions rendering them of no practical legal relevance[83]—giving another meaning to the more familiar method of "establishing a hedge about the Torah" by way of enlarging its restrictions marginally to protect their core intent. The court that issued a single death sentence in seven years was known as the bloody Sanhedrin (*Makkot* 1.10).

In similar spirit it was held that breaching of any commandment save those against idolatry (specifically, public and symbolic desecration of the core principles of the Law), incest (construed to include adultery), and murder was permissible for the sake of saving a human life. The proof text: "You shall observe My institutions and My ordinances, which a man shall perform and live by. I am the Lord." The biblical conception of a law of life is taken here in a distinctive sense that makes explicit the idea that the service of life—its preservation and enhancement—are cardinal and overriding principles of the Law.[84] Thus it is permissible to break the Sabbath in order to save or even to protect a human life or to relieve pain.[85] It is obligatory that cattle should be milked on the Sabbath, to prevent "the suffering of living beings." The cravings of a pregnant woman allow violation of the fast of the Day of Atonement, on the theory that such promptings of the appetite might be signals of vital significance. And, in general, the demands of ravenous hunger are to be answered, even if meeting such needs requires violation of the dietary laws.[86]

Rabbinic humanism is typified in the Mishnaic implementation of the agricultural laws by which the Torah had sought to put into practice the requirements of fellowship, cementing the Israelite community as a nation: seeking definition for the biblical requirement that the corners of the field are left unharvested for the poor, the rabbis discover that the size of the corner, like the measure of good deeds in general, is one of the few things upon which the biblical law places no upper limit. The rabbis specify a minimum but leave the upper limit open and praise the practice of one community in harvesting with a rope (presumably as a labor-saving expedient), and adding to the 'corners' left for the welfare of the poor the extra portion of unharvested grain. Rabbinically, again, the laws of the 'corner' are extended to vineyards and orchards as well as fields.[87] The rabbis were confident that they understood the nisus of the law and thus could act to expand its coverage without concern that they might unwittingly undermine some unknown and unfathomable hidden object.

Using as their axiom the principle that biblical laws exist to promote and enhance human lives, the rabbis laid down rules for the regulation of wages, hours, commerce, prices and profits.[88] Their mandate as 'interpreters' came from the spirit of the biblical laws which forbade retention of a day worker's wages overnight or taking a millstone in pledge.[89] Even the so-called natural laws of self-preservation were modified by the requirements of ethical principle. To kill a would-be murderer was to prevent his sin, not merely to protect the victim; and one could not commit a murder even to save one's own life—for example, if ordered to murder another or die oneself. One must rather die, the Talmud ordains, "for who knows that your blood is redder than his. Perhaps his blood is redder than yours."[90] Even to save an entire group one could not single out one to be given up for death or defilement.[91]

The talmudic rabbis find basis in the Torah for the institution of free universal education,[92] and Maimonides finds a clear basis, in the rabbinic program of eliciting the life-affirming values of the Torah, for rejecting the ethos of asceticism, which exerted so powerful a hold upon Hellenistic, late ancient, and medieval thought and practice.[93] Guiding the entire progress of rabbinic elaboration is the delicately balanced assumption that perfection of the individual human life is the Law's concern, but that no human individual can live an adequate or fulfilled life in isolation. Rather, our condition is one of universal interdependence, and its quality, the very possibility of human dignity, depends upon mutal recognition, generosity of thought and action.[94]

The rabbis took seriously their role as arbiters of the meaning of the Law at its immediate point of applicability. They did not hesitate to use their authority, which in their theory was Sinaitic, even to reverse the plain sense of biblical commandments, where they saw a literal interpretation to produce rulings which would run counter to the larger thrust of the Law as they understood it on the basis of its specific themes. They proudly pictured Moses as unable to follow the technical debates of rabbinic jurists and argued that even signs from Heaven had no authority against the majority vote of the duly constituted court: the Torah was no longer in heaven but on earth, and the task of interpreting it was unavoidably man's, not God's.[95] Reading the biblical accounts of actions which seemed lawless by their standards, the rabbis did not hesitate to embroider their own legalism and proceduralism over entire episodes, using that amazing synchronicity which at once ironed flat the sense of history and opened the entire corpus of scripture to them as a living florilegium of exempla. From the biblical injunction against destruction of fruit trees in time of siege they derive the categorical commandment which they perceive as its underlying premise: "Thou shalt not wantonly destroy" (*Bal tashchit*).[96] The inference typifies the rabbinic approach: the laws separating meat from dairy foods and utensils elaborate upon the repeated biblical injunction against seething a kid in its mother's milk;[97] the laws of slaughter (*shekhittah*) elaborate again upon biblical requirements, reaching an optimum, Maimonides argues, in balancing concerns of humaneness and household economy.[98] The Holy One, blessed be He, the rabbis urge, is not too lofty to be concerned with the accessibility and cost of meat to the humblest household.

The dimension and direction of rabbinic elaboration is never arbitrary. To elaborate a law one must first grasp its intention, apprehend the values it seeks to serve. Without such understanding one could as easily forbid joining the *names* of milk and meat or prohibit the *purchase* of leather from improperly slaughtered animals. With an understanding of the relation of the dietary laws to the symbolization of purity (as specified biblically), the modalities of their elaboration become clear enough to suggest themselves for discussion. One rabbi asks: "What difference does it make to the Holy One, blessed be He, whether one slaughters animals by cutting their throats or chopping off their heads? One must say that the *mitzvot* were given only to purify humankind" (*Bereshit Rabbah* 44). Purification can be read in two ways here: as an arbitrary discipline or as a discipline with a content relevant to its outcome. The former reading is that of legal positivism; the latter, of rationalism. Regardless of what I say, each reader of this essay will decide individually which interpretation bears more truth or value. I justify my preference for the rationalist view on the grounds that the purification produced by an arbitrary discipline is only that of obedience to authority, a virtue in Platonic 'auxiliaries,' but not in a people whose task it is to become a kingdom of priests and a holy nation (Exodus 19:6). Nachmanides glosses more trenchantly: "The commandments were given "to purify men"—that is, to make them like refined silver. For one who refines silver does not act arbitrarily or capriciously, but to remove any impurity. So the *mitzvot* serve to purge from our hearts all corrupt notions, to awaken us to the truth and remind us of it continually. . . . Their benefit accrues not to God . . . but to us—to instill compassion in us . . . develop a soul that is purified and refined, so that we grow wise and alive to the truth."[99]

Every symbol contains something of the arbitrary, without which there would be nothing to signal that it was a symbol rather than simply an unmeaning act. But symbols address intelligence and invite the effort to interpret and understand. To obey out of love is to obey in the understanding that grows from love and enhances love in turn. To obey for the sake of obedience is not to purify but often simply to stultify by isolating act from understanding and thought from the love that might have been its motive.

5. Conclusion

If we draw together and sum up the values encountered in the Mosaic, Prophetic and rabbinic articulations of Judaic concepts about the individual and the community, we find an emphasis on economic autonomy as a root and fruit of freedom, a recognition of the moral and spiritual irreducibility of the individual to any social or economic function—we are valued for what we are, not solely for what we do as 'useful' or 'productive' members of society—a central emphasis on the ethical responsibility of the individual as the author of choice, and an attendant dignity in choicemaking and accountability, a strict legalism and proceduralism, placed in the service not merely of social order but of individual rights, conceived of as positive deserts. The conception of individual interest does not excuse but explicitly includes moral, social and spiritual dimensions of growth and per- fectibility. As a means to such growth, particular, often distinctive institutions—laws, rituals, symbolic expressions—are placed in the service of human moral development and spiritual evocation. And dialogue, criticism and comparison run a tireless course through his- tory, striking off, as they pass, the most protrusive or disharmonious edges of tradition, while actually sharpening the more central and integrated categories, values and intellectual distinctions. The living tradition of rabbinic humanism, in the values it articulates and in its subtle shifting in the angle of a judge's seat from that of arbiter to that of arbitrator, still has much to offer to the larger world culture from which it has sprung and to which it has already given much.

The life which the Law was given to preserve, promote and per- fect is the life of the human individual. The rabbis underscore the value of that life when they write homiletically that whoever slays a single human being is as though he had destroyed the world; whoev- er saves a single human life, as though he had saved the world. They argue not only from the progeny who might have descended from one couple, but from the fact of human uniqueness: Ordinary mortal craftsmen form things in a mold, and every exemplar is alike. But when the Holy One, blessed be He, sets about to form humanity, no two individuals from the human mold are identical.[100] Each is a unique and irreplaceable world of possibilities, and as such each is sacred. Shmuel Sambursky, the Israeli physicist and historian of theo- ries of nature, used to compare this teaching of the rabbinic sages with the immense difficulty thinkers in the Greek philosophic tradi- tion had in accepting and situating the idea of uniqueness: from Plato, who placed value, truth, being, and even unity at the level of the uni- versal, to Aristotle, who argued that there is no science of the individ- ual and that all that individuates particulars is accidental to their true being, down to the late neo-Platonists, who struggled with the notion of a universal yet individual 'guardian spirit', and Averroes, who held that you and I are one individual save for the matter that divides us, all of the thinkers who followed the gnomic advice of Heraclitus, "Look to the common," were bemused at the fact of individuality and tended to regard uniqueness as tantamount to idiosyncrasy and hence irrationality.

But following their biblically mediated intuitions, the rabbis dis- covered value in the very fact of uniqueness: if man is created in the image of God, that is in part because each human being, like God, will be unique. The value discovered in this uniqueness, we might say, is like that of an entire living species, which in its way exhausts, explores and gropes to transcend its own world of possibilities. The value of community is attendant on this prior value. Aristotle showed the value of the community by arguing that man by nature is a social animal. It is because of the social (and resultant cultural) side of human biology that so many of the Aristotelian virtues and vices are (culturally mediated) social dispositions—affability, niggardliness, magnificence, magnanimity. The Torah, which the rabbis structure into system not only as a legal but as a cultural foundation, addresses the same fact, man's social nature, in its own language. It mediates the gap between individuality and community, as Aristotle does, but in its own idiom, which is mythic where Aristotle is conceptual, historic and particular where Aristotle is scientific and universal, intimate and normative where Aristotle is objective and descriptive. It records (Genesis 2:18): "And the Lord God said, 'It is not good for the man to be alone'."

Notes

1. *Sefer Ha-Chukkim* (The Statutes of Israel) 1980, 163; cited by jurists as *S.H.*, officially translated in corresponding volumes as *Laws of the State of Israel*, (*L.S.I.*). The principle legislated in 1980 was founded on the doctrine of the Israel Declaration of Independence, 1948 (1 *L.S.I.* 3): "The State of Israel . . . will foster the development of the country for the benefit of all its inhabitants; it will be based on freedom, justice and peace as envisaged by the prophets of Israel. . . ." The Supreme Court of Israel ruled that the Declaration did not have constitutional or legal force but did express "the vision of the people and its credo" and contains "the guiding principles for the interpretation of statutes." Ze'ev *v.* Acting District Officer of Tel Aviv, *H.C.* 10/48, in *Selected Judgments of the Supreme Court of Israel* 68, and Shtreit *v.* the Chief Rabbi of Israel, *H.C.* 301/63, 18 *P.D.* 11/598.

2. *Haggadah shel Pesach: Ve-hayu sham le-goy . . .*—"And there they became a nation."

3. See Becker 1968 (1932); Cuddihy 1974; Gay 1978; Kamenka 1972 (1962); Carlebach 1978.

4. Exodus 21:1–6, Deuteronomy 15:12–18. Some modern commentators claim that the law (Deuteronomy 23:16) forbidding return of fugitive

slaves could never have been enforced, as its effect would be to abolish involuntary servitude. But that, surely, was the intention.

5. Leviticus 25:8–18.

6. Numbers 18:20–24; cf. 34–35.

7. Deuteronomy 23:20–21; Exodus 22:24.

8. Deuteronomy 15:1–10; Leviticus 25:1–7.

9. See Soss 1973, pp. 323–44; cf. Henry George's appreciation of Moses.

10. 1 Kings 4:25, 2 Kings 18:31, Zechariah 3:10; cf. Proverbs 27:18, etc. For the rabbinic continuance of the ideal of economic self-sufficiency, e.g., *Avot de Rabbi Natan* 31: 29a (Cohen).

11. Hillel established the device of transposing private debts into public obligations. This device, known as the *prosbul* (lit. "for the Court"), mitigated the effects of biblical remission (*shemittah*), allowing the continuation of credit even in the face of the sabbatical year. His authority was Deuteronomy 15:9. See Mishnah *Shevi'it* 10.3: 51 (Danby).

12. See Deuteronomy 25:5–10; cf. Genesis 38:8–26. The Torah refers to the preservation of one's brother's name as the basis of the levirate obligation. The effect is to preserve his widow's house. Thus she is the claimant who must grant release when her brother-in-law is unable to fulfill the obligation. The inability becomes regularized with the rise of monogamous norms and exogamous tendencies. Such regularization is provided for in the biblical law of *chalitzah*, levirate release.

13. See Deuteronomy 15:7–8 and *Sifre* Re'eh, *ad loc.*: 116 (Fine and Rosenkrantz); Proverbs 3:27; Ben Sirah 4:3, 34:21; Josephus, *Antiquities* 20, 9.7: 9:505 (Feldman), *Against Apion* ii. 27; Isaiah 10:1, 16–17, 3:14–15; Deuteronomy 27:19. "A community that has no synagogue and no shelter for the poor must first provide for the poor," Judah ben Samuel he-Chasid (d. 1217), *Sefer Chasidim*: 374–5 (Wistinetzki). Cf. *Tosefta Peah* 4.9: Refusal to give charity is tantamount to idolatry. *Shabbat* 104a: charity must "run after the poor," not passively await them.

14. Maimonides' *Code* 7.2, Gifts to the Poor 10.7: 91 (Klein): "The highest rank, than which none is higher, is that of one who upholds the hand of an Israelite reduced to poverty by giving him a grant or loan, or entering into partnership with him or finding work for him, in order to strengthen his hand, so that he will have no need to beg from other people. Of this Scripture says, "Thou shalt sustain him; as a client and a resident shall he live with thee" " (Leviticus 25:35). I translate the Biblical verse according to Mai-

monides' emphasis and Saadiah's conception of the *ger* as a client, which the Rambam here adopts. Cf. Isaac Napaha, *ad* Isaiah 58:8ff. in *Baba Batra* 9b.

15. See Goodman 1990; Agus 1978, chapter 8.

16. Deuteronomy 23:8; cf. Isaiah 19:25. The *fact* that Israel were strangers in Egypt is the reason stated for the commandment. The character of their sojourn is morally irrelevant to the treatment due to descendants of the Egyptians.

17. Leviticus 19:17.

18. Exodus 23:9—"for you know the heart of a stranger." The commandment against mistreating the stranger is repeatedly biblically 36 times. See *Baba Metzia* 59b, Maimonides, *Book of the Commandments*, Introduction, Rule 9: 2:400 (Chavel). Rabbinically the commandment was interpreted as forbidding discriminatory practices, attitudes and expressions. Cf. Deuteronomy 24:17–18, Exodus 22:20.

19. Deuteronomy 10:19, Leviticus 19:34. Relations between Jews and non-Jews in rabbinic legal thought are treated extensively and sensitively in Novak 1983. Valuable historical insights and findings about the early differentiation of group identities between Jews and Christians are contained in Neusner and Frerichs 1985.

20. Leviticus 19:18 and 19:34.

21. Leviticus 18:26; cf. 16:29, 24:22, Numbers 15:30. Cf. Cohen 1919.

22. See Maimonides, "Eight Chapters," 4: 231 (Goodman).

23. Deuteronomy 4:1, 16:20, 30:6, Leviticus 18:5; cf. Deuteronomy 5:33, 8:1, 30:16, 19. And see Mishnah *Avot* 4.24: 79 (Hertz)/ 4.19: 455 (Danby).

24. Deuteronomy 12:8, 13:19; cf. Judges 17:6, 21:25.

25. Leviticus 19:15; see Maimonides' *Code* 14.1, Sanhedrin 20.4–5: 60–61 (Hershman). The proof text for the prohibition against favoring merit is Exodus 23:6: "Thou shalt not wrest the judgment of thy poor in his cause." Maimonides glosses: "Even though he is poor in piety, do not wrest his judgment."

26. Thus in Hammurabi's Code the death penalty for theft was commuted to thirtyfold restitution if the theft was from a royal estate, tenfold if from a gentleman, fivefold if from a commoner. The rules were constant by class, but not uniform. See Driver and Miles 1955, 2, pp. 16–17, article 8; note also the presumption of guilt in article 7.

27. Exodus 23:2–3, Leviticus 19:15 and see note 25 above. Cicero abused Republican principle in claiming that Catiline's conspiracy voided his right of access to the machinery of law.

28. See Exodus 12:49, Leviticus 24:22, Numbers 15:16, 29.

29. See Exodus 24:7, Deuteronomy 17:11; 27:3, 8; 31:11–12, 24–26; etc.

30. The rabbis note at Genesis 1:31 that it is only after the creation of humanity that the world is described as "*very* good."

31. Exodus 21:23–26, Leviticus 24:17–22, Numbers 35: 29–34.

32. Exodus 21:13, 18–19, Numbers 35:9–34.

33. Exodus 21:12, 14; Numbers 35:16–21. Moshe Greenberg 1976 sees an important parallel in adultery, which is deemed a crime by a couple against God (Genesis 20:6, 39:8), not simply by a wife against her husband, Thus there is "no question of permitting the husband to mitigate or cancel the punishment" (see Leviticus 20:10, Deuteronomy 22:22–3), just as there is no royal pardon for murderers. In the sharp Mosaic division between crimes against persons and crimes against property, the latter are never capital.

34. Deuteronomy 24:16. Contrast Hammurabi's rule (230) that the *children* of a negligent builder shall die or that a creditor's son is killed, if a distrained son of a debtor dies on his account (116); an assailant's daughter, if he causes the death by miscarriage of another man's daughter (209–14). See Driver and Miles 1955, 2, pp. 83, 47, 79.

35. Leviticus 26:3 ff.

36. Genesis 18:23 ff.—crucially, there is no acceptance of the notion that all deserve to die. For the mission of Israel: Genesis 22:18.

37. The (circumstantial) agreement of two witnesses, required in capital cases, tilts the presumption in favor of the accused and against the accuser. See Numbers 35:30, Deuteronomy 19:15. Cf. note 81 below for the rabbinic elaborations of biblical proceduralism.

38. Job 10:2, 15; 13:15, 18; 14:17; etc. Cf. *Shevu'ot* 31a. For the legal imagery of Job see my commentary on Saadiah's *Book of Theodicy*, introduction (1988) p. 35, n. 8.

39. Deuteronomy 4:26; cf. 32:1, 31:28, 32:40.

40. See Talcott Parsons et al. 1955, pp. 101–03, 113, 305–06, 356; 1964, pp. 3–8, 43–46, 51 57–77, 97–101, 264; 1966, p. 36. For the ethical principles behind the biblical incest laws see Goodman 1986.

41. Leviticus 18.

42. Genesis 9:20–27; 10:6, 15–20; 9:18.

43. Thus the idiom: *lo' tigalleh 'ervat . . .*—"thou shalt not expose the nakedness of . . ."—the same idiom used to describe Ham's offense in Genesis 9:22–23.

44. For further elaborations on the theme of the sanctity of the individual, see Philo, *The Decalogue* 10.36–43: 7:23–29 (Colson); with *On the Confusion of Tongues* 37.183–198: 4:111–119 (Colson); Brandeis 1915, p. 5; Buber 1947, p. 200; Einstein 1950, p. 23: "The highest principles for our aspirations and judgments are given to us in the Jewish-Christian religious tradition. It is a very high goal which, with our weak powers, we can reach only very inadequately, but which gives a sure foundation to our aspirations and valuations. If one were to take that goal out of its religious form and look merely at its purely human side, one might state it perhaps thus: free and responsible development of the individual, so that he may place his powers freely and gladly in the service of all mankind. There is no room in this for the divinization of a nation, of a class, let alone of an individual. . . . It is only to the individual that a soul is given. And the high destiny of the individual is to serve rather than to rule, or to impose himself in any other way." Cf. Bergson 1977 (1935), p. 95; *Midrash Tanchuma* Nitzavim 25a (S. Buber); Yehiel Michael of Zlotchov in M. Buber 1950, p. 17; and Zusya in M. Buber 1947–8, 1, p. 251.

45. For Job's monogamy, see Ginzberg 1968 (1909), 2:241.

46. Exodus 20:5, 34:14, Deuteronomy 4:24, 5:9, 6:15, 1 Kings 19:10, 14; Joel 2:18, Zechariah 1:14, 8:2.

47. See Goodman 1991, chapter 1.

48. Modern detractors of the ethical affinities of Kantian and Mosaic ethics should recall that the expression of the categorical imperative as a command to treat humanity in self and others as an end and never merely as a means is a restatement of 'love thy neighbor as thyself' in a formulation designed to highlight its humane material content and its formal connection with the ideal of law. Kant's celebrated call for ethical autonomy expresses a revulsion with externalizations of the idea of duty. When Kant rejects hedonism as heteronomy he is turning the tables on an old Epicurean charge, that the morality of duty (exemplified in Stoicism) is inherently immoral because it roots obligation in an external standard. The argument worked well against Stoics, dialectically, because it played upon their Cynic heritage of naturalism and candor. But it assumed that only pleasures can be proper (true or honest) motives of our own. The Stoics derived human virtue from a sublimation of mere appetites or interests, in which higher values are appropriated to the self—which is in some measure constituted as a moral identity by that act of appropriation. See Cicero, *De Finibus* 3.621: 239 (Rackham). Kant remains in the Stoic tradition. But by that very token, he ought to recognize that if Stoics can treat duties as proper to the self while Epicureans treat duties as external and only pleasures as proper motives, religious sensibility, adopting the will of God as its own, interpreting its own perfect expression as action in accordance with God's will, can constitute itself as a moral and spiritual identity by that very act, obviating the claim that religious duties are hereronomous. Kant might have adverted to this fact, had he not been distracted by the reli-

gious pretensions of institutions that do externalize the will of God—in much the way that the Kantian concept of duty itself was later externalized despite Kant's recognition that the moral law as such must be self-legislated. Kant's point about autonomy was that duty, when properly appropriated, cannot be conceived as alien. The Torah means nothing different when it commands us to love God with all our hearts and to express our love of God by setting His commandments upon our hearts. Kant in turn, despite his romantic restiveness with externalized notions of duty (the same authoritarian notions he is sometimes accused of truckling to), does not violate but fulfills the biblical idea of right when he defines religion as regarding all our duties as divine commands. See *Metaphysic of Morals*, 2, The Doctrine of Virtue: 105–06 (Gregor); cf. *Religion within the Limits of Reason Alone*: 170ff. (Greene and Hudson). Compare Kant's notion that godliness can be a useful propaedeutic to morality with Maimonides' affirmation that moral perfection is a necessary prerequisite of prophecy.

49. See "Eight Chapters," 4; Goodman 1978. *Mishneh Torah*, 1.2 Ethical Laws 6.8: 55b (Hyamson).

50. *Crito* 53d–54b with *Apology* 30–31.

51. Biblical history adopts a universal perspective by taking the creation of the world as its starting point and by situating the history of Israel in context among the history of the nations. All nations are blood relations (Genesis 3:20), all cultures and languages disperse from a common origin (Genesis 10, 11) and coalesce (in the vision of the Prophets) to a common end. All are subject to the same moral laws: hence, God's concern for the lawlessness of Noah's generation (Genesis 6:11–13), His visitation of judgments—liberations and punishments—upon all nations. See Genesis 13:13, 15:14, Deuteronomy 27:16–26; and in the Prophets: Amos 1:3 – 2:9, 9:7. Biblical history is objective in that its goal is not to celebrate the nation and still less its leaders, but to record the insights, acts and failings of a people and its leaders in the context of an emerging order of meaning. See Vogelin 1976, pp. 116–87.

52. *Guide* 3.26–28, 2.40: 3:57–62, 2:85–87 (Munk).

53. *Guide* 3.33: 3:73–74 (Munk). Cf. Plato, *Laws:* 719E–720.

54. *Guide* 3.28: 3:60b–62 (Munk); cf. Ibn Ṭufayl, *Ḥayy Ibn Yaqẓân*: 156, 161–5 (Goodman).

55. *Guide* 1.46–47 ff., 3.13: 1:49b–54, 3:22–26b (Munk); "Eight Chapters," 5.

56. *Guide* 3.35: 3:75–77 (Munk).

57. *Guide* 2.6, 12, 3.17.5, 18, 2.36–38: 2:16–18, 24b–26b, 3:34b, 37b–39, 2:77b–83b (Munk).

58. Maimonides, *Sefer Ha-Mitzvot* (Chavel). Mishnah Commentary (Rosner). Maimonides' Code, *Mishneh Torah*, familiarly the *Yad Chazakah.* The volumes of the Code have been appearing in English translations by various hands in the Yale Judaica Series over an extended period.

59. *Guide* 3.12: 3:18–22 (Munk).

60. *Guide* 3.34, 2.40, 3.26–28, 32, 1.2: 3:74b–75, 2:85–87, 3:57–62, 69–73, 1:13–14b (Munk).

61. See Proverbs 10:2, 11:4–5, 19; 13:6, 14:34, 15:9, 16:12, 25:5.

62. Saadiah Gaon, *Book of Beliefs and Convictions*, I, Exordium: 38–40 (Rosenblatt).

63. See *Sifre* to Numbers 27:7.

64. Hamilton 1949, pp. 99–100. To develop in detail the juridical articulations in rabbinic law of the Biblical norms about relations between the sexes would be the work of many volumes. In the crucial areas of sexual and reproductive relations, we have a model study: Feldman 1975 (1968).

65. Cf. 2 Samuel 15, Hosea 6:3; Jeremiah 22:16, 31:34. See Simlai in *Makkot* 23b–24a: "Moses was given 613 commandments. David summed these up in eleven (Psalm 15), Isaiah in six (33:16–17), Micah in three (6:8), Isaiah again in two (56:1), and finally Habakkuk founded them all in one principle, fidelity."

66. Exodus 24:7, Deuteronomy 27, 1 Kings 1:36, 1 Chronicles 16:36, Nehemiah 5:13, 8:6.

67. Isaiah 50:1, 54; Jeremiah 2:2; cf. Deuteronomy 2:7, 32:11, 18; Jeremiah 31:20; Hosea passim, esp. 11:1–11, 13:8, Ezekiel 23, 33, etc., Isaiah 66:11–13, 42:14, 49:15, Job 38:28–9. See Trible 1973; cf. Trible 1978 and Mollenkott 1984.

68. Genesis 9:1–17. Cf. Goodman 1981, p. 115.

69. Malachi 1:11. God visits justice upon all nations: Damascus, Philistia, Tyre, Edom, Moab are not immune (Amos 1–2). Israel is not alone in being saved from slavery: The Syrians, Cushites, and Philistines are equally the subjects of divine redemption (Amos 9:7). For universal peace: Isaiah 11:6–9, 2:4; Micah 4:3, mimicking and reversing Joel 4:10.

70. Isaiah 2:3, 11:6; with Maimonides' exposition in the famous closing passages of his *Code* 14 Kings and Wars, 11–12: 238–42 (Hershman).

71. See *Shabbat* 92a, *Nedarim* 38a with Genesis Rabbah 27 and Maimonides *Guide* 1.46, 2.36, 38, cf. 3.18: 1:49b–53, 2.77b–80, 82–83b, 3.38–39 (Munk).

72. See Neusner 1981.

73. See Mishnah *Yoma* 2.6, and consider the Mishnaic role of the *parhedrin* (palhedrin) in advising the High Priest, *Yoma* 1.1, a projection of the rabbinic role. For "disciples of Aaron," Talmud *Yoma* 91b, with Mishnah *Avot* 1.12; and Urbach 1977, pp. 89–90.

74. *Guide* 1.59. Yet he saves the rabbis' Midrashic (homiletic) anthropomorphisms as *allegories* by accounting them as uninhibited rabbinic participations in the poetic license accorded to prophetic boldness by the exigencies of emanation/inspiration; *Guide* 1.46.

75. Mishnah *Peah* 1.1: 10 (Danby); Mishnah *Avot* 6.1, 2.9 (Hertz), but cf. 1.17, 2.2: 459, 448, 447 (Danby).

76. See Ecclesiastes 1.17–18; 6:8, 12; cf. 2:15–23.

77. Mishnah *Avot* 2.12, cf. 1.3, 2.4 (Hertz)/ 449, 446, 448 (Danby).

78. Mishnah *Avot* 2.19 (Hertz)/449 (Danby); *Shulchan Arukh*, passim. For the commercial aspects of the codes, see, e.g., Passamaneck 1983.

79. See I. Heinemann 1949; Solomon Ibn Adret of Barcelona (1235–1310), the Rashba, Responsum no. 94, cited in Jacobs 1975, p. 64. But note that the Rashba's positivism, directed against a rationalism he feared was reductionistic, did not excuse a spiritual or mystical rationale attaching to the aura of intrinsic value assigned to the *mitzvot* (especially the ritual *mitzvot*) as commands of God.

80. See Genesis 1:26, *Genesis Rabbah* 8:8–9; 1.1; 13: 59–60; 1, 12 (Freedman); cf. *Berakhot* 55a, and Philo, *De Opificio Mundi* 4.15–16: 1.15 (Colson and Whitaker); Maimonides, *Guide* 2.6: 2.16–18 (Munk). The imagery is reversed but the theme held constant in Mishnah *Avot* 4:10, 454 (Danby): Only God can judge alone.

81. *Sanhedrin* 33b–34a, 84b, etc. For the procedural protections of Mishnaic law in capital cases, see Mishnah *Sanhedrin* 4.1; for the banning of hearsay, 4.5: 387 (Danby). *Sanhedrin* 4.1 also disallows reversal of acquittals in capital cases. For the exclusion of circumstantial evidence, *Tosefta* to *Sanhedrin* 8.3. See also *Baba Kamma* 73a: "Evidence voided in part is voided altogether." Cf. Urbach 1977, pp. 104–08.

82. Raba in *Sanhedrin* 96; cf. Mishnah *Ketubot* 2.9: 247 (Danby); Maimonides' *Code* 14, *Hilkhot Sanhedrin* 18.6: 14:52–53 (Hershman): "Perhaps he was one of those who are in misery, bitter in soul, who long for death. . . . The principle that no man is to be declared guilty on his own admission is a divine decree."

83. See Numbers 5:12 as qualified by the rabbinic requirements: warning by the husband before two witnesses, with the suspected third party

named explicitly, ignoring of the warning, certified by the testimony of two witnesses not including the husband (that the suspected wife continued secretly to consort in private with the individual warned against), and consent by the wife to the ordeal. Refusal of the ordeal made a suspected wife subject to divorce without return of the marriage settlement. But insufficient warning or inadequate testimony as to its violation left divorce the only remedy, _with_ return to the wife of her marriage settlement. Cases regarding the bitter waters were to come only before the full Sanhedrin of 71 high court judges in Jerusalem. Renewal of sexual relations between the married couple during the period between the warning and the ordeal voided the efficacy of the ordeal and required divorce with return of the marriage portion. So did the husband's decision to relent in the demand for the ordeal. Any premarital or extramarital affairs on the husband's part nullified his demand for the ordeal; so did any significant physical handicap on the wife's part or on the part of her husband. See Mishnah _Sotah_: 293–298 (Danby); Maimonides, _Code 4 Sotah_: 341–364 (Klein); Chill 1974, pp. 322–24. The requirement of the wife's consent sufficed to ensure that the ordeal would be little practised. The ordeal was magical even in its enactment (see Goodman 1986, n. 14)—the only commandment, Nachmanides remarks, that depended on a miracle—and the Mishnah treats it as a legendary matter: the ordeal was expected to produce identical effects on the lover as on the woman who drank the waters. Maimonides is rather casual about the composition of the waters themselves: "some bitter ingredient like wormwood or the like" (p. 356) and implies (p. 358) that the efficacy of the ordeal rested on popular belief in it. In Second Temple times, following a hint in Hosea (4:14), the Sanhedrin abolished the ordeal completely, on the grounds that adultery was too widespread to allow presumption of the necessary innocence on the part of husbands.

84. See _Sanhedrin_ 74a, with Leviticus 18:5 as the proof text. For the preservation and enhancement of life as cardinal principles of the Law: Deuteronomy 5:30, 6:3, 18, 4:40, 5:26. If the quality of life is understood to include the preservation of communal and sacred values, the preservation and enhancement of life may be called _the_ cardinal principles.

85. Mishnah _Yoma_ 8.6: 172 (Danby), and Talmud _Yoma_ 84a, 85b; cf. Mishnah _Shabbat_ 2.5: 102 (Danby); Talmud _Shabbat_ 30, 32a, _Kiddushin_ 39b. Babes were to be delivered normally on the Sabbath and circumcised if male even if the day of circumcision fell on the Sabbath, _Shabbat_ 18.3. Similarly no sick child was to be circumcised until recovered, _Shabbat_ 19.5.

86. _Yoma_ 8.5–6: 172 (Danby), and Gemara _ad loc._

87. See Leviticus 23:22, Deuteronomy 14:28–29, 24:19–22, 26:12; Mishnah _Peah_ 1.1–2: 11 (Danby). For gleanings see _Peah_ 4.10: 14 (Danby) and Gemara _ad locc._

88. *Baba Batra* 8b.

89. Exodus 22:25–26, Deuteronomy 24:6, 10–12.

90 *Sanhedrin* 74a. For the justification of deadly force in self-defense, see Mishnah *Sanhedrin* 8:6; for the construal of the use of deadly force against a potential murderer or rapist as a saving of the would-be perpetrator from sin, *Sanhedrin* 8:7. The use of deadly force to prevent murder or rape is not, of course, deemed murder; see Exodus 22:1.

91. *Terumot* 8.12: 62–63 (Danby) and *Tiferet Israel* (commentary by Israel Lipschutz, 1782–1860) *ad loc.*

92. *Pesachim* 72b, *Ketubot* 105a; cf. Bokser 1942, pp. 151–52.

93. See Maimonides' "Eight Chapters" 4; Code I *Hilkhot De'ot* 3.1: 49b (Hyamson); cf. Saadiah *Book of Beliefs and Convictions* 10.4: 364–67 (Rosenblatt), and Goodman 1980, p. 409. Both Maimonides and Saadiah reject hedonism as well, of course.

94. See *Yevamot* 62b–63a on Genesis 5:2; Midrash *Tanchuma* 12. Mishnah *Avot* 5:13: 457 (Danby) presents the maxim "What's mine is mine; what's thine is thine" as defining the ethos of Sodom—against which the Law deploys its compulsory requirements as well as its powers of persuasion and habituation. Cf. *Berakhot* 29b; *Eruvin* 49a, *Ketubot* 103a, *Baba Batra* 12b, 59a, 168a. For the practical application of the rabbinic principle "*Kofin 'al Midat Sedom*" ("We enforce against the ethos of sodom") see Shilo 1980, pp. 49–78; on "*Lifnim mi-shurat ha-din*" (supererogation in the law) see Shilo 1978, pp. 359–90.

95. See *Baba Metzia* 59b, citing Deuteronomy 30:12. God Himself is said to have rejoiced at this: "My children have triumphed over Me."

96. Deuteronomy 20:19–20. See Hirsch 1837, chapter 56 *ad loc.* 2, 279–82.

97. See Mishnah *Chullin* 8: 524–5 (Danby), elaborating the laws of Exodus 23:19, 34:26, Deuteronomy 14:21.

98. *Chullin* 1:513–15 (Danby); *Guide* 3.26: 3.58 (Munk).

99. See Nachmanides *ad* Deuteronomy 22:6.

100. See *Sanhedrin* 4.5: 387–88 (Danby). *Avot de Rabbi Natan* 31.2–3: 291 (Cohen); characteristically, this Midrash argues that a single precept, a single Sabbath, is also tantamount in value to the world at its creation. Cf. *Mekhilta*: 1, p. 113 (Lauterbach).

References

Avot de R. Natan. Translated by A. Cohen. 1984. London: Soncino.

Agus, Jacob. 1978. *Jewish Identity in an Age of Ideologies.* New York: Ungar.

Becker, C. L. 1968 (1932). *The Heavenly City of the Eighteenth Century French Philosophers.* New Haven: Yale University Press.

Bergson, Henri. 1977 (1935). *Two Sources of Morality and Religion.* Translated by R. A. Audra and C. Brereton. Westport: Greenwood.

Bokser, Ben Zion. 1942. "Democratic Aspiration in Talmudic Judaism." In *Science, Philosophy and Religion,* ed. L. Bryson and L. Finkelstein. New York: Harper and Row. Reprinted in *Judaism and Human Rights,* ed. M. Konvitz. New York: Norton, pp. 145–55.

Brandeis, Louis. 1915. *The Jewish Problem and How to Solve It.* New York: Zionist Essays Publication Committee.

Buber, M. 1947. *Between Man and Man.* Translated by R. G. Smith. New York: Macmillan.

Buber, M. 1947–48. *Tales of the Hasidim.* Translated by O. Marx. New York: Schocken.

Buber, M. 1950. *The Way of Man According to the Teachings of Hasidism.* London: Routledge.

Carlebach, Julius. 1978. *Karl Marx and the Radical Critique of Judaism.* London: Routledge.

Chill, A. 1974. *The Mitzvot.* Jerusalem: Keter.

Cicero. *De Finibus.* Edited and translated by H. Rackham. 1971 (1914). Cambridge: Harvard University Press.

Cohen, Hermann. 1972 (1919). *Religion of Reason out of the Sources of Judaism.* Translated by S. Kaplan. New York: Ungar.

Cuddihy, J. M. 1974. *The Ordeal of Civility.* New York: Oxford University Press.

Driver, G. R. and Miles, J. C. 1955. *The Babylonian Laws.* Oxford: Clarendon Press.

Einstein, Albert. 1950. *Out of My Later Years.* New York: Philosophical Library.

Feldman, David. 1975 (1968). *Marital Relations, Birth Control, and Abortion in Jewish Law.* New York: Schocken.

Gay, Peter. 1978. *Freud, Jews and other Germans.* New York: Oxford University Press.

Genesis Rabbah. Translated by H. Freedman. 1961 (1939). London: Soncino. 2 vols.

Ginzberg, Louis. 1968 (1909). *Legends of the Jews.* Translated by Henrietta Szold. Philadelphia: Jewish Publication Society.

Goodman, L. E. 1978. "Maimonides' Philosophy of Law." *Jewish Law Annual 1:* 72–107.

Goodman, L. E. 1980. "Saadiah's Ethical Pluralism." *Journal of the American Oriental Society* 100: 407–19.

Goodman, L. E. 1981. *Monotheism.* Totowa, N.J.: Allenheld.

Goodman, L. E. 1986. "The Biblical Laws of Diet and Sex." *Jewish Law Association Studies* 2: 17–57.

Goodman, L. E. 1990. "Three Meanings of the Idea of Creation." In *God and Creation: An Ecumenical Symposium*, ed. D. Burrell and B. McGinn. Notre Dame: Notre Dame University Press, pp. 85–113.

Goodman, L. E. 1991. *On Justice.* New Haven: Yale University Press.

Greenberg, Moshe. 1976. "Some Postulates of Biblical Criminal Law." In *The Jewish Expression*, ed. Judah Goldin. New Haven: Yale University Press, pp. 18–37.

Hamilton, Edith. 1949. *Spokesmen for God: The Great Teachers of the Old Testament.* New York: Norton.

Heinemann, I. 1949. *Ta'amei Ha-Mitzvot.* Jerusalem: Histadrut.

Hirsch, S. R. 1837. *Horeb.* Translated by I. Grunfeld. 1968 (1962). London: Soncino. 2 vols.

Jacobs, Louis. 1975. *Theology in the Responsa.* London: Routledge.

Josephus. *Antiquities.* Edited and translated by L. H. Feldman. 1965. Cambridge: Harvard University Press.

Judah ben Samuel he-Chasid. 1924. *Sefer Chasidim.* Edited by J. Wistinetzki. Frankfurt: Wahrmann.

Kamenka, Eugene. 1972 (1962). *The Ethical Foundations of Marxism.* London: Routledge.

Kant, Immanuel. 1797, 1803. *The Metaphysic of Morals*, II, The Doctrine of Virtue. Translated by Mary Gregor. 1964. Philadelphia: University of Pennsylvania Press.

Kant, Immanuel. 1793, 1794. *Religion within the Limits of Reason Alone.* Translated by T. M. Greene and H. H. Hudson. 1960. New York: Harper and Row.

Maimonides. *Book of the Commandments.* Translated by C.B. Chavel as *The Commandments.* 1967. London: Soncino.

Maimonides. *Code* 1. The Book of Knowledge. Edited and translated by Moses Hyamson. 1967. Jerusalem: Feldheim.

Maimonides. *Code* 4. The Book of Agriculture. Translated by I. Klein. 1979. New Haven: Yale University Press.

Maimonides. *Code* 7. The Book of Women. Edited by I. Klein. 1972. New Haven: Yale University Press.

Maimonides. *Code* 14. Book of Judges. Translated by A. M. Hershman. 1967 (1949). New Haven: Yale University Press.

Maimonides. "Eight Chapters" in *RAMBAM—Readings in the Philosophy of Moses Maimonides.* 1976. Edited by L. E. Goodman. New York: Viking Press.

Maimonides. Mishnah Commentary, *Kitâb al-Sirâj* or *Perush ha-Mishnah.* Translated by Fred Rosner. New York: Feldheim, 1975.

Maimonides. *Guide.* (*Dalâlat al-Hâ'irin: Le Guide des Égarés.* Edited with French translation by S. Munk. Paris, 1855–66; reprinted, Osnabrück: Zeller, 1964, 3 vols.)

Mekhilta. Edited and translated by J. Z. Lauterbach. 1933. Philadelphia: Jewish Publication Society. 3 vols.

Michael, Yehiel. 1950. *The Way of Man According to the Teachings of Hasidism.* London: Routledge.

Midrash Tanchuma. Edited by S. Buber. 1913. Wilna: The Widow and Brothers Ram.

The Mishnah. Translated by H. Danby. 1977 (1933). Oxford: Oxford University Press.

Mishnah *Avot.* Edited by J. Hertz. 1945. New York: Berhrman.

Mollenkott, Virginia R. 1984. *The Divine Feminine: The Biblical Imagery of God as Female.* New York: Crossroads.

Neusner, Jacob. 1981. *Judaism: The Evidence of the Mishnah.* Chicago: University of Chicago Press.

Neusner, J. and Frerichs, E. S. 1985. *"To See Ourselves as Others See Us"—Christians, Jews, "Others" in Late Antiquity.* Chico: Scholars Press.

Novak, David. 1983. *The Image of the Non-Jew in Judaism: An Historical and Constructive Study of the Noahide Laws.* New York: Mellen.

Parsons, Talcott, et al. 1955. *Family, Socialization and Interaction.* Glencoe: Free Press.

Parsons, Talcott, et al. 1964. *Social Structure and Personality*. Glencoe: Free Press.

Parsons, Talcott, et al. 1966. *Societies, Evolutionary and Comparative Perspectives*. Englewood Cliffs: Prentice Hall.

Passamaneck, Stephen. 1983. *The Traditional Jewish Law of Sale: Choshen Mishpat 189–240*. Cincinnati: Hebrew Union College–Jewish Institute of Religion.

Philo. *The Decalogue*. Edited by F. H. Colson. 1958 (1937). Cambridge: Harvard University Press.

Philo. *On the Confusion of Tongues*. Edited and translated by F. H. Colson and G. H. Whitaker. 1958 (1932). Cambridge: Harvard University Press.

Philo. *De Opificio Mundi*. Edited and translated by F. H. Colson and G. H. Whitaker. 1962 (1929). Cambridge: Harvard University Press.

Saadiah Gaon. *K. al-Mukhtâr fî 'l-âmânât wa 'l-I'tiqâdât (Book of Critical Selection among Beliefs and Convictions)*. Translated by S. Rosenblatt, 1967 (1948), as *The Book of Beliefs and Opinions*. New Haven: Yale University Press.

Saadiah Gaon. *Book of Theodicy* (Commentary on the Book of Job). Translated by L. E. Goodman. 1988. New Haven: Yale University Press.

Shilo, Shmuel. 1978. *"Lifnim mi-shurat ha-din" Israel Law Review* 13: 359–90.

Shilo, Shmuel. 1980. *"Kofin 'al Midat Sedom." Israel Law Review* 15: 49–78.

Sifre. Edited by S. Zuckerman and S. Luria. 1866. Wilna: Fine and Rosenkrantz.

Soss, Neal M. 1973. "Old Testament Law and Economic Society." *Journal of the History of Ideas* 34: 323–44.

Trible, Phyllis. 1973. "Depatriarchalizing Biblical Interpretation." *Journal of the American Academy of Religion;* reprinted in *The Jewish Woman: New Perspectives*, ed. Elizabeth Koltun. New York: Schocken, 1976, pp. 217–41.

Trible, Phyllis. 1978. *God and the Rhetoric of Sexuality*. Philadelphia: Fortress.

Urbach, E. 1977. "Jewish Doctrines and Practices in the Hellenistic and Talmudic Periods," and "Jewish Doctrines and Practices in Halakhic and Aggadic Literature." In *Violence and Defense in the Jewish Experience*, ed. S. W. Baron and L. E. Goodman. Philadelphia: Jewish Publication Society, pp. 71–112.

Vogelin, Eric. 1976 (1956). *Israel and Revolution, 1: Order and History*. Baton Rouge: Louisiana State University Press.

The Elimination of Perplexity: Socrates and Maimonides as Guides of the Perplexed

Daniel H. Frank

1. Introduction

Euthyphro and Meno in the Platonic dialogues named for them are perplexed, brought into such a state by Socrates. For his part, R. Joseph ben Judah, Maimonides' erstwhile student, does not need anyone to lead him into perplexity; he is *already* perplexed. And, of course, Maimonides' *Guide* is written for R. Joseph (and those like him) in order to lead him out of his perplexity. In sum, perplexity, a state in which one finds oneself at least temporarily incapable of (intellectual) egress, plays a significant role in Plato and Maimonides. For the former, *aporia* (perplexity: lit. "no exit") is a standard feature of the Socratic *elenchus*, that method by which Socrates examines the views of an individual who claims knowledge and expertise in some area. Furthermore, the early Platonic ('Socratic') dialogues invariably end in perplexity, at least to the extent that the major question under discussion, e.g. "What is courage?" (*Laches*), "What is piety?" (*Euthyphro*), "What is virtue?" (*Meno*), is left unanswered. For Maimonides, we need merely reiterate that the *Guide* itself is framed as an attempt to resolve the perplexity that young R. Joseph feels as a result of having studied some science and philosophy and (then) having attempted to square such study with his own traditional religious beliefs.

In this essay I propose to analyze the nature and structure of perplexity in Plato and Maimonides. Although Plato highlights the *inducing* of perplexity as the first step in the attainment of knowledge, both thinkers agree that the *resolution* of perplexity is a major task of the philosopher. For both, the philosopher is a therapist, helping the (temporarily) helpless out of his perplexity. Furthermore, Plato and

Maimonides are concerned to link perplexity, intellectual impasse, with (concurrent) *moral* failure and its resolution with moral reform. For both thinkers, a defect in character necessitates perplexity. As we shall see, for Plato, perplexity is mandated by, and the antidote for, moral failure, specifically the conceit of wisdom. Both Euthyphro and Meno are vain men, self-proclaimed experts. This is their (moral) failing, and Plato is concerned to point out the necessity of their being perplexed, if they are ever to be rid of the conceit. For Plato, perplexity is a good thing, for it can engender self-reflection. Only by being perplexed do Euthyphro and Meno have a chance to reflect upon and remove that character flaw which stands in the way of intellectual progress. This, as much as attempting to provide specific answers to specific questions, is Plato's intent in the 'aporetic' dialogues. For Maimonides too, perplexity is linked with moral failure. The root cause of R. Joseph's perplexity is a defect (or defects) in his character. The efficient cause, as it were, of his incapacity to square the truths of science and philosophy with those of his tradition is his misplaced optimism regarding the powers of the human intellect and an overweaning desire to learn metaphysics before he has been fully prepared. This exuberance and impetuosity, indeed the mark of youth, is a moral failing, and it leads to his perplexity. And as with Euthyphro and Meno, it is only upon elimination of the moral failing that learning can proceed. We must understand the *Guide* in light of this. It is written for R. Joseph (and those like him), not merely to respond to his intellectual perplexity, to reveal to him the deep harmony between science/philosophy and Judaism, but also with a view to eliminating the moral failing which leads to his perplexity and (currently) stands in the way of his intellectual progress.

2. Euthyphro's and Meno's Perplexity

Euthyphro is a self-acknowledged expert on piety and impiety; furthermore, he has the strength of his convictions, for he is prosecuting his own father for murder.[1] Naturally enough, Socrates, on trial for his life and charged with impiety, wishes to learn from Euthyphro that knowledge which he claims to possess. Akin to his incessant questioning of noteworthy Athenian politicians and poets, Socrates asks Euthyphro: "What is the pious, and what the impious?"[2] The self-proclaimed expert and would-be teacher of Socrates responds in a variety of ways which need not detain us here, but all of his responses are, for various reasons, inadequate. Euthyphro's claim to know what piety is is ill-founded. Upon (cross)examination, Euthyphro is unable to sustain any of his claims as to the nature of piety, e.g., that piety is "what all the gods love."[3] The Socratic *elenchus* has revealed that the self-proclaimed teacher is a fraud. To be sure, this relevation is not Socrates' intended goal, for he wished merely to learn what Euthyphro claimed to know, in order to better defend himself at his impending trial for impiety.[4] Nevertheless, the unfrocking of Euthyphro is a by-product of the Socratic *elenchus*.

After a number of unsuccessful attempts to 'define' piety, i.e., to teach Socrates the nature of piety, Euthyphro becomes exasperated. However, he becomes exasperated not with himself, as he ought, but with his 'student,' Socrates. He likens Socrates to Daedelus,[5] one who has the capacity to unsettle things, to literally dislocate the apparently stable. Euthyphro refuses to take the blame for his own obvious shortcoming; he does not have the courage to own up to his own ignorance. And so he blames Socrates, who for his part denies that he consciously intends to refute Euthyphro and reiterates his desire to learn from Euthyphro the nature of piety. With this, Euthyphro is (temporarily) pacified and the dialogue resumes.[6] But, alas, Euthyphro soon departs and the dialogue ends in *aporia* and failure, at least to the extent that Socrates does not learn what piety is. Socrates' search for a teacher has been frustrated. The dialogue is a failure in another way as well. Not only does Socrates not learn what piety is, but Euthyphro's abrupt departure, with no hint that he will desist from prosecution of his father, betokens Euthyphro's failure to learn anything from his encounter with Socrates. Although repeatedly shown to be ignorant of what he claims to know, Euthyphro has not learned, as he ought to have, that one ought not to act in ignorance. In persisting in the prosecution of his father and, *a fortiori*, in his claim to know what piety is, Euthyphro makes it clear that he has not learned that it is the conceit of wisdom, the persisting in one's false beliefs and the refusal to own up to one's ignorance, which is the greatest impediment to knowledge and right action.[7] Euthyphro's failure is at root one of character.

Although ultimately incorrigible, there is one (very) brief moment in which Euthyphro is honest with himself. At 11b, after having been encouraged by Socrates to try (again) to disclose what piety is, Euthyphro says: "Socrates, I have no way of telling you what I have in mind . . ." (*ouk echō egōge hopōs soi eipō ho noō . . .* ; 11b6–7). Here, for the first and last time in the dialogue, Euthyphro is perplexed. Indeed, Euthyphro's perplexity leads immediately to his accusing Socrates of being a Daedelus, but the fact remains that he has become (ever so slightly) cognizant of his ignorance and, at least implicitly, of the falsity of his position as an expert, as one who knows. Again, this awareness is fleeting and is not highlighted by Plato in the dialogue, nor is Euthyphro in any way finally changed by it; nonetheless, we must understand Euthyphro's perplexity as a glimmer of self-awareness, an opening for a concerted meditation upon the falsity of his life as an expert.

I do not want to read too much into this passage in the *Euthyphro*, for Plato is quite explicit in the *Meno* and, much later, in the *Sophist* about the role of perplexity in the quest for (self-)knowledge. Nevertheless, when read in the light of the *Apology*, the following emerges. In the *Apology* Socrates is dumbfounded to learn that the oracle at Delphi has declared him to be the wisest of men.[8] Henceforth, he lived his life as an attempt to refute the oracle. But he was unsuccessful. Everyone whom he questioned, politicians, poets and craftsmen, in his (on-going) attempt to disprove the oracle *thought* himself possessed of wisdom. But Socrates found them all wanting in the sort of (moral) wisdom which they claimed to possess. As a result, the oracle was vindicated, for Socrates, unlike his interlocutors, did not have the conceit of wisdom. He did not think himself to be wise when he was not; and because of *this* he was possessed of a certain wisdom (as well as an eagerness to learn). As Socrates reflected upon his questioning of men like Euthyphro who boldly claimed to have knowledge about piety (or courage or temperance), he came to the following conclusion: "I am wiser than this man; it is likely that neither of us knows anything worthwhile, but he thinks he knows something when he does not, whereas when I do not know, neither do I think I know; so I am likely to be wiser than he to this small extent, that I do not think I know what I do not know" (*Apology* 21d).

Disbelief in and perplexity at the verdict of the oracle led Socrates into the agora to question those who claimed to know, to be wise in matters of courage, piety, etc. And after repeatedly being disappointed in his desire to refute the oracle, i.e., to be instructed in the 'wisdom' of the 'wise,' Socrates concluded (was led to reflect) that the wisdom of which the oracle spoke was nothing but his lack of the conceit of wisdom, i.e., his not supposing himself to be possessed of a knowledge about something of which he was in fact ignorant. Socrates' initial perplexity at the oracle's message led him on a voyage of self-discovery. And what he discovered was that the conceit of wisdom, a sort of vanity, a moral failing, was the bar to wisdom. What we see in the *Euthyphro* and other 'Socratic' dialogues is Socrates' discovery writ large. Euthyphro is vain from beginning to end, and his vanity is a bar to wisdom; indeed, his final departure and continued prosecution of his father in light of his abysmal ignorance about the nature of piety is ample evidence. If only he would act upon the (momentary) perplexity he feels at 11b; then, and only then, would Euthyphro, like Socrates, embark on a voyage of self-discovery, a journey which would disabuse him of his conceit, force him to evaluate his false character, and prepare the way for knowledge.

The *Meno* is explicit in a way that the *Euthyphro* is not about the role of perplexity in the Socratic *elenchus*. The *Meno* commences with the questions "Can virtue be taught? Or is it not teachable but the result of practice, or is it neither of these, but men possess it by nature or in some other way?" (70a), but these questions quickly resolve themselves into the (logically prior) question "What is virtue?"

Meno proceeds, like Euthyphro, to give a variety of incorrect responses to the question at hand. Finally, at 80a–b Meno, although not so conceited as Euthyphro, but, nonetheless, one who has "made many speeches about virtue before large audiences on a thousand occasions, [and] very good speeches as I thought" (80b), falls into perplexity. He is "benumbed" (80b) and speechless. He likens Socrates to a torpedo fish (a sting ray) which numbs everything with which it comes into contact. But not only is Meno, the man who has "made many speeches about virtue . . . on a thousand occasions," now incapable of saying what virtue is; he no longer even *thinks* he knows what it is.[9] Both his mind and his tongue are dumb, paralyzed; not only does Meno have nothing to say, but his mind is also a blank.

Forthwith, Meno despairs of ever attaining the knowledge about what virtue is, which he and Socrates are seeking. It is in this context that Meno presents his famous "paradox of inquiry," a paradox which entails not merely the impossibility of attaining knowledge, but also the utter futility of even trying.[10] The paradox need not detain us. What is of special interest, however, is Socrates' commentary on his illustration of the *falsity* of the paradox. In an aside to Meno during an examination of a slave boy's mathematical prowess, an examination which is supposed to illustrate that Meno's "paradox of inquiry" is spurious, Socrates in effect reprises in brief compass his entire previous discussion with Meno concerning the nature of virtue. I quote the passage in full:

Socrates: You realize, Meno, what point he [the slave boy] has reached in his recollection. At first he did not know what the basic line of the eight foot square was; even now he does not yet know, but then he thought he knew, and answered confidently as if he did know, and he did not think himself at a loss, but now he does think himself at a loss, and as he does not know, neither does he think he knows.

Meno: That is true.

Socrates: So he is now in a better position with regard to the matter he does not know?

Meno: I agree with that too.

Socrates: Have we done him any harm by making him perplexed and numb as the torpedo fish does?

Meno: I do not think so.

Socrates: Indeed, we have probably achieved something relevant to finding out how matters stand, for now, as he does not know, he would be glad to find out, whereas before he thought he could easily make many fine speeches to large audiences [cf. 80b] about the square of double size and said that it must have a base twice as long.

Meno: So it seems.

Socrates: Do you think that before he would have tried to find out that which he thought he knew though he did not, before he fell into perplexity and realized he did not know and longed to know?

Meno: I do not think so, Socrates.

Socrates: Has he then benefited from being numbed?

Meno: I think so.

Socrates: Look then how he will come out of his perplexity while searching along with me. I shall do nothing more than ask questions and not teach him. Watch whether you find me teaching and explaining things to him instead of asking for his opinion. [*Meno* 84a–d (Grube)]

This passage is very explicit about the role that perplexity plays in the Socratic *elenchus*. The following pattern emerges: from an initial state in which the slave boy (or Meno) has the conceit of wisdom he is brought by the Socratic *elenchus* to a point in which he is at a loss, 'benumbed' as it were. He is perplexed, and though in no way currently possessed of knowledge, the slave boy has progressed to the extent that he no longer *thinks* he knows (sc. what in fact he is ignorant of). And this is progress. At least the slave boy has become aware of the vacuousness of his previous (self-)confidence; he has been disabused of his conceit of wisdom. In this way perplexity breeds reflection and entails moral reform. Now, in his perplexity and because of the elimination of his false conceit, "he would be glad to find out [the truth]," whereas "before [he fell into perplexity] he would [not] have tried to find out that which he thought he knew though he did not. . . ." Upon this eagerness, the dialogue (within the dialogue) resumes and the slave boy makes steady progress toward true opinion.[11] Again, this is only possible because of the elimination of that bar to progress—vanity.[12]

What is important to note in this passage is that perplexity is a good thing. Although Euthyphro and Meno are frustrated by it, perplexity has the power to engender self-reflection, and self-reflection has the capacity to overcome that odious conceit of wisdom which is the most significant bar to wisdom. As Richard Robinson puts it: "The *elenchus* changes ignorant men from the state of falsely supposing that they know to the state of recognizing that they do not know; and this is an important step along the road to knowledge, because the recognition that we do not know at once arouses the desire to know, and thus supplies the motive that was lacking before. Philosophy begins in wonder, and the assertion here made [in *Meno* 84] is that *elenchus* supplies the wonder."[13] Philosophy, the desire to understand, commences only when the conceit of wisdom has been eradicated. Given this, we can understand Socrates and his *elenchus* as, respectively, a doctor (to the soul) and his purgative. Indeed, as noted, Socrates does not consciously set himself up as a therapist; rather, he wishes merely to apprentice himself to a self-proclaimed expert. Nonetheless, via his indefatigable search for the expert's 'wisdom' and the subsequent *aporia* engendered by the *elenchus*, Socrates, the 'student' is in effect transformed into Socrates, the deliverer from false conceit. We ought to note, however, that such delivery from conceit would, if successful (i.e., if the interlocutor's character is reformed), eradicate any 'teacherstudent' dichotomy, for it would establish the interlocutor on an equal footing with Socrates as a copartner in the search for truth. Neither Meno nor Socrates knows what virtue is or whether it is teachable, and now that Meno does not even think he knows, a true search, a true dialogue, may commence.[14]

A final passage from a late dialogue provides Plato's most explicit statement about the therapeutic function of the Socratic *elenchus*. The passage is from the *Sophist:*

Stranger: Of teaching in arguments, one method appears to be rougher, another smoother.

Theaetetus: How are we to distinguish the two?

Stranger: There is the time-honored method which our fathers often practised toward their sons, and which many still use today: either of angrily reproving their errors or of gently exhorting them. This method as a whole may correctly be termed "admonition."

Theaetetus: True.

Stranger: But some appear to have arrived at the conclusion that all ignorance is involuntary, and that no one who thinks himself wise is willing to learn the things in which he regards himself so. It follows that the admonitory sort of education gives much trouble and does little good.

Theaetetus: They are quite right.

Stranger: So they try to eradicate this conceit in another way.

Theaetetus: What?

Stranger: They question someone when he thinks he is making sense but really isn't. They easily show that such opinions are like those of people who wander. In their discussions they collect these opinions, and placing them side by side, show they contradict one another. . . . Seeing this, the subject becomes angry with himself and gentle toward others. In this way, he is relieved of the inflated and severe opinions he has of himself. This process is quite pleasant to the listeners, but produces the most lasting benefit on the subject himself. For just as physicians believe that the body will receive no benefit from food until the internal obstacles have been removed, so the purifier of the soul believes that his patient will receive no benefit from the application of knowledge until he is refuted, and by being refuted, is made to feel shame. He must be purged of the opinions

	which obstruct knowledge so he will think he knows only what he in fact knows, no more.

Theaetetus: This is certainly the best and wisest state of mind.

Stranger: For all these reasons, we must admit that refutation is the greatest and most proper purification. He who has not been refuted, though he be the great King himself, is in an awful state of impurity. He is ignorant and deformed in those things in which he who would be truly happy ought to be fairest and purest. [*Sophist* 229e–230e (Seeskin)]

In this passage, which doubtless has reference to Socrates (and, furthermore, unhesitatingly describes him as a "purifier of the soul"),[15] a distinction is made between two pedagogical methods, admonition (nouthetētikē) and *elenchus*. The former, a "time-honored method," is, however, of little use against someone like Euthyphro (or even Meno), "who thinks himself wise" (230a7), i.e., who has the conceit of wisdom. Given that Euthyphro thinks he knows what piety is and is unwilling to countenance the possibility that he might be wrong, admonition, whether angry or gentle, is useless. It does not get to the root of the problem, a moral failing, the conceit of wisdom, but merely treats the symptoms, ignorance and error. In order to 'purge' the vain man of his conceit, Socrates used a wholly different method, the *elenchus*. Only this method forces the (conceited) respondent to 'take stock' of his beliefs in such a way that he *also* takes stock of himself and his false position. Only the *elenchus* can induce perplexity of the sort that first 'angers,' next 'shames' and finally 'purges' the subject of his conceit; contrarily, the admonitory method, focusing as it does upon the 'correctness' and 'incorrectness' of opinions and actions and not upon the character of the agent, has no abiding effect, engenders defensiveness and at best substitutes (for a time) one opinion for another, but without the requisite moral reform.

In the *Sophist* passage the analogy between the questioner (Socrates) and the physician is perspicuous. Both believe that their respective patient's system is 'clogged' and that no benefit can be derived "until the internal obstacles have been removed." Health or knowledge (virtue) cannot be realized until the system has been 'purged'; and, to continue the analogy, purgative drugs are to the physician as the *elenchus* is to the philosopher. Only upon application of the moral 'drug,' the 'sting' of refutation, is there a chance that the vain man will take stock of his own (false) beliefs and (false) life and as a result "think he knows only what he in fact knows, no more."

Indeed, as Socrates famously declared, "the unexamined life is not worth living" (*Apology* 38a). Complacency, moral and intellectual, renders a life worthless. Without the (*aporia*-producing) examination of one's beliefs, one's life is as false (and dishonest) as the life of Camus's Clamence. For Socrates, ignorance may be a moral sin; but complacency and the conceit of wisdom surely are.

We have now examined those passages in which Plato assesses the role of perplexity in knowledge acquisition and the reform of one's character. In this latter regard, Socrates' role as a moral reformer, in spite of himself, is clear.[16] Left to himself and without Socrates, Euthyphro would never entertain the thought of his *not* knowing what piety is; even *with* Socrates, he barely entertains the possibility, so conceited is Euthyphro. Only Socrates (the philosopher) escaped this conceit. This is why it was Socrates who was enjoined by the god to 'pester' (cf. *Apology* 23d) the Athenians, to 'sting' (like a gadfly) the 'sluggish mare' (i.e., the Athenians; ibid. 30e). And importantly, once stung, Socrates' task was to minister to the wound. This necessity for Socrates to both sting and then minister to the wound betokens a particular view of human nature and a certain (political) theory about the role of philosophy and the philosopher in (the reformation of) society. In brief, it suggests that left to itself mankind (Socrates excluded) is intellectually lazy and morally deficient, and in need of reformation, and that the reformation can only be achieved through philosophy. Euthyphro and Meno, not to speak of Protagoras and Gorgias, are vain and conceited crowd pleasers. Only Socrates (the philosopher) is willing to discount reputation and the approbation of the crowd, and to seek truth wherever it may be found.[17] Unwilling to accept conventional wisdom or the views of those of high repute simply because of their source, Socrates nonetheless viewed himself as Athens' greatest friend.[18] And Socrates (the philosopher) *was* Athens' greatest benefactor even while (or, better, precisely because) he *seemingly* stood outside of it and refused to play by *its* rules. For Plato, then, the *elenchus* and the inducing of *aporia* has a political motivation.[19] It is the means whereby Socrates produces a better citizen. Meno, like the slave boy, is no worse off for having been benumbed. And, as a result, his city is a better community for his having been stung.

3. R. Joseph's Perplexity

The perplexity of R. Joseph ben Judah, an erstwhile student of Maimonides, and those like him is the raison d'etre for Maimonides' writing the *Guide*. R. Joseph came from abroad to study under Maimonides. And:

Maimonides found him to be an intelligent student with a strong desire to learn, but he feared that Joseph's thirst for knowledge might exceed his mental capacity. A good pedagogue, Maimonides insisted on an orderly course of study. "Truth," he told his student, "should be established in your mind according to the proper methods and . . . certainty should not come to you by accident" (*Guide*, Dedication: 4). He first set Joseph to work on mathematics, and then proceeded to teach him astronomy. His pupil showed a special liking and aptitude for mathematics, so Maimonides let him continue this subject on his own. Joseph next read texts in the art of logic under Maimonides' guidance. . . . At this stage Maimonides was so pleased with his pupil's progress that he began to give him glimpses of the secrets of the Jewish scriptures. Joseph, however, became impatient and asked his teacher to instruct him in metaphysics, especially the system and method of the Muslim Mutakallimūn. . . . Joseph had received some intimations of their metaphysical ideas from others, causing him to be perplexed by apparent conflicts with his religious beliefs. Maimonides was now convinced that his pupil's desire to learn did indeed exceed his grasp. Joseph wanted to hurry on to metaphysics without being properly prepared for it. He had not yet been taught physics, which Maimonides considered to be a necessary preparation for metaphysics. No wonder Joseph felt perplexed about his religious beliefs, despite the help that Maimonides tried to give him. Joseph then left his teacher without reaching the study of metaphysics. But Maimonides' experience with his pupil bore some fruit, for he decided to write a guide for Joseph and those like him, who, having studied the sciences and philosophy, and being firm believers in the Jewish religion, were bewildered by the ambiguous and figurative language of its sacred writings.

[Maurer 1988, pp. 206–207]

If the efficient cause of the *Guide* is R. Joseph's perplexity, its formal and final cause is the *partial* elimination of that perplexity[20] by clarifying for R. Joseph (and those like him), "one who has philosophized and has knowledge of the sciences, but believes at the same time in the matters pertaining to the Law" [1, Introduction: 10

(Pines)], those terms and parables in the Bible which, if taken in their literal sense, cause perplexity. As Maimonides himself puts it:

For the purpose of this Treatise and of all those like it is the science of Law in its true sense. Or rather its purpose is to give indications to a religious man for whom the validity of our Law has become established in his soul and has become actual in his belief—such a man being perfect in his religion and character, and having studied the sciences of the philosophers and come to know what they signify. The human intellect having drawn him on and led him to dwell within its province, he must have felt distressed by the externals of the Law and by the meanings of the above-mentioned equivocal, derivative, or amphibolous terms, as he continued to understand them by himself or was made to understand them by others. Hence he would remain in a state of perplexity and confusion as to whether he should follow his intellect, renounce what he knew concerning the terms in question, and consequently consider that he has renounced the foundations of the Law. Or he should hold fast to his understanding of these terms and not let himself be drawn on together with his intellect, rather turning his back on it and moving away from it, while at the same time perceiving that he had brought loss to himself and harm to his religion. He would be left with those imaginary beliefs to which he owes his fear and difficulty and would not cease to suffer from heartache and great perplexity.

This Treatise also has a second purpose: namely, the explanation of very obscure parables occurring in the books of the prophets, but not explicitly identified there as such. Hence an ignorant or heedless individual might think that they possess only an external sense, but no internal one. However, even when one who truly possesses knowledge considers these parables and interprets them according to their external meaning, he too is overtaken by great perplexity. But if we explain these parables to him or if we draw his attention to their being parables, he will take the right road and be delivered from his perplexity. That is why I have called this Treatise "The Guide of the Perplexed." [1, Introduction: 5–6 (Pines)]

The *Guide* is an elitist work, written for a select audience.[21] Only such a group has acquired the kind of knowledge which appears to be at odds with the Law. Only such a group of 'thinkers' is liable to be perplexed. For Maimonides, then, perplexity arises from knowledge. But more than this, and as the case of R. Joseph plainly indicates, perplexity arises from knowledge too hastily gained, or perhaps better, knowledge gained in a haphazard fashion.[22] And this latter is itself due to a moral failing, a flaw in R. Joseph's character. That R. Joseph's (self-induced) perplexity arises from his (youthful) exuberance, the reckless and premature desire which leads him to study metaphysics before he has properly studied God's creation, the natural world,[23] and that the beginning of its resolution awaits elimination of the moral failing is the Maimonidean analogue to Plato's (moral) point that perplexity is mandated by the conceit of wisdom and that it is a flaw in one's character which is the bar to intellectual progress. For both Plato and Maimonides, perplexity is the result not merely of intellectual error, but also of moral failing. Euthyphro and, in his own way, R. Joseph are vain. For his part, R. Joseph thinks he has the capacity, at a stage when in fact he does not, for embarking upon a study of metaphysics. Indeed, R. Joseph's "desire to learn did exceed his grasp" (cf. 1, Introduction: 3).

Although Maimonides asserts that the student for whom the *Guide* is written is "perfect in his religion and character" (*din w'akhlaq/de'ot v'middot*; 1, Introduction: 5), this cannot be entirely correct. If it were, the just-mentioned reasons for R. Joseph's perplexity would be inexplicable. R. Joseph's perplexity is self-induced. Unlike those conceited characters whom Socrates encounters and brings to perplexity, R. Joseph's perplexity is very much of his own making and, as noted, due to his premature desire to commence upon a study of metaphysics. As a result, the *Guide* is a treatise devoted (necessarily) not only to showing the deep harmony between Judaism and philosophy and thus alleviating the intellectual perplexity which R. Joseph feels, but also to tempering, in ways which we shall soon discuss, the enthusiasm of R. Joseph (and those like him), the young traditional Jew ("for whom the validity of our Law has become established in his soul and has become actual in his belief;" 1, Introduction: 5), who, because of his too early study of "the sciences of the philosophers" (ibid.), has become perplexed. Maimonides has R. Joseph in mind in 1.34 when he argues strongly against the teaching of metaphysics to the young:

It is accordingly indubitable that preparatory moral training should be carried out before beginning with this science [metaphysics], so that man should be in a state of extreme uprightness and perfection. . . . For this reason the teaching of this science to the young is disapproved of. In fact it is impossible for them to absorb it because of the effervescence of their natures and of their minds being occupied with the flame of growth. When, however, this flame that gives rise to perplexity is extinguished, the young achieve tranquillity and quiet; and their hearts submit and yield with respect to their temperament. They then may call upon their souls to raise themselves up to this rank, which is that of the apprehension of Him, may He be exalted; I mean thereby the divine science that is designated as the Account of the Chariot. (1.34: 77)

The reason here offered why one ought not to teach metaphysics to the young is perfectly illustrated by the case of R. Joseph.[24]

This 'moral' aspect of the *Guide* which I have been emphasizing reveals itself early in the work, in Maimonides' remarks about the *limited* goal of the *Guide*, that it cannot remove *all* the difficulties of the subject at hand and that in the final analysis the deep scientific and metaphysical truths it reveals are not (and cannot be) "fully and completely known to anyone among us" (1, Introduction: 6–7).[25] Given human nature and the finitude of man's intellect, mere flashes of truth are the best we can hope for. God's nature is beyond human ken, and similarly is His design for the world. Furthermore, such knowledge as we may achieve of our own end and goal comes only after a prior study of metaphysics, which itself depends upon a prior study of the principles of natural science.[26] Not only does Maimonides (attempt to) temper the boundless optimism of the young intellectual by outlining the limits of human knowledge (and the *Guide* itself), but he also does so by insisting that such (metaphysical) knowledge as R. Joseph hopes to attain cannot be achieved without prior study of that very subject, physics, which he wished to hurry over. R. Joseph's exuberance, natural but dangerous and ultimately self-defeating, and based upon a youthful, limitless intellectual optimism, is the immediate cause of his 'overlooking' the necessity of studying physics prior to metaphysics and, as a result, the root of his perplexity. And it is a major part of the *Guide* to root out this *moral* failing.

Viewed this way, Maimonides is, as much as Socrates, a moral teacher, an improver of men's souls. Of course Maimonides is interested in eliminating the intellectual perplexity which R. Joseph feels; and in this regard he proceeds to demonstrate the deep harmony between philosophy and Judaism. But at the same time Maimonides also wishes to root out the moral failing inherent in R. Joseph's too eager desire to learn truths for which he is not yet prepared. In fact, the *Guide's* double purpose, intellectual stimulation and moral improvement, is manifested in the very order of its presentation. The "Account of the Beginning" (physics) in part 2 precedes the "Account of the Chariot" (metaphysics) in part 3, and, given Maimonides' remarks in his Introduction to part 1 (9), this is hardly surprising. But preceding both physics and metaphysics is Maimonides' account of the nature of God (esp. 1.50–60), an account which is offered in the main, it seems to me, to show how 'other' God is from man and how slight man is relative to the divine. The entire discussion in 1.50–60, those famous chapters devoted to the human *in*capacity to know and to speak about God, is striking for the radically minimalist position Maimonides adopts. There is no direct way for us to know or to speak about God; given God's nature and human finitude, epistemic and linguistic periphrases are a necessity.[27] And *this* point, I suggest, has as much to do with inculcating a proper (moral) attitude (humility?) in R. Joseph as it does with making 'theoretical' points in epistemology and philosophy of language. Maimonides' remarks are offered with a view to deflating R. Joseph's pretentions about the infinite capacity of human wisdom. The *Guide*, then, via the order of its presentation, has the dual goal of humbling as well as instructing the perplexed. It chastens as it edifies. It forces a self-reflection upon the would-be learner. Unlike Euthyphro and Meno who (hopefully) learn that the conceit of wisdom is the greatest impediment to wisdom, R. Joseph learns that, although there is a deep harmony between philosophy and the foundations of his religion, there is an equally deep chasm between human wisdom and divine.[28] My claim is that for Maimonides this latter lesson, directed to the character of the student, is no less important than the former. Indeed, for Maimonides it precedes the former.

4. Individual and Community: Some Political Implications of the Maimonidean Elimination of Perplexity

Part 3, chapter 51 of the *Guide* adds nothing new to what has preceded, as Maimonides explicitly asserts. This chapter, indeed the final four chapters of the *Guide* (chapters 51–54) are "only a kind of conclusion, at the same time explaining the worship as practised by one who has apprehended the true realities peculiar only to Him after he has obtained an apprehension of what He is; and it also guides him toward achieving this worship, which is the end of man. . . ." (3.51: 618). But even if the final chapters of the *Guide* add nothing new to what has preceded, they do present Maimonides' final and most considered thoughts about the worship and knowledge of God, the *summum bonum*, and as such have much to do with the topic at hand, namely the ultimate goal which Maimonides as a moral reformer and teacher of the perplexed R. Joseph (and those like him) hopes to achieve.

Guide 3.51 initiates Maimonides' final discussion about the worship and knowledge of God. It does so in the form of a famous parable, likening God to a ruler in his palace and mankind to the ruler's subjects, some of whom dwell within the royal city, while others dwell outside the city's walls. The parable is as follows:

The ruler is in his palace, and all his subjects are partly within the city and partly outside the city. Of those who are within the city, some have turned their backs upon the ruler's habitation, their faces being turned another way. Others seek to reach the ruler's habitation, turn toward it, and desire to enter it and to stand before him, but up to now they have not yet seen the wall of the habitation. Some of those who seek to reach it have come up to the habitation and walk around it searching for its gate. Some of them have entered the gate and walk about in the antechambers. Some of them have entered the inner court of the habitation and have come to be with the king, in one and the same place with him, namely, in the ruler's habitation. But their having come into the inner part of the habitation does not mean that they see the ruler or speak to him. For after their coming into the inner part of the habitation, it is indispensable that they should make another effort; then they will be in the presence of the ruler, see him from afar or from nearby, or hear the ruler's speech or speak to him. (3.51: 618)

Maimonides' interpretation of the parable reveals, not surprisingly, his intellectualist prejudices. Proximity to the ruler is proportionate to the subject's scientific and philosophical capacity and achievement.[29] In the present context that part of Maimonides' interpretation which is of interest is his placement of those who fit the description of R. Joseph. Maimonides asserts:

Know, my son,[30] that as long as you are engaged in studying the mathematical sciences and the art of logic, you are one of those who walk around the house searching for its gate. . . . If, howev-

er, you have understood the natural things, you have entered
the habitation and are walking in the antechambers. If, however,
you have achieved perfection in the natural things and have
understood divine science, you have entered in the ruler's place
into the inner court and are with him in one habitation. This is
the rank of the men of science; they, however, are of different
grades of perfection. (3.51: 619)

As these remarks make plain, especially if we recall the description
which Maimonides gives of R. Joseph in the dedication to the *Guide*,
R. Joseph and those like him are far removed from the ruler's inner
sanctum, far removed even from the knowledge of the natural scien-
tist, not to speak of prophetic wisdom and true worship of God. Inasmuch as R. Joseph has not yet made a proper study of natural science,
he has not yet reached even the penultimate stage of wisdom. In fact,
Maimonides seems to equate the level of apprehension at which R.
Joseph currently is with that of those "jurists who believe true opinions on the basis of traditional authority and study the law concerning the practices of divine science, but do not engage in speculation
concerning the fundamental principles of religion and make no
inquiry whatever regarding the rectification of belief" (3.51: 619).
Although R. Joseph has studied mathematics and logic with Maimonides—and in this perhaps he had gone beyond those talmudists
who were innocent of such knowledge—his premature forays into
metaphysics, divine science, did not convince his teacher that his
intellectual acumen was beyond that of the nonphilosophically mind-
ed talmudist. In any event, neither is asserted to have yet gained
access to the ruler's antechambers.

At the acme of cognition, far removed from R. Joseph, are the
prophets. They are metaphysicians of the highest order, possessed of
a knowledge of God and consumed with a love for Him. These are
men "who set their thought to work after having attained perfection
in the divine science, turn wholly toward God, . . . renounce what is
other than He, and direct all the acts of their intellect toward an examination of the beings with a view to drawing from them proof with
regard to Him, so as to know His governance of them in whatever
way possible" (3.51: 620). And Maimonides completes his intellectualist ideal by asserting that "it is clear that after apprehension, total
devotion to Him and the employment of intellectual thought in constantly loving Him should be aimed at. Mostly this is achieved in soli-
tude and isolation." (ibid.: 621).

This intellectualist ideal, a deep religious devotion grounded in a consummate knowledge of natural science and metaphysics, seems to entail that the *summum bonum* for man is, according to Maimonides, isolationist. For Maimonides, as for his fellow countryman and near contemporary, Ibn Bājja, there would appear to be, in the final analysis, a deep cleavage between the individual's (true) good and his (political) role as a citizen in a society.[31] The elimination of R. Joseph's perplexity would seem to be purchased at the expense of his playing an active role, indeed any role, in his community.

But we would be wrong to reach this conclusion. I have argued previously and at some length against this 'apolitical' reading of Maimonides' view of the *sumum bonum*.[32] While I am not suggesting that there is no tension between the individual's good qua individual and that of the community, I believe that it can be attenuated to a large degree, and, further, that Maimonides is at pains to do so. As Maimonides argues in the final chapter of the *Guide* (3.54; cf. 1.54), the knowledge of God that one may hope to attain is knowledge of God's *acts* of (moral) goverance (sc. over nature, incl. man). Furthermore, "the way of life of such an individual, after he has achieved this apprehension [of a God who acts with loving kindness, justice and righteousness; cf. Jeremiah 9:23], will always have in view loving kindness, righteousness and justice, through assimilation to His actions" (3.54: 638). In sum, what R. Joseph learns at the end of the *Guide* is that God "delights" (*"chafatzti"*: Jeremiah, ibid.; cf. 3.54: 637) in acts of loving kindness, justice, etc., and, as a result, He demands such actions from man. In this way the intellectualist ideal entails moral and political action. I cannot, however, agree with Pines who asserts that "[t]he practical way of life, the *bios praktikos*, is superior to the theoretical,"[33] unless by "theoretical" Pines means "isolationist." Maimonides' 'intellectualism' is uncompromising; the talmudist who does "not engage in speculation concerning the fundamental principles of religion" (3.51) is, as we have seen, far removed from the antechambers of the ruler, i.e., from knowledge of God. But, although Maimonides' intellectualism is uncompromising, the *summum bonum* does entail practical activity. In this way the aforementioned tension is attenuated. Although *we* may distinguish between (theoretical) knowledge of God and (practical) imitation of ("assimilation to") His actions, the distinction is for Maimonides not sharp. For him, one does not have (true) knowledge of God if one does not imitate His ways. For Maimonides, the prophets were philosopher-kings.

The elimination of R. Joseph's perplexity is thus not purchased at the expense of his playing an active role in his community. By the end of the *Guide* R. Joseph has learned that, although God is utterly 'other' than man and man himself is possessed of merely a finite intelligence, knowledge of God, to the extent that that is humanly possible, necessitates moral and political activity. Properly reformed (*ex hypothesi*), sober and realistic in outlook and deliberate in his manner of study, R. Joseph has learned that it is only men like himself, morally virtuous and intellectually astute, who are capable of attaining that sort of wisdom upon which the well-being of his community depends.

5. Conclusion

The elimination of perplexity is for both Plato and Maimonides not merely the elimination of an intellectual worry. For both thinkers, it is concerned as much with moral reform, reform of character, for it is a defect in character which necessitates the initial perplexity. Indeed, for Plato the very *inducing* of perplexity is the first step in moral (and intellectual) progress. For him, perplexity is mandated, rendered necessary, because it is the only way by which, e.g., Euthyphro may (begin to) be disabused of his moral failing, the conceit of wisdom. So long as Euthyphro is emboldened by his conceit to lay claim to a knowledge which he in fact does not possess and to live a life which is at root a lie, a true search for wisdom, indeed the living of a good life, is precluded. Hence, the need for the Socratic *elenchus*, which elicits not only inconsistencies in the interlocutor's beliefs, but also in his life. In this regard Socrates stands revealed as a moral reformer, concerned to force all with whom he comes into contact to take stock of their lives. And in this regard too Socrates may be viewed as a *political* reformer, concerned to help his beloved Athens to live up to its reputation as "the greatest city with the greatest reputation for both wisdom and power" (*Apology* 29d).

In his own way Maimonides is also a moral reformer and the *Guide* his analogue to the Socratic *elenchus*. R. Joseph has attempted too much too soon, and this reckless impetuosity, a moral failing, even if understandable, leads to his perplexity. As a result, my suggestion has been that the *Guide* was written not only to remove his intellectual perplexity by providing explicit answers to specific problems (e.g., the compatibility of the account of creation in Genesis with the Aristotelian belief in the eternity of the world, the intelligibility of the *mitzvot*), but also to inculcate, in part by means of the very order of its presentation, the appropriate attitude or moral stance with which to achieve the *summum bonum*. By virtue of a discussion of the human incapacity to fathom God's essence, indeed of man's finitude relative to the divine, Maimonides indicates that the boundless optimism of R. Joseph is misplaced, in fact a sign of vanity, if it were not a sign of youth. Maimonides' discussion of the limits to human understanding, beyond which even Moses could not pass,[34] provides R. Joseph with the moral lesson that a kind of humility, a proper appreciation of man's finitude, is imperative before true learning commences.

That there are limits to human understanding does not drive Maimonides into scepticism. Knowledge is possible, even an indirect knowledge of God. In this regard Maimonides reveals himself, perhaps surprisingly, as a man of action. Although the *summum bonum* is knowledge of God, an intellectual achievement, such knowledge entails imitation of God's actions, deeds, moral and political, of loving kindness, justice and righteousness. In the final analysis, R. Joseph's perplexity as to the apparent unintelligibility of his religion is overcome not only by his being shown the deep harmony between Judaism and philosophy, but also by his coming to realize that humility before God provides the means whereby a man such as he can in due course achieve such knowledge of God and His creation that he becomes convinced that the foundations of his religion are intelligible and that the performance of the *mitzvot* is itself a *mitzvah*.[35]

Notes

1. *Euthyphro* 4a.

2. *Euthyphro* 5d.

3. *Euthyphro* 9d–e.

4. *Euthyphro* 5a–b, 15e–16a.

5. *Euthyphro* 11c–d.

6. *Euthyphro* 11e.

7. *Euthyphro* 15d.

8. *Apology* 21a.

9. *Meno* 80b.

10. *Meno* 80d–e.

11. *Meno* 85c.

12. Seeskin 1987, p. 100.

13. Robinson 1953, p. 11; Seeskin 1987, pp. 84–85.

14. *Meno* 86b–c with Seeskin 1987, pp. 125–26.

15. Kraut 1984, p. 295; Seeskin 1987, p. 134, n. 19.

16. Robinson 1953, p. 14.

17. Seeskin 1987, p. 81.

18. *Apology* 30a.

19. *Apology* 29d–30b. Note that Socrates views his mission as political, even as he is debarred by his *daimonion* from taking part in political life; cf. *Apology* 31c–d.

20. "Partial": 1, Introduction: 6–7 (Pines).

21. See also 1, Introduction: 16–17.

22. Dedication: 4; 1, Introduction: 9.

23. 1, Introduction: 9; 1.34: 75 with L. Strauss, "How to Begin to Study *The Guide of the Perplexed*," in *Guide* (Pines) 1963, p. xvii.

24. We might note in passing that Plato himself as well as Aristotle, like Maimonides and Aquinas after them, also warn against the too early study of metaphysics: Plato: *Republic* 497e–498c, 539b–540b; Aristotle: *Nicomachean Ethics* 1142a11–20 with *Rhetoric* 2.12; Aquinas: see the references in Maurer 1988, pp. 211–15 with notes 19–26.

25. Cf. 1.31–32.

26. See note 23 above.

27. For some recent remarks, see Harvey 1988, pp. 65–68 with note 26.

28. Again, 1.31–32 are important to read in this connection; see also 1.56: 130 and 1.58: 137.

29. 3.51: 620–21.

30. "My son" must certainly have reference to R. Joseph.

31. For Ibn Bājja, see *The Governance of the Solitary* 17.2: 78–9 (ed. Asin Palacios); cf. Pines, "Translator's Introduction," in *Guide* 1963, p. civii.

32. Frank 1985; Jospe 1986, pp. 188–91; Kreisel 1984, pp. 21–26.

33. Pines 1979, p. 100.

34. 1.54: 123.

35. Roslyn Weiss and David Shatz forced me to clarify some issues in an earlier version of this paper, and for this I thank them.

References

Frank, D. 1985. "The End of the *Guide*: Maimonides on the Best Life For Man." *Judaism* 34: 485–95.

Harvey, W. 1988. "Maimonides and Aquinas on Interpreting the Bible." *Proceedings of the American Academy for Jewish Research* 55: 59–77.

Jospe, R. 1986. "Rejecting Moral Virtue as the Ultimate Human End." In *Studies in Islamic and Judaic Traditions*, ed. W. Brinner and S. Ricks. Atlanta: Scholars Press, pp. 185–204.

Kraut, R. 1984. *Socrates and the State*. Princeton: Princeton University Press.

Kreisel, H. 1984. "Maimonides' View of Prophecy as the Overflowing Perfection of Man." *Daat* 13: 21–26.

Maimonides. 1963. *The Guide of the Perplexed*, 2 vols. Translated by S. Pines. Chicago: University of Chicago Press.

Maurer, A. 1988. "Maimonides and Aquinas on the Study of Metaphysics." In *A Straight Path: Studies in Medieval Philosophy and Culture* (Essays in Honor of Arthur Hyman), ed. R. Link-Salinger et al. Washington D.C.: Catholic University of America Press, pp. 206–15.

Pines, S. 1979. "The Limitations of Human Knowledge According to Al-Farabi, ibn Bajja, and Maimonides." In *Studies in Medieval Jewish History and Literature*, ed. I. Twersky. Cambridge, Mass.: Harvard University Press, pp. 82–109.

Robinson, R. 1953. *Plato's Earlier Dialectic*, 2nd ed. Oxford: Clarendon Press.

Seeskin, K. 1987. *Dialogue and Discovery: A Study in Socratic Method*. Albany: State University of New York Press.

Autonomy, Community, Authority: Hermann Cohen, Carl Schmitt, Leo Strauss

Martin D. Yaffe

1

Undoubtedly Carl Schmitt (1888–1986) intended his *The Concept of the Political* (Berlin, 1932; trans. 1976) as a corrective to twentieth-century philosophical discussions of, *inter alia*, autonomy and community.[1] Consider, for example, the book's concluding remark, concerning the interdependence of ethics and economics and their mutual dependence in turn on politics:

> the polarity of ethics and economics [is] a polarity astonishingly systematic and consistent. But this allegedly nonpolitical and even antipolitical system serves existing or newly emerging friend-and-enemy groupings and cannot escape the logic of the political.[2]

Schmitt insists that no coherent account of ethics and economics—nor hence of autonomy and community—can dispense with an adequate notion of political authority, which he finds missing in the liberalism of his thoughtful contemporaries. One suspects, perhaps, that Schmitt's own political shadow, his *quondam* or *quasi* Nazi past,[3] darkens any light his argument would cast on autonomy and community in Judaism nowadays. Even so, Schmitt's argument deserves attention, whatever its (or his) final merits. Consider the following mitigating or pressing circumstances.

First, Schmitt himself is a former Neo-Kantian,[4] an apostate of that philosophical school whose prominent representative, Hermann Cohen, remains arguably the leading systematizer of Judaism (rivaled

only by Cohen's epigone Franz Rosenzweig). May not Schmitt's
implicit inhouse critique of Neo-Kantianism, though not addressed
primarily either to Cohen or to Judaism, nevertheless prove instruc-
tive concerning the possible scope and limits of a Jewish systematics?

Second, Schmitt's critique touches the nerve-center of Cohen's
own synthesis of Judaism and Kantianism, insofar as Cohen on the
one hand construes the Torah's legislation governing the moral
behavior of the *community* as legislation intended above all to benefit
the (economically) poor, and on the other hand views morality as the
law-governed *autonomy* of the individual, i.e., as the individual's prin-
cipled (ethical) behavior dictated by a—or the—categorical imperative.[5] Would not Schmitt's critique then warrant our reexamining the
putative compatibility of Judaism and Kantianism, especially in light
of the former's traditional insistence, *contra* Cohen, on the harshness
or heteronomy of divine authority?[6]

Finally, Schmitt's book has occasioned at least one other noteworthy defection from Neo-Kantianism, namely Leo Strauss's return,
by way of an intricate polemic against Cohen, to the thought of Maimonides and his predecessors.[7] Does not Strauss's passing debt to
Schmitt therefore suggest at least the partial validity of Schmitt's critique in Maimonidean terms, i.e., in terms of the traditional conflict of
authority between classical political philosophy and the Torah's
divine law as understood by Maimonides?[8]

We plan to pursue the foregoing questions as follows. First, we
shall summarize Cohen's argument concerning the interdependence
of autonomy and community in his magnum opus *Religion of Reason
out of the Sources of Judaism* (1919),[9] insofar as it may be said, correctly,
to rest on the interdependence of ethics and economics. Second, we
shall outline Schmitt's implicit critique of Cohen in *The Concept of the
Political*, insofar as it points to the absence in Cohen et al. of an adequate notion of political authority. Third, we shall evaluate Schmitt's
critique from Strauss's newfound Maimonidean perspective by considering Strauss's own comments on Schmitt (1932), which Strauss
himself considered his first written expression of doubt concerning
the supposition of Cohen et al. that a return to premodern thought is
impossible.[10]

2

Does the systematic connection which Cohen would establish
between ethics and economics supply an adequate basis for under-

standing autonomy and community in Judaism? The connection sur-
faces in three central chapters of *Religion of Reason*: "The Discovery of
Man as Fellowman" (ch. eight), "The Problem of Religious Love" (ch.
nine), and "The Idea of the Messiah and Mankind" (ch. thirteen).
Cohen's argument throughout appeals for support to authoritative
Jewish texts (or "sources"), including of course the Torah and the
Prophets. Characteristically, Cohen 'idealizes' his sources.[11] That is, he
interprets them in the light of what he regards as their highest ethical
(and economic) possibilities. Accordingly, those sources are seen to
point the way toward a socially homogeneous and politically cosmopolitan mankind, whose individual members are linked above all
by their common respect for one another's moral autonomy, i.e., for
the presence or possibility of the categorical imperative in each.[12]
Even so, by idealizing his sources in this way, Cohen leaves doubt as
to whether he has adequately taken into account the possible truth of
their plain meaning—at least as understood by their original
addressees.

Chapter eight of *Religion of Reason*, for example, traces the original connecting of ethics with economics to the biblical Prophets:

> The great achievement of the prophetic teaching, and that which
> shows its inner connection with true morality, consists in this: . . .
> prophetic thought puts aside [the] questions of life and afterlife
> in the face of the life whose meaning is in question because of
> the evil which is represented by *poverty. Poverty becomes the main
> representation of human misfortune.*[13]

Cohen's argument here aims to show that what might be considered
the intellectual weakness of the Prophets is rather their moral
strength. The Prophets are said to ignore strictly theological questions, such as that of the relation between earthly life and an afterlife,
in favor of the single most pressing question affecting all human
beings as such, i.e., human beings without distinction of social class
or political loyalty. The Prophets question the meaning of the human
suffering occasioned by economic poverty. This question proves
inseparable from that of the moral worth of human life itself, for the
poor man (to say nothing of others around him) must inevitably consider whether his misfortune is somehow his own fault. The prophetic "achievement" is therefore to sever any presumed (or metaphysical)
correlation between individual suffering and individual guilt, and to
substitute a practical (or moral) correlation between that suffering

and what Cohen calls "the objective social contradictions which upset the balance of society."[14] Accordingly, individual suffering, notably in the person of the poor, calls not for society's blame but for its compassion; the poor man himself is to be thought of no longer as the anonymous 'next man' to whom we may remain indifferent, but instead as our 'fellowman,' whom we are bidden to love or treat as ourselves (cf. Lev. 19:18 and context). Rabbinic as well as pentateuchal texts are found to bolster Cohen's construction of the Prophets' meaning here. For example, Cohen cites the controversy between Akiba and Ben Azai over whether Leviticus 19:18 (*v'ahavta l'rey'acha kamocha*) or Genesis 5:1 (*zeh sefer toldot adam*) is the greater principle of the Torah, and endorses Ben Azai's preference for the latter on the grounds that the "moral concept of the fellow countryman [*reya'*] has as its indispensable condition the general concept of man [*adam*]"[15]—though we observe that Cohen's argument does not dispose of Akiba's practical point that the human beings whom the Torah directly addresses relate to one another in the first instance as fellow countrymen. Cohen further argues for the cosmopolitanism of the Torah's understanding of the 'fellowman' (*reya'*) by virtue of the latter term's connoting in addition the impoverished 'stranger-sojourner' (*ger toshav*), to whom the Torah grants legal equality in its stipulations concerning, e.g., uniform lawcourts (Ex. 12:49; Lev. 24:22; Num. 15:15–16; Deu. 1:16, 24:17–18), moneylending (Lev. 25:35ff.), slavery (Ex. 21:26–27; Lev. 25:47), and cities of refuge (Num. 35:5ff.)—albeit the texts themselves which Cohen cites seem to speak of the stranger-sojourner, if not exclusively, at least primarily as a temporarily dispossessed Israelite (cf. Lev. 25:8ff.). Finally, Cohen's idealizing stance towards the Prophets' teaching concerning the undeserved suffering of the poor allows or requires him to maintain near-total silence concerning the divine blessings and curses of Leviticus 26 and Deuteronomy 27–28, which include the threat of national impoverishment for disobedience to the Torah. Evidently the social homogeneity and cosmopolitanism which Cohen ascribes to the prophetic synthesis of ethics and economics do not rest on his appeal to authoritative texts alone.

What Cohen brings to (or takes from) his sources may be seen in chapter nine of *Religion of Reason*, which treats the Torah's "social legislation."[16] This term covers not only laws specifically benefiting the poor—including curtailment of property rights (Deu. 23:5), tithe (Deu. 14:28), first fruits (Deu. 26:6–10, 12ff.), gleaning (Lev. 19:9–12; Deu. 24:19ff.), sabbatical and jubilee years (Lev. 25:1–24), year of release (Deu. 15:1ff.), and debt regulations (Ex. 22:25; Deu. 24:6, 10,

14ff.)—but above all the Sabbath, which Cohen calls "the quintessence of the monotheistic moral teaching."[17] According to Cohen, the Prophets consider the Sabbath equivalent to the entire exercise of morality (cf. Is. 56:2, 58:3; Jer. 17:27), inasmuch as it aims at an equality of condition for all human beings by way of its bringing about a weekly equality of rest from work.[18] Cohen does not mention the additional or alternative possibility that the biblical Sabbath promotes communal cooperation and trust among Israelites in particular, by linking that weekly equality with common memories of the creation of the world and of the exodus from Egypt (cf. Ex. 20:11; Deu. 5:15). He does suggest the restorative benefit of the Sabbath for the poor man's soul when he remarks in a different context that "in poverty . . . the entire man is torn out of the equilibrium of his culture," and infers that religious love or compassion must therefore come to fill the "cultural consciousness" of the Torah's addressees in order to overcome poverty's culturally destructive effects.[19] Nevertheless, to speak of the Sabbath in terms of "culture," as Cohen does, is to separate its purported significance from whatever authority, divine or human, warrants its observance in the first place. We cannot help noting the similarity between Cohen's speaking here of the Sabbath in terms of culture and his speaking in chapter eight of human suffering in terms of economics. In either case, by construing his sources so as to conform with the presumed emancipation of the cultural and the economic from the theological and the political, Cohen betrays his approach to those sources as 'liberal' in the sense subsequently diagnosed by Schmitt (and Strauss).[20]

Chapter thirteen of *Religion of Reason* extends Cohen's idealized identification of suffering with poverty to an interpretation of the messianic passages in the Prophets. The Prophets themselves are now said to idealize poverty as piety: poverty becomes piety insofar as the pious in turn are the "forerunners of the Messiah."[21] Cohen argues dialectically against christological interpretations of Deutero-Isaiah's suffering servant passages, which would make the pious sufferer the scapegoat, not just the index, of mankind's ethical (and economic) shortcomings. On the contrary, the coming of the Messiah, according to Cohen, must never blur or compromise mankind's ongoing ethical responsibility toward the poor, but must sharpen and promote it. Awareness of his messianic task thus distinguishes the pious from the merely "eudaimonistic" or selfish. Because the pious man consciously "suffers from the injustice of the world's economy,"[22] it follows that his experience of poverty entitled him to infer the moral guilt of mankind, at whose hands, or negligence, he suffers. Even so, his piety originates in that he suffers not just from them but for their sake: his suffering would alert others to their need for moral repentance (and their concomitant redistribution of wealth to favor the poor). To this extent, then, the pious man's suffering is freely chosen, or partakes of the virtue of humility.[23] Nor is this all, for the relevant passages in Deutero-Isaiah et al. identify God's servant further with the people of Israel, which "to this day suffers vicariously for the faults and wrongs which still hinder the realization of monotheism."[24] Israel's messianic vocation is thereby opposed to vulgar nationalism, the political equivalent of eudaimonism for Cohen.[25] Yet does not Cohen exaggerate the antinationalistic animus of the Prophets when he claims, e.g., that Ezekiel paves the way for Deutero-Isaiah's "messianic leveling of all national contrasts and inhibitions for the sake of the uniform worship of God"?[26] According to Cohen, the depreciation of the nation in favor of mankind, or of the political in favor of the messianic, "is nowhere else formulated with such precision" as in Isaiah 49:5–8:

> And now, saith the Eternal that formed me from the womb to be His servant . . . "it is too light a thing that thou shouldst be My servant to raise up the tribes of Jacob and to restore the offspring of Israel; I will also give thee for a light of the nations, that My salvation may be unto the end of the earth . . . and give thee for a covenant of the people."[27]

Cohen rightly gathers from Deutero-Isaiah the superior merit of Israel's ideal messianic task of becoming a "light of the nations," as compared to its strictly political task of "rais[ing] up the tribes of Jacob and restor[ing] the offspring of Israel"; nevertheless, as we have already remarked concerning Cohen's reading of the "fellowman" and "Sabbath" passages of the Torah, the superiority of Israel's messianic task need not imply that its political task has no merit in its own terms. Cohen maintains in general that Israel's "historical dignity," like that of the economically poor, rests on its "tragic" suffering at the hands of the other nations of the world, whereby it "*acquires the right to convert them*"; yet surely this claim overlooks Deuteronomy 4:5–6, where the other nations are said to find Israel's ways intrinsically attractive by virtue of the Torah's "statutes and ordinances" (which are called "your wisdom and your understanding in the eyes of the nations"), i.e., by virtue of Israel's divinely revealed law rather than its putatively mandated suffering.[28] "What other solution is there," Cohen asks rhetorically in his own defense, "for the discrepancy between Israel's historical mission and its historical fate"?[29] Cohen's answer, it appears, is purchased at the price of the loss of the political.

3

In attempting to restore the dignity of the political in the face of contemporary liberalism, Schmitt resembles a twentieth-century Hobbes. Like Hobbes, he holds to the premise that man is, as Schmitt puts it, a "dynamic and dangerous" being.[30] Hence Schmitt's political thought looks first and foremost not to the greatest or most desirable human good, but to the worst or most terrible human evil: following Hobbes, he traces the need for the political community to each man's deep-set fear of his own violent and agonizing death at the hands of others.[31] Schmitt goes so far as to stress that a political community can properly protect its members from violent and agonizing death only when it understands itself in its own terms, unmarred by extraneous economic, ethical, or aesthetic considerations. Thus, for example, Schmitt is not content with merely endorsing the Neo-Hegelian Erich Kaufmann's criticism of the Neo-Kantian Rudolf Stammler's claim that the "social ideal" is the "community of free willing individuals"; after quoting Kaufmann as saying that "not the community of free willing individuals, but the victorious war is the social ideal: the victorious war as the last means toward that lofty goal," Schmitt immediately adds that the very term "social ideal," a hallmark of Neo-Kantian ethics, is nevertheless incommensurate and incompatible with an understanding of the political.[32] Inasmuch as Cohen himself uses the term "social ideal" as equivalent to what he takes to be the goal of Judaism's prophetic messianism,[33] we limit our account of *The Concept of the Political* to showing Schmitt's reasons for rejecting that term. We may conveniently gather Schmitt's argument under the three headings mentioned in the title of our paper—autonomy, community, authority.

Schmitt on Autonomy. Schmitt deliberately limits his overall argument to clarifying the distinguishing feature of the political.[34] Accordingly, neither economic nor ethical nor even aesthetic considerations enter into his concomitant understanding of autonomy. Autonomy for Schmitt properly characterizes only the political community. What then distinguishes the political? As economics stands or falls with the concept of the profitable (as opposed to the unprofitable), ethics with the concept of the good (as opposed to evil), and aesthetics with the concept of the beautiful (as opposed to ugly), so too the political has its underlying concept. It is the concept of the friend as opposed to the enemy. A friend is whoever defends the particular way of life established by a given political community; an enemy is whoever threatens it. The difference between friend and enemy is not merely conceptual, though, but "concrete and existential,"[35] since the very existence or survival of the political community depends on its knowing who its friends and enemies are. In a crisis, a friend is whoever will fight on behalf of that community; an enemy, whoever will fight against it. The autonomy of the political community is thus its ability "to treat, distinguish, and comprehend the friend-enemy antithesis independently of other antitheses."[36] Schmitt does not draw the inference that politics, given its fullblown autonomy, is altogether amoral. "The connection of politics with thievery, force, and repression is, in the final analysis, no more precise than is the connection of economics with cunning and deception."[37] Politics, like economics, though superfically amoral, permits the exercise of morality—nay, as Strauss will comment approvingly concerning Schmitt, is the condition for its possibility.[38] It follows that moral action always takes place within the horizon of one's political loyalties. Consider, for example, how Schmitt might resolve the ethical controversy as Cohen cites it between Akiba and Ben Azai over whether the Torah's legislation concerning the "fellowman," etc., covers above all one's fellow Israelite or all mankind. Were Schmitt's own political allegiance (or counsel) first and foremost to ancient Israel, then he might well agree with Akiba, on the grounds that economic solidarity with one's fellow Israelite is morally necessary for insuring Israel's purely political survival, and vice versa (cf., e.g., Jeremiah 34). On the other hand, given that his political allegiance is to a modern 'liberal' state, within which Jews are nevertheless afforded certain liberties, his endorsement of either Akiba's practical parochialism or Ben Azai's "ideal" universalism—or more grimly, his own "existential" animus against both—would depend on his judgment concerning whether *tsedakah* in the form of Jewish self-help or in the form of general philanthropy—or in any form at all!—were morally preferable for the good of, say, Weimar Germany's political survival.

Schmitt on Community. Still, modern political communities according to Schmitt are not fully autonomous, but "liberal."[39] Schmitt argues that the notion of liberal politics is a contradiction in terms: liberalism can supply no more than a critique of politics, or a set of policies which would hinder and control the political, since it is animated by a "critical distrust of state and politics . . . whereby the individual must remain *terminus a quo* and *terminus ad quem*."[40] Liberalism's radically individualistic premises in no way justify the political community's need, in the extreme case, for the sacrifice of life on the part of its members. "For the individual as such there is no enemy with whom he must enter into a life-and-death struggle if he does not want to do so."[41] Because liberalism thus limits itself to "securing the conditions for [individual] liberty and eliminating impediments on [individual] freedom," its repertory of concepts remains entirely "demilitarized and depoliticized."[42] Liberalism would then replace the bond uniting the members of a given political community, their common fear of a potentially deadly enemy, by supplying instead a "rationally constructed social ideal," i.e., a "program, a tendency or an economic calculation."[43] Liberalism would thereby transform "the state" into "society" by blurring the fundamental, intuitively understood distinction between war and peace, and appealing instead to individuals' common apolitical self-interest, especially in the economic and the ethical. Economically, what unites individuals would be the common system of production and exchange of consumer goods and services; ethically, individuals' common "cultural" interests as supported by various humanitarian ideologies. Disregarding the life-and-death, existential struggles which beget the human need for political authority, then, liberalism would reduce human confrontation to a mere "dynamic of perpetual competition and perpetual discussion."[44] The core of Schmitt's critique of liberalism's supposition of a "social ideal" would thus seem to be the systematically rational or constructive—hence arbitrary or willful—character of that ideal, as opposed to the "self-understood" character of the political. In this respect, Schmitt remains less beholden to Hobbes, the putative founder of liberalism,[45] than to Nietzsche, who like Schmitt discerns the irrational character of rationality when the latter is viewed as a merely constructivist or willful activity.[46]

Schmitt on Authority. To see the political plausibility, at any rate, of Schmitt's argument concerning mankind's continuing need for political authority, it is sufficient to consider his answers to the following two questions: (1) How would the "ideal" global society come about? (2) How would it run? Regarding the former question, its coming about would seem impossible without the elimination of political enmities which now abound and which thereby justify the need for political communities. If their elimination will not be spontaneous or fortuitous, then by what further justification will men accomplish it?

Liberalism's "social ideal" provides no adequate warrant for the threat or use of force presumably required, inasmuch as "no program, no ideal, no norm, no expediency confers a right to dispose of the physical life of other human beings"—a right justified only by a "real," albeit potentially ever-present, emergency.[47] To argue that, say, a global war to abolish trade barriers is necessary so that the survivors or their grandchildren may live in peace and economic abundance is "sinister and crazy"; similarly, "to condemn war as homicide and then demand of men that they wage war, kill and be killed, so that there never again will be war" is a "manifest fraud"; etc.[48] Regarding the second question, then, about how the purportedly politically neutralized society would run, Schmitt considers the claim that cooperation would be no less smooth than within any interest group nowadays, e.g., among tenants of the same apartment building, or subscribers to the same utility company, or passengers traveling on the same bus.[49] Schmitt, of course, is not convinced. The "belief that everything would then function automatically, that things would administer themselves, and that a government by people over people would be superfluous because human beings would then be absolutely free," he argues, remains just that—a "belief," or what he also calls "an anthropological profession of faith" in an "optimistic" view of man, as opposed to the "pessimism" assumed by all genuinely political thinkers.[50] Schmitt thereby pits himself against the unargued or barely argued "optimism" which may be said to permeate liberal thinkers like Cohen.[51]

4

Though persuaded by Schmitt's strictly political critique of liberalism, Strauss wonders in turn about its philosophical implications, which Schmitt fails to address fully. While Schmitt polemicizes against liberalism, he remains by his own admission a prisoner of it, and so in the last analysis fails to supply an alternative by which its effect may be more fully understood.[52] That alternative, according to Strauss, is the thought of Maimonides and his predecessors—including on the one hand what Strauss later came to call classical political philosophy, as found in the writings of Plato et al.,[53] and on the other hand the Torah itself.[54] Despite fundamental disagreements or tensions among Maimonides' sources, and hence within Maimonides as Strauss understands him, they all seem to agree both among themselves and with Schmitt on the continuing need for strong political authority.[55] They divide over whether that authority is justified in terms of the irreducibly political character of human nature (Plato et al.) or the irreducibly revealed character of the divine law (the Torah) or whether some rapproachement is possible (Maimonides).[56] In any case, Strauss's own critique of Schmitt seems guided in great measure by the foregoing agreements and disagreements.

Contra Schmitt on Autonomy. As Strauss points out, Schmitt himself admits that it is not enough merely to show the incoherence of liberalism as it abandons the possibility of justifying political authority. "What is required," says Strauss, quoting Schmitt's words, "is to replace the 'astoundingly consistent systematics of liberal thought,' which reveals itself in the inconsistency of all liberal *policies*, by 'a different system,' by a system that does not negate the political, but brings the political into full recognition."[57] Why then is Schmitt himself unable to supply that "different system"? According to Strauss, Schmitt too has succumbed to liberalism's failure to understand the political. On the one hand, Schmitt acknowledges the almost total victory of liberalism since Hobbes in "depoliticizing" the concepts by which human affairs are to be understood; on the other hand, Schmitt's own principle of attending above all to "concrete" political existence prevents him from further considering the principles appealed to and articulated by the political participants themselves, which might conceivably "bring the political into full recognition." In other words, Schmitt is not sufficiently attentive to the fact that "liberalism did not banish the political from the world, but only concealed it."[58] If Strauss is correct, then, the need to reintroduce the notion of political authority is not merely polemical but philosophical, i.e., to "clear the obfuscation of reality which liberalism has caused."[59]

Contra Schmitt on Community. Philosophically speaking, the proper starting-point for appraising Schmitt's critique of liberalism, as Strauss reads it, is his rejection of the flawed Neo-Kantian attempt to understand the political community as a species or product of 'culture'.[60] Strauss's reading of that rejection is as follows. Given that the need for the political community is grounded in the extreme case, in those existential confrontations where human life itself is at stake, it follows that Schmitt is correct in insisting that the political is not simply analogous to other supposed products of 'culture' (like economics, morality, art, etc.) but is *sui generis*, fundamental, and authoritative with respect to its understanding of human life. 'Culture', on the other hand, originally means the cultivation of human 'nature' (by an analogy with 'agriculture', the cultivation of the soil). Even so, Schmitt here fails to notice an important ambiguity, which might have led him to a more philosophical understanding of the need for the political community, namely, does 'cultivation of nature' mean the development of human dispositions by looking to nature as a guide or model to be imitated, or does it mean instead the overcoming of those dispositions by conceiving of nature as a mere inconvenience or disorder to be removed? Unfortunately, post-Hobbesian liberals tend to take for granted the latter alternative. Hence arises the danger, among those liberals and others, of forgetting that nature is the indispensable basis for 'culture'. To that extent, Strauss therefore approves of Schmitt's returning to Hobbes, for whom the political community is justified in terms of nature, albeit in order to overcome the so-called 'state of nature', which Schmitt like Hobbes conceives as a state of war.[61] If Schmitt nevertheless differs from Hobbes, it is in identifying the 'natural' state of war with enmity among communities rather than among individuals. Thus he is able to justify the community's demand for sacrifice of individual life, as Hobbes cannot. For both Hobbes and Schmitt, though, the authority of the political community remains conditional, i.e., the function of politics is said to be the protection of civilized life against 'natural' violence. In any case, Strauss finds Schmitt correct in holding Hobbes to be superior to post-Hobbesian liberals for his maintaining the connection between the political community and nature. As Strauss remarks, Hobbes' own "liberal ideal of civilization" is polemically directed against "not corrupt institutions or the ill will of a ruling stratum, but man's natural malice."[62]

Contra Schmitt on Authority. And yet Strauss approves of Schmitt's refusal to consent to Hobbes' 'liberal' premise that man's natural malice, or what Schmitt calls man's "dangerousness," ought to be entirely removed by "civilization." He does so at least in part for the sake of morality itself. He argues that a completely "civilized" or pacified globe, a world without life-or-death conflicts (the world, we may say, of Nietzsche's 'last man'), would be a world where human acts themselves would lack serious consequences.[63] It would be a world without morality, hence a less-than-human world. Yet if morality is to be understood as 'autonomy' in the (Neo-)Kantian (and liberal) sense, then what serious alternative remains for preserving it against liberalism's onslaught? Here Strauss sees the limits of Schmitt's own position. Schmitt "accepts his opponents' view of what constitutes morality instead of questioning the claim of humanitarian-pacifist morality to be the true morality."[64] Strauss himself does not spell out that alter-

native in his present "Comments," which are limited rather to analyz-
ing Schmitt's own "simple and elementary presentation" of the political.[65] Nevertheless Strauss's incidental references to Plato's *Euthyphro*
(7b–c) and *Phaedrus* (263a) indicate the decisive premise which separates the post-Hobbesian morality or politics from the pre-Hobbesian
alternative which he has in mind, namely, the latter's openness or def-
erence to a higher, supramoral or suprapolitical authority.[66] The
Euthyphro passage to which Strauss refers suggests that serious moral
disagreements, along with the resulting enmities which human
beings face, far from being self-contained or adequately intelligible in
themselves, derive instead from human beings' practical inability to
come to adequate understandings about the highest things, such as
what is just and unjust, noble and base, good and bad. Strauss's impli-
cation, *contra* Schmitt, is that while human beings may need friends,
and hence morality, etc., in order to help themselves defend against
enemies, they need friends even more in order to help themselves
pursue wisdom concerning the highest things, i.e., to philosophize.
Similarly, as we have already mentioned in connection with Cohen
(and as Strauss himself notes elsewhere), the Torah too seems to set
its standards by reference to wisdom—although not necessarily of a
philosophical kind.[67] However else the moral teachings of the pre-
Hobbesian political philosophers may disagree with the authority of
the Torah, they agree that the harshness of political life is made necessary, or at any rate plausible, by human beings' ongoing need for wisdom.

Notes

1. The German original of Strauss's essay (1932) is republished in
Strauss 1965a, Anhang, pp. 161–81, and in Meier 1988, pp. 99–125. The
English translation first appeared in Strauss 1965b, Appendix, pp. 331–51.
Subsequent references to *The Concept of the Political* and to Strauss's Com-
ments on it will be to Schwab's edition (Schmitt 1976).

2. Schmitt 1976, p. 79.

3. Cf. Bendersky 1983 and Schwab 1989.

4. Cf. Schwab 1989, p. 14, with pp. 49f. and 73f.

5. Cf. "Innere Beziehungen der Kantischen Philosophie zum Judentum," in Cohen 1924, vol. I, pp. 284–305, esp. p. 300f., or abridged translation
in Cohen 1972b, pp. 77–89, esp. p. 86f.; with Cohen 1966, pp. 69, 123f., 281f.,

339ff., 385f., 400ff., 416ff., 525ff., or Cohen 1972a, pp. 60, 106, 240f., 291ff., 331, 344f., 357ff., 455ff.

6. Cf., e.g., *Pirkei Avot* I.7, II.19–21, III.1–2, 11, 15, IV.13, 24, 29, V.11–12, 26.

7. Strauss 1935 or 1987; with Yaffe 1989.

8. Cf. Strauss 1979.

9. See note 5, above.

10. See note 1, above, with Strauss 1965b, p. 31. The preface is republished in Strauss 1968, pp. 224–59; see p. 257.

11. Cohen 1966, pp. 89ff., 172, 303f., 307, 313, 329, 390f., 404, 422, 434, 462f.; or Cohen 1972a, pp. 77ff., 148, 260f., 263, 268, 282f., 335f., 347, 363, 374, 398f.

12. E.g., "The national peculiarity [of the Jewish people] in its stateless isolation is the symbol for the unity of the confederation of mankind, as the ultimate of world history. It is the unity of mankind in monotheism and in the morality founded upon it." Cohen 1966, p. 296, or Cohen 1972a, p. 254.

13. Cohen 1966, p. 155, or Cohen 1972a, p. 134; the emphasis is Cohen's.

14. Cohen 1966, pp. 155 ("die grosse Tat der Prophetismus"), 154, or Cohen 1972a, pp. 134, 133.

15. Cohen 1966, p. 137f., or Cohen 1972a, p. 119.

16. The term itself occurs only in later chapters: Cohen 1966, pp. 499, 512; or Cohen 1972a, pp. 430, 444.

17. Cohen 1966, p. 180, or Cohen 1972a, p. 155.

18. Cohen 1966, p. 182f., or Cohen 1972a, p. 157.

19. Cohen 1966, p. 170 ("seines Kulturbewusstseins gerissen"), Cohen 1972a, p. 146.

20. Cf. Schmitt 1976, pp. 48, 53ff.; Strauss 1976, pp. 85ff., with Strauss 1935, p. 31 (n. 1), or Strauss 1987, p. 114 (n. 7).

21. Cohen 1966, p. 309, or Cohen 1972a, p. 264.

22. Cohen 1966, p. 310, or Cohen 1972a, p. 265.

23. Cf. Cohen 1966, pp. 309ff., 493ff., or Cohen 1972a, pp. 265ff., 425ff.

24. Cohen 1966, p. 313, or Cohen 1972a, p. 268.

25. Cf. Cohen 1966, p. 308f., or Cohen 1972a, p. 264f.

26. Cohen 1966, p. 328, or Cohen 1972a, p. 281f.

27. Cohen 1966, p. 329, or Cohen 1972a, p. 282; the emphasis is Cohen's.

28. Cohen 1966, p. 330, or Cohen 1972a, p. 283; the emphasis is Cohen's. Cf., however, Cohen 1966, p. 91, or Cohen 1972a, p. 78, with Cohen 1924, vol. III, p. 201.

29. ibid.

30. Schmitt 1976, p. 61. Cf. *Leviathan*, ch. 12, in Hobbes 1960, pp. 80–84.

31. Schmitt 1976, pp. 26ff.

32. ibid., p. 33 (n. 13).

33. E.g., Cohen 1966, p. 512, or Cohen 1972a, p. 444. Cf. "Das sozial Ideal bei Platon und den Propheten," in Cohen 1924, vol. III, pp. 306–18, or abridged translation in Cohen 1972b, pp. 66–77.

34. Schmitt 1976, pp. 25ff.

35. ibid., p. 27.

36. ibid.

37. ibid., p. 77.

38. ibid., p. 99.

39. ibid., pp. 69ff.

40. ibid., p. 70f.

41. ibid., p. 71. Cf. *Leviathan*, ch. 21, in Hobbes 1960, p. 142f., with Strauss 1976, pp. 88ff.

42. Schmitt 1976, p. 71.

43. ibid., p. 72.

44. ibid.

45. Cf. Strauss 1986, pp. 89, 105.

46. Cf. *Twilight of the Idols*, "Maxims and Arrows," Aphorism 26, in Nietzsche 1976, p. 470.

47. Schmitt 1976, p. 48.

48. ibid.

49. ibid., pp. 57ff.

50. ibid., p. 57f

51. Cf. Cohen 1966, pp. 33ff., 213, 503, 524, with 108, 111f., 314ff., 432ff., 459ff., 512f., 518, 523ff.; or Cohen 1972a, pp. 17ff., 182, 434, 454, with 98f., 102f., 269ff., 372ff., 396ff., 444, 448f., 453ff. Meier indicates that Schmitt's own pessimism is ultimately grounded in a "political theology" heavily indebted to a belief in original sin; 1988, pp. 77ff. Cf. Schmitt 1985, esp. pp. 36ff.

52. Strauss 1976, pp. 84ff., 103f.

53. Cf. Strauss 1959, pp. 78–94.

54. Cf. Strauss 1983, pp. 147–73.

55. Cf. Strauss 1963, p. 205, or Strauss 1959, p. 111.

56. The rapprochement may be to a considerable extent, though not entirely, rhetorical. Cf. Strauss 1935, pp. 68–122, esp. 121f., or Strauss 1987, pp. 59–110, esp. 109f., with Strauss 1952, pp. 38–94, and Strauss 1979.

57. Strauss 1976, p. 83.

58. ibid., p. 82.

59. ibid.

60. Cf. ibid., p. 84.

61. ibid., pp. 91ff., 101, with note 30, above. Cf. Strauss 1936, pp. 168ff.

62. ibid., p. 89.

63. *Thus Spoke Zarathustra*, Part I, Prologue, sec. 5, in Nietzsche 1976, pp. 128–31.

64. Strauss 1976, p. 102.

65. Cf. ibid., p. 81.

66. ibid., p. 100. The *Euthyphro* passage reads as follows: "Then what would we differ about and what decision would we be unable to reach, that we would be enemies and angry at each other? Perhaps you have nothing ready to hand, but consider while I speak whether it is these things: the just and the unjust, and noble and shameful, and good and bad. Isn't it because we differ about these things and can't come to a sufficient decision about them that we become enemies to each other, whenever we do, both I and you and all other human beings?" (trans. West 1984, p. 49).

67. Cf. Deu. 4:6–8, with Maimonides, *Mishneh Torah*, Laws of Kings and Their Wars, XII.4–5.

References

Bendersky, J.W. 1983. *Carl Schmitt: Theorist for the Reich*. Princeton: Princeton University Press.

Cohen, H. 1924. *Hermann Cohens Jüdische Schriften*. 3 vols. Berlin: C.A. Schwetschke & Sohn.

——. 1966. *Religion der Vernunft aus den Quellen des Judentums*. 2nd ed. Darmstadt: Joseph Melzer Verlag.

——. 1972a. *Religion of Reason out of the Sources of Judaism*, trans. by S. Kaplan. Introductory essay by L. Strauss. New York: Frederick Ungar.

——. 1972b. *Selections from the Jewish Writings of Hermann Cohen*, trans. and ed. by E. Jospe. New York: Viking.

Hobbes, T. 1960. *Leviathan*, ed. by M. Oakeshott. Oxford: Basil Blackwell.

Meier, H. 1988. *Carl Schmitt, Leo Strauss, und "Der Begriff des Politischen": Zu einem Dialog unter Abwesenden*. Stuttgart: J.B. Metzler Verlag.

Nietzsche, F. 1976. *The Portable Nietzsche*, trans. and ed. by W. Kaufmann. New York: Penguin Books.

Schmitt, C. 1963. *Der Begriff des Politischen. Text von 1932 mit einem Vorwort und drei Corollarien*. Berlin: Dunckler & Humblot.

——. 1976. *The Concept of the Political*, trans. by G. Schwab, with comments on Schmitt's essay by L. Strauss. New Brunswick, N.J.: Rutgers University Press.

——. 1985. *Political Theology: Four Chapters on the Concept of Sovereignty*, trans. by G. Schwab. Cambridge, MA: MIT Press.

Schwab, G. 1989. *The Challenge of the Exception: An Introduction to the Political Ideas of Carl Schmitt between 1921 and 1936*. 2nd ed. New York: Greenwood Press.

Strauss, L. 1932. "Anmerkungen zu Carl Schmitt, *Der Begriff des Politischen*." *Archiv für Sozialwissenschaft und Sozialpolitik* 67: 732–49.

——. 1935. *Philosophie und Gesetz: Beiträge zum Verständnis Maimunis und seiner Vorläufer*. Berlin: Schocken Verlag.

——. 1936. *The Political Philosophy of Hobbes*, trans. by E.M. Sinclair. Oxford: Clarendon Press.

——. 1952. *Persecution and the Art of Writing*. Glencoe, Ill.: The Free Press.

——. 1959. *What is Political Philosophy?* Glencoe, Ill.: The Free Press.

——. 1963. *On Tyranny*. rev. ed. Ithaca, N.Y.: Cornell University Press.

———. 1965a. *Hobbes' politische Wissenschaft*. Neuweid: Hermann Luchterhand Verlag.

———. 1965b. *Spinoza's Critique of Religion*. New York: Schocken Books.

———. 1968. *Liberalism Ancient and Modern*. New York: Basic Books.

———. 1976. Comments on Schmitt, in Schmitt 1976.

———. 1979. "The Mutual Influence of Theology and Philosophy." *The Independent Journal of Philosophy* 3: 111–18.

———. 1983. *Studies in Platonic Political Philosophy*. Chicago: University of Chicago Press.

———. 1987. *Philosophy and Law: Essays toward the Understanding of Maimonides and his Predecessors*, trans. by F. Baumann. Philadelphia: Jewish Publication Society.

West, T.G. and G.S. 1984. *Four Text on Socrates: Plato's* Euthyphro, Apology of Socrates, *and* Crito, *and Aristophanes'* Clouds. Ithaca, N.Y.: Cornell University Press.

Yaffe, M.D. 1989. "On Leo Strauss's *Philosophy and Law*." *Modern Judaism* 9: 213–25.

A Jewish Context for the
Social Ethics of Marx and Levinas

Robert Gibbs

If ethics can no longer originate in an autonomous self, then ethical responsibility need not dissolve into a puddle of ideological constraints. Rather, ethics stands in need of a reorientation, one which can loosely be called social ethics; that is, responsibility emerges in an already social interaction. The responsible person is already bound with others in a material nexus. Thus economics is neither irrelevant nor consequent to ethics, but constitutes the very plane in which responsibility occurs. Ethics must address economic injustice neither by quitting nor by transcending the field, but by redressing injustice within the economic world.

This paper presents a parallel reading of two valuable resources for reconstruing ethics as that sort of social ethics: Levinas and Marx. I will draw out a common agenda of social ethics focusing on the material needs of others. I will explore the ground shared by three views: Levinas's social ethics, Marx's emphasis on economic justice, and a generic articulation of Jewish thought. I propose to give an economic reading of Levinas focusing on questions that would arise from some Marxian perspectives, and also to give a social ethical reading of Marx, drawing out Levinasian implications in his texts. Following those readings, I will situate both within a context of Jewish concepts. I will coordinate the three views by exploring the argument against the state.

1. In the Face of the Other

The central issue in Levinas's thought is how we come into society. He argues not only that we are social beings, but that even our freedom to join society is itself the result of a previous interhuman relationship. Thus the freedom which founds social institutions itself rests upon a previous sociality—a face-to-face relationship with an other. That previous relationship is the ethical, because in that confrontation with another person, with the face of another, I become infinitely responsible (able to respond) for the other person. My freedom is what the other invests in me, and so my responsibility for the other constitutes my own self. Thus my identity, my independence, and my rationality are social for Levinas.

My interest here is to focus on Levinas's concept of economic justice. Even though Levinas places greatest emphasis on the one-to-the-other social relation, I will coordinate my discussion around the theme of the third person. And while I do not wish to suggest a radical developmental theory of Levinas's thought, there are also significant variations. I will note the change in the roles that justice and economics play in his thought. On the basis of the roles of justice and economics I will raise the question about social institutions and the state.

Critique of Privacy

My point of departure for Levinas will be an essay published in 1954: "Le Moi et la Totalité" (MT). The purpose of this essay, and indeed of all of Levinas's mature work, is to describe the moral conditions for thought, to identify moral experience prior to thinking which itself calls forth thinking and reason. Levinas inverts the question of much ethical theory, as he asks not, Is it rational to be ethical? but, Is it ethical to be rational? His answer involves tracing rationality back to a prerational moral experience of looking at another face-to-face (see also SAS, 58). In this essay Levinas posits economic justice as the very moral condition for thought. However, he contests two alternate claims: (1) that love, particularly in an I/you relationship, is that condition, and (2) that reason provides its own condition for thought.

In more recent work Levinas has made room for the concept of love, but at that time he criticized it. The problem is simply that love creates an intimate society of two and only two persons. It makes no allowance for unintentioned consequences of actions. In the context of love, I can always redress and repent any wrong to the beloved, and so be forgiven, because the harmed person is a present you. But if a third person comes on the scene, then by restoring your due to you, I may deprive the third of its due. In French grammar, there is no informal plural of the second person: two *tu*'s must be addressed as *vous*. Levinas calls the relationship between two not justice, but rather beyond or before justice (MT, 358/31).

Society, in opposition, involves the permanent risk of alienation of my freedom. Society is a relationship where most of the others are not present, not known by me. What I do to them I will never know, nor can I remedy the harm I do to them. They do not have a personal relationship with me. Justice becomes an issue only with the possibility of a wound, or a tort, which cannot be repaired—in a situation where repair would cause other torts. Structural inequalities and market distortions of our works are the primary forms of injustice, because I cannot find the others whom I have oppressed in order to redress the wrong. Levinas even goes so far as to speak of the harm to a third precisely by the love of two—that their exclusivity can be this very sort of tort.

This theme recurs throughout Levinas's works, although purged of its strongly economic tone. In later works, he rejects a romantic, privatized interpretation of the face-to-face interaction. Levinas distances himself from the popular appropriation of Buber by insisting that the other is not to be a *tu* but a *vous*. Indeed, Levinas rejects the notion of an intimate relationship with God, an infinite *tu*, and prefers instead the emphasis on *il*, (he), going so far as to coin a term for the thirdness of the face-to-face relationship: *illeity*. Thus, while Levinas hones in on a face-to-face encounter, which appears to be a I/you relationship, he retains this critique of the privacy of love as not just.

In this early essay Levinas also presents an argument that will later move more and more to the center of his work, an argument that reason cannot be the foundation for ethics nor consequently for society. The basic argument is a reformulation of Rosenzweig's, from the *Star*, II, 2—that ethics 'appears' first in language, in speech. Spoken speech itself is an address from one person to another, but the I that speaks is a singular (even unique) person, while rational knowledge is general, based on the subordination of specific characteristics to concepts. Thus the knowing I is an I that speaks/thinks in order to know its own *ipseity*, but in knowing it loses that *ipseity*. The foundation of reason is the singularity of the I. Levinas asks, Can reason found the unique worth of each individual in his individuality? But, if we allow this standard trope of existentialist critique of reason, we can follow the claim that reason will rest on linguistic practice, and that linguistic practice itself will originate in a speech of an I to an other. For Levinas the primary encounter which precedes and indeed demands speech is of the I with its other.

The Face and Proximity

In the same essay, Levinas develops at length the concept of the face (*le visage*) which is his central concept. He later transformed it into the concept of proximity. I indicated above that Levinas claims that there is a moral condition for thought, that ethics precedes rationality. That moral condition is the one-on-one encounter, in which the other commands me by his face. The face is not some cluster of nose and eyes and ears, but is rather the nudity of his vulnerability. He shows his face, by showing that his freedom is vulnerable to my will. But at the same time, his face is a nonviolent limitation on my freedom. The face of the other commands me, "You shall not murder." His face affirms my freedom, by way of his *alterity*/his freedom.

In later writings, Levinas backs away from his strong commitment to a visible presence of the other in his face, and changes to an emphasis on proximity and touch, where again the other's vulnerability nonviolently commands a prohibition of my possible violation of the other. The proximity to touch of a naked face becomes the central phenomenon, as Levinas tries to refuse claims that the other becomes a presence for my consciousness.

But what remains constant from the earliest discussions of the face is that it is not simply an I/you relationship. Indeed, the point is that it does not depend on any intimacy and does not necessarily create intimacy. Thus one of the strongest tendencies of misinterpretation in Levinas must be checked: the isolation of two people in this moment where my responsibility arises is not a withdrawal from others. This is critical precisely because of the exorbitance of Levinas's rhetoric concerning this responsibility. He began his rhetorical descriptions with a reciprocal responsibility in "The Ego and the Totality," but he soon made it asymmetric, in *Totality and Infinity*, where I am responsible to the other. Then in ever heightened rhetoric: I am responsible for the other, for the other's persecution of me, and ultimately I am hostage for the other, even in his persecution of me (*Otherwise than Being*).

The Third

The intensification of the responsibility in this ethical 'experience' prior to reason, prior to intentionality, even to consciousness, produces an infinity of obligation. It is, moreover, an infinitizing spiral where the more I do, the more I accept responsibility for, the more I find myself accused and called upon to accept more. It is not long before one raises the question of how I can be infinitely responsible to two people at once, particularly in so far as each responsibility is independent of universal norms or principles. Since reason is derived from ethics, how can ethics be based on infinite obligations—unless we return to that tempting misinterpretation that Levinas is talking on the basis of love.

Levinas insists repeatedly that negotiation and measuring, even calculation of responsibilities begins with the entrance of a third person into my relationship with the other. In *Otherwise than Being*, he refers back to *Totality and Infinity*, (AE, 201/158) and there he all but quotes from his discussion in that earlier essay (TI, 188/213). There he discusses how the other is a third, that he institutes not an intimate love affair, but a society of freedom and of respect. In this early essay, Levinas had not discovered the asymmetry of responsibility, the fundamental nonreciprocal quality that he develops so persuasively in the major works. Thus the other is capable of being both a face and a third, and so requiring of me that I become a third by respecting the other and so myself.

> To respect is not to bow down before the law, but before a being who commands a work of me. But for this command not to allow any humiliation—which would take from me the very possibility of respecting—the command which I receive must also be a command to command him who commands me. It consists of commanding a being to command me. This reference from a command to a command is the fact of saying We, of forming a party. Because of this reference from a commandment to the other [*à l'autre*], We is not the plural of I. (MT, 371/43)

This command to command is what makes me also into a third, a person capable of giving commands. Whereas the intimacy of I/you would seem to consist of two independent selves in relationship to each other, the possibility of a We requires that we reciprocally invest each other with the freedom to command each other, for the sake of a third. In this essay Levinas articulates his strongest concept of mutuality and of community in his longest treatment of the We. He insists that we give each other commands, we do works, all for the sake of social justice (MT, 371/44). Justice requires an equality of the persons. Mutual relation accomplishes this equality.

Afterwards, when he develops the concept of the face, or proximity, when the ethical relationship is focused more exclusively on the one-to-one relationship, he avoids this We more and more, and distinguishes the asymmetric nature of ethicality from mutuality. But Levinas retains the importance of the third in order to avoid the honeymoon ethics he dismissed here. Despite the radical asymmetry of responsibility, that the other is higher than me, is master, teacher, and commander of me, Levinas still insists on an equality.

> The poor one, the stranger presents himself as equal. His equality in this essential poverty consists in referring to the *third*, thus present at the encounter and whom, in the midst of its destitution, the Other [*Autrui*] already serves. He joins himself to me. But he joins me to him in order to serve. He commands me as a Master. This command can concern me only so far as I myself am a master. Thus, this commandment commands me to command. The *you* [*tu*] is posited before a *we*. (TI, 188/213)

The equalization of the other with me occurs by reference to the third, for whose sake we must both serve. "The presence of the face—the infinity of the other—is destitution, a presence of the third (which is to say of all humanity which looks at us) and a command which commands commanding." (ibid.) Thus the other as the face is not only a concrete individual, but also obligates me with the whole world watching, as it were. Not only with his eyes am I seen and accused, but his eyes imply the eyes of everyone. I am not free to serve him in such a way as to harm a third. Thus we are in public, in the strongest sense. In *Otherwise than Being* Levinas writes, "[I]n the proximity of the other, all the others than the other obsess me and that obsession already cries out for justice." (AE, 201/158). Here is the emphatic denial of a private tryst, but the affirmation of a one-to-one relationship which, in its imperative of responsibility, is before the eyes of the world. While I am obligated beyond measure by the other, by the face or proximity, that responsibility is a public duty.

Levinas interprets this interposition of the third as the very speaking of language. Words, instead of being idiosyncratic tokens of love, are universals, referring to all humanity as their potential audience (TI, 184/208, 196/221). I speak to the other in response to the nonverbal command of "Thou shall not kill" in an attempt to justify myself, to apologize in the Socratic sense. I speak to the other as a response, but I cannot make a private deal with the other. By speaking I establish a public relationship, a relationship which reveals its intrinsic sociality. I speak because I cannot appropriate the other to myself. The third is the intrusion of language in responsibility.

Economics Before and After the Face

To balance duties to the thirds requires calculation, which itself is a further demand for reason. Justice requires that quantified duties replace infinite duties, and so produces an economics. "Justice can have no other object than economic equality" (MT, 372/44). In the early essay, Levinas introduces the concepts of work and of money as the means of accomplishing justice. He claims both economic works and money are intrinsically social. What is noteworthy is that seven years later, in *Totality and Infinity*, Levinas moves economics prior to the experience of the fact, to a pre-ethical world. The role that works played in the essay is now performed by the will and its freedom. By the time of *Otherwise than Being*, economics is eclipsed totally and has no place in the discourse. This eclipse of economics, of work and labor, and of money is in some ways only a measure of Levinas's developing focus on the confrontation which is the face, but it also is a move away from an analysis of the material world and its social reality. Levinas retains some rhetorical gestures towards material needs, but he is no longer interested in exploring them philosophically.

What is most interesting is not the eclipse but the shift from an economic theory which was linked to justice and to ethics, to an economic theory which is pre-ethical. In the earlier theory Levinas insisted that labor and will are not conditions for thought, but that they rest on thought. This depends on his interpretation of thought as itself resting on sociality—on the third and on the ethical. In that essay, we work in order to establish the justice commanded in the face of the other. Working, as opposed to enjoyment, is to risk alienating myself in the work produced. We consign the work to others, and abandon our control over it. Work is the production of something which will have social consequences beyond my intentionality, and thus depends on a previous trust in the society. Money, moreover, serves to measure the immeasurable—the other. The very calculation and balancing of duties instituted with the third requires an economic calculus, and money serves for that. Money allows for a social commerce to replace the vendetta for unintentional wrongs. But to use money is to trade what is in itself useless but what we trust others to honor in the future. Money is intrinsically social and is the key tool for instituting social justice.

In *Totality and Infinity* Levinas creates a moment of enjoyment prior to the ethical. We live for the sake of the Same, for assimilating what is other to ourselves. Independent of others, we stake a claim and make a home. We enter the world from our home, and go home when the day is through. Labor is the acquisition of what is other, transforming it into property, which can be stored at home. Labor now occurs in this pre-ethical world as my triumph over the resistance of matter, furnishing me with good things to eat, a house to be home in, clothes to protect me from the elements, etc. The key moment is the making mine by labor, the bringing it home—economics, in an etymological sense.

This economic theory, of labor and enjoyment, is pre-ethical, before the experience of the face, in order to make the other break into my self-centered world. At that moment I must feed him with my food and bring him into my home. Without a non-ethical economic life, I would not be capable of hospitality, of receiving the other, of giving from myself. The key move of ethics for Levinas is the inversion of the self from the one who brings other things home, making them its own, into a self which is bound to the other and gives to the other those same things. Moreover, the ethical demand is not in a different realm, in a nonmaterial realm. The demand from the other is not for some spiritual good, but for my material possessions. Economics is the milieu not only of pre-ethical experience, but also of ethical experience. Again, the demand for justice is a demand for economic justice.

In parallel fashion, Levinas has relocated justice. In the earlier essay, justice was the very goal of his project, and ethics was identical to economic justice. In the major works, justice becomes a third moment. First there is economics as the pre-ethical demand of the same, then the face and its infinitizing responsibility, and third, justice as a negotiation and weighing of those infinite responsibilities due to the presence of the third. It is not that Levinas no longer cares about justice, but that he focuses on the second moment (indeed, in *Otherwise than Being*, not only is the third moment of justice pushed to the boundary, but the first pre-ethical moment all but disappears). Levinas narrows his perspective to the complexities of that moment of obligation, the meeting with the other as the face or as proximity. For this paper, the relevant point is that although Levinas insists on the sociality of ethics, his focus draws ever more narrowly on the asymmetry and nonreciprocity of the face or proximity. But that is not a moment of justice, but a moment which precedes justice. Economics becomes a prior moment, and in so doing creates a permanent context for ethics and politics, and religion, while justice becomes the desired result, but not the question which most concerns him.

Religion vs. Politics: (1) Love and Paternity

In *Totality and Infinity* Levinas develops two contrary forms of social institutions. Starting from the face he moves in two opposed directions: (1) through love to fecundity and paternity, which he calls religion, and (2) through reason and the will to freedom, culminating in the state, which he calls politics. The first is truer to ethics discovering the self living beyond its own death in the continuity of generations. The second is at best an ambivalent transformation of ethics, as politics betray ethics as it translates it into an overcoming of time and its change.

Perhaps after criticizing private love as nonsocial, an invocation of love seems out of place, and yet, it is love that Levinas draws upon for the positive sociality of religion. He asserts again that love is antisocial (TI, 242/264–5), but he then explores love's ambiguity. Love is at once ethical and pre-ethical. On the one hand it is a pre-ethical desire for assimilation, of one's own enjoyment, but on the other hand it is an ethical relationship with an other. As merely love, the relationship to an other is exactly that isolated, private relationship I began by criticizing. The culmination of Levinas's analyses of voluptuosity, however, is the moment of sexual reproduction, the fecundity creating a child.

This discussion of fecundity is at once astonishing and obvious in Levinas. It appears in *Time and the Other* (1947) and more fully in *Totality and Infinity*, and it disappears in *Otherwise than Being* altogether. It is astonishing because Levinas argues that the father/son relationship displays a positive form of sociality based on the face. My child is me, although I am not him. That is, I am responsible for him, but not the converse. The very separation of the other from me here appears as unconquerable, but at the same time as constructive for responsibility. Indeed, Levinas sees time as infinitized with this responsibility, as the continuity of the generations creates a true time, an infinite future.

Despite the fantastic claims for sexual reproduction, Levinas is at the same moment making a quite obvious claim: that the responsibility we have for the other as free and independent (our children) can be the form for all ethical experience. Just as we would die to save our children, as we would pay their ransom—even if they were ungrateful, indifferent, or even hostile to us—so must we be responsible for others in a nonreciprocal and unilateral way. All encounter with the other, with the face, is of this basic form. The child is to be my survivor. Its freedom overcomes my own mortality. But all responsibility is responsibility for the other beyond my own death.

Moreover, fraternity arises from fecundity. The equality instituted by the third is a correlate of fraternity, just as the infinitizing responsibility is one of paternity. Levinas states that "fraternity is the very relation with the face where both my election and my equality are accomplished at the same time, which is to say, the mastery exercised by the other over me" (TI, 256/279). Just as the one-to-another relation involves the third, so fecundity creates fraternity; ethics is the inception of true equality.

Levinas devotes much of *Totality and Infinity* to discovering a sociality which will preserve the ethical. His discovery of the family as a positive institution is contrary to Hegel's analysis in *The Philosophy of Right*, where the family is an immediate social structure overcome in civil society. For Levinas, the family is a nonimmediate sociality. Moreover, in the family structure Levinas finds the possibility of the asymmetry and infinitizing of obligation that lies at the core of ethics, as well as the equality of justice. He is not canonizing the nuclear family as much as finding it as a model for all sociality. But a fuller appreciation of this positive institution depends on a contrast with the other form: the political.

Religion vs. Politics: (2) Reason and the State

Politics rests on freedom, on the will. The will, for Levinas, is the engine of the economic life. However, in *Totality and Infinity* Levinas discusses the will nearly as extensively as the face because what I make, my works, the fruit of my labor, is given over to others. My will becomes contradictory in my works, because it shows both the alienability of my will to others and also my attempt to make something my own (TI, 202/227). By cooking bread I appropriate it and prepare to assimilate it, but I also then exchange a second loaf for some cheese. Thus my loaf is now the other's loaf; my labor is now at the other's disposal; my will is lost. Commerce itself displays the interdependence of oneself and the others, not just as an exchange of complementary needs, but as entrusting one's work, and so one's will, to others.

Moreover, my will is not satisfied by hiding at home, within myself. It has no choice but to make works, to externalize itself. My will to survive, to live, to enjoy life, requires that I perform works for others. In one of the few simple appropriations from Hegel, Levinas's archenemy, Levinas agrees that a good will requires means outside itself to realize true freedom (TI, 218/241). The very equality which the third brought to the other and to me now becomes a foundation for exercising freedom. Freedom, like the third, brings a universality. Moreover, this universality is the prerequisite for reason.

Thinking, because of its abstraction and formalization in representing, allows for the balancing of competing wills and even of infinite responsibilities. As represented, as known, those infinities are reduced. In order to institute justice we must reason, we must use universal principles and concepts. The face cannot appear within rational discourse, but the face is the originating cause of that discourse. When the will expresses itself, it preserves freedom. In the expression, the will stays with its product: its word. A person stands behind his word, while he sells or commits his works to others. Reason and language function together to create the social realms of freedom.

But freedom requires institutions in order to survive. The will is molded into written texts. Written laws preserve freedom by universalizing it. Reason is the tool for this task. We put an end to violence. The state is the visible power of reason and universality.

And yet Levinas criticizes this realm of reciprocal freedom, of universal rational order. The very objectivity of this order is based on the reduction of the infinite responsibility I have towards the other. The universal discourse of reason cannot hear the unique apology of the I, the excess of responsibility which rests on me. I become a person, one of a species, with the universal duties which rest on us all. But I have lost the origin of the desire for freedom: the unique and personal responsibilities which devolve on me and for which I cannot be replaced. The rationalizing of responsibility is necessary in society, but it also betrays the prior sociality of the face. The state, as an institution of reason and of universality, is always drawn towards totalitarianism. In Levinas's terms, politics, as opposed to religion, is intrinsically a mistranslation, a betrayal of ethics.

The key point, at least in *Totality and Infinity*, is that the state is based on a universal reason which reduces the infinity of responsibility, which barters away its own foundation. The family, on the other hand, is a model for a positive sociality wherein not only is the infinity of responsibility preserved, but also where eternity can arise. Levinas elevates the family over the state, and indeed suggests that it is unlike the state, even when the state makes room for it (TI, 283/306). Thus there is a social program of sorts, based on the discontinuity and separation of selves in the family, which can stand as an alternative institutionalization of the responsibility demanded for by the face.

Critique: Skepticism and Philosophy

In this last section on Levinas, I take up what is one of the most challenging themes in his work: the derivation of reason from the ethical, and the consequent necessity for a skeptical interruption of philosophy. This dialectic of skepticism and philosophy is bound to a parallel dialectic of ethics and politics. In later works, such as *Otherwise than Being*, Levinas calls the ethical, proximity. In proximity to the other I discover my inalienable responsibility for what the other does. This responsibility precedes consciousness and intentionality. I have been assigned, accused, from before in a moment which is in principle immemorial. And yet, the third enters, or rather, in proximity to the other I am called before all others.

The relation with the third is an incessant correction of the asymmetry of the proximity where the face is faced. There is weighing, thought, objectification and by that, an order which betrays my anarchic relation to the Him [*l'illéité*], but where my relation is translated before us. Betrayal of my anarchic relation with the Him, but also a new relation with it: it is only *thanks* to God that I am a subject incomparable to the Other, that I am approached as other among the others, which is to say "for myself." . . . The "passing" of God, of whom I can speak only by reference to this help or to this grace, is precisely the reverting of the incomparable subject into a member of society. (AE, 201–02/158)

From the perspective of society, the obsession and 'infinition' of proximity is impossible. But absolute responsibility cannot be divested. God appears in a reflective judgment. God's agency cannot be specified, but the emergence of rational society out of the 'dead-end' of infinite responsibility requires this role. But once we gain reason, we start to think in terms of a society of three equals. Justice emerges from the previous ethical relation. The judge, upon whom the universal rational law depends is still a person, a person who is not outside the society, but within it—face-to-face with the criminal or the plaintiff. "The law is in the midst of proximity. Justice, Society, the State and its institutions—labor and markets—are intelligible from proximity: which means that nothing escapes verification by the responsibility of one for the other" (ibid.). Ethics verifies politics, the infinite is the measure of the finite.

Clearly, society is the society of politics, not that of religion. Religion's role has now been limited to the absent God who was here. Indeed in his later writings, Levinas seems ever more interested in the theological issues of an absent infinite God. Throughout *Otherwise than Being*, Levinas abandons the discussions of family and its alternate sociality. In *Totality and Infinity*, Levinas writes of the violation of individuals in politics, and claims that justice centers on the right to speak, to offer an apology. "Perhaps it is here that the perspective of a religion opens. It moves out of political life to which *philosophy does not necessarily lead*." (TI, 274/298; italics mine). But in *Otherwise than Being*, we find that philosophy now leads only down the path to the state. Politics remains as the essential form of sociality.

The disappearance of religion transforms the discussion of reason and the state. The ethical critique of reason and the state become focal, with no appeal to the more ethical social structure. But at the same time, we make room for an irresistible critique of philosophy. Philosophy, with no possibility of a detour into religion and social justice, must now become the rationale of the reduced responsibility of the state, and of written laws.

What saves philosophy, and the state itself, is that philosophy is not only what is thought, but that the act of philosophizing is speech to another, to someone else. The interruption of the philosopher's reasoning, the freedom of the interlocutor, transforms philosophy into apology. Philosophy's other is skepticism, which disrupts the system and universal reasoning. What skepticism objects to is not important; what is important is the perennial need for philosophy to apologize, to justify its answers to another. In that dialogue, proximity breaks up reason's government, and reason is criticized by the ethical moment. Thus the very vulnerability of the political to the objection of the ethical is the privilege of skepticism to demand an apology, a justification by philosophy.

At that point in his thought, Levinas focuses all of his sociological concern on a doubled dialectic within the state. Due to the freedom of the other, the ethical encounter remains both the origin and the perpetual interruption and critique of politics and its discourse, philosophy. But any full sociality of responsibility has become impossible, as the family and its positive sociality is gone. Social institutions are now limited to the political. We are left with an inevitable emergence of the state, and a demand that the state always be subjected to critique. As long as the family could be held out as an alternative, we could claim that Levinas rejects the state. Now that the ethicality of the family is gone, Levinas sees sociality producing an intrinsically unethical state whose fortunes are linked to philosophy. There no longer is a positive model for social institutions, and so Levinas chooses in a consistent way to focus on the moment before reason, the ethical moment which subtends the demand for justice.

I would add that these moves are paralleled in several of his essays on Jewish topics—the most important of which are his commentaries on *Sanhedrin* 99a (DL2, 89ff.) and the essays on Zionism in *L'Au-delà du Verset*. In an essay written in 1971, Levinas affirms the state, but, after tracing the theology of the Davidic kingship, he limits it to an almost Hobbesian role of protecting us from each other as wolves. He then explores messianic politics and the question of whether it takes us beyond the politics of war and beyond the politics of oppression (ADV, 216f.). Levinas's affirmation of Zionism is both dovish and religious, in both cases because he sees it as an attempt to transform politics towards a messianic politics, and he insists on distancing it from nineteenth century nationalism and realpolitik. He sees Israel's political arena as especially open to the critique of ethics. The question of Zionism, however, is not my concern here. Rather, the affirmation of a very limited politics, a state which establishes order, but which must be vulnerable to ethical critique, is the issue. Even in his writings about Israel, Levinas invokes what he calls religion (see "Pièces d'identité", DL2, 78f.) against mere politics. But in his later philosophical thought he insists on the inevitability of politics, and abandons the earlier hope for a religious social form.

2. Fully Human Sociality

While the focus on the third and on economics provided a somewhat unusual perspective on Levinas, the parallel overlap in reading Marx's work is more common. Not only are there Levinasian readers of Marx today both in Latin America and in France, but a general emphasis on Marx's social thought and earlier writings are a well-established trend. Levinas himself makes very few references to Marx. While the reading I now present is hardly a definitive reading of Marx, it serves to highlight the social ethics at the heart of the whole body of his thought. If the historical dialectic and the economic analyses receive short shrift here, it is only in order to identify an important and challenging common ground, and not in any sense to exhaust Marx's thought.

Social Humanity

Marx opposes the interpretation of the person as a self-sufficient individual, free to pursue his own interests, competing with all other individuals in order to maximize his own pleasure. In place of that view of the person [*der Mensch*], Marx offers the view of a social [*gesellschaftliche*] human.

> Therefore, the universal character of the whole movement is the *social* character; as society produces the *human* as *human*, so is it [society] *produced* by he/she. Activity and enjoyment in both content and *mode of existence* are *social: social* activity and *social* enjoyment. The *human* essence of nature is first that of the *social* human; because here for the first time nature is there for the person as a *bond* with *people*, as an existent for the others and the others for it, as the element of life of human reality. Here for the first time nature is there as *foundation* of its own *human* existence. Here for the first time its *human* existence become its *natural* existence and what is nature to it become human. (MS, 537–38/136–37)

Marx locates this positive concept of sociality in the communist society after the revolution; but I wish to begin here with a few essential qualities of that society, because it serves as a norm in Marx's thought. First and foremost, proper sociality is where one exists for others and they exist for one. This deep solidarity, that one's very existence is for the sake of others, is the heart of social ethics. It easily contrasts with the form of human existence in civil society: "Society—as it appears for National economists—is civil society, in which each individual is a whole of needs and is for others only, as the others are for it, in so far as each can be made a reciprocal means" (MS, 557/159). Thus society appears to be either a set of isolated individuals, who use each other as means, or a locus of solidarity, in which existence itself is interpersonal. Civil society is the illusion of people who exist only as means for others. It is a reduction of humanity from its fundamental social form.

Second, Marx claims that all forms of human society are intrinsically social. Even the businessman competing in the marketplace for his own interest participates in a socially defined practice. We are always social, but in all previous historical forms we have not been fully conscious of our mutuality, our solidarity. The illusion of isolated individuals making free choices to enter into contracts, as in Hegel's discussion of Abstract Right, is an illusion, confusing a small sphere of autonomy with the image of a radically nonsocial agent. The right to do what we want with our property is merely the right to ignore the social reality of our property and the social consequences of our choice (JF, 365/53).

Thus, third, the emphasis on the communist society as natural reveals the sense in which Marx considers human nature to be social. Only when existence becomes existence-for-others do I become what I am by nature. This moment of conscious appropriation transforms my inherent sociality, from alienation under the sway of unreflective institutions, into a rational and liberating sociality. Nature is to be reunited with humanity; rather, the fulfillment of human nature is to discover the full nature of humanity—that we are social, essentially. ("The individual *is* the *social Essence*" (MS, 538/138.)) Hence, the reconciliation of our nature with our humanity is possible only when we become fully social—and every form of society without that conscious reconciliation allows for oppression and false consciousness.

Fourth, and critical, this reconciliation occurs through the universality of the human race. "The universal character of the whole movement" is the discovery of the consciousness of the human race as the correlate in thought of the social life of the individual. This universality is an affirmation parallel to Levinas's third, as both Levinas and Marx are similarly sensitive to the need for universality. However, for Levinas such universality also brings with it a violence against individuality, in the name of the totality.

The Dissolution of Private Community

Marx opposes the positive sociality not only to the illusion of individuality in civil society, but also to the limited social forms of earlier society. He does not rest positive sociality on the community (*Gemeinschaft*), and indeed is somewhat reluctant about the very immediacy of the community. Rational thought, in which I have no immediate community, is a stronger principle for the universality of social life. By thinking in universal categories, I discover myself as fully social.

Like Levinas's critique of the privacy of love, Marx seems suspicious of any private, immediate community. True sociality requires the intervention of universality—what Levinas called the third. And civil society has made it its business to dissolve immediate communities, the family and other 'natural' associations (MS, 531/129). Marx describes in the *Communist Manifesto* how the bourgeoise has destroyed feudalism, the guilds, the dignity of the professions, etc. In civil society all value is reduced to a price. But Marx sees this as a positive move in history, precisely because the earlier direct communities are arbitrary and exclusivist. The integrity of landed property, to take an example, bestows value on the gentry, but it is hardly a rational or fully social value. Like Hegel, Marx accepts that the emergence of the rationality of modernity and of the destructive universality of civil society serves to sweep away these arbitrary social structures. The modern state serves the interests of civil society, in place of the feudal state which served the interest of the ruling class. But to replace the one state by the other required the dissolution of the communities upon which the feudal state rested (JF, 368/55). Like Levinas's third, this dissolution is accomplished by a weighing and calculation of the value of each thing—a commodification of all values, where the price determines worth.

The Universal Class

Marx claims that civil society will culminate in a capitalism so rampant that it will engender a universal class of laborers, a class which will hold no capital. The universality of civil society thus prepares humanity for the emergence of a fully social universality, that full sociality with which I began. While Hegel affirmed the state serving civil society, Marx claims that even that state cannot stabilize the universalization of competition and the destruction of communities. Even the artificial community of capitalists will fall prey to the competition of the market. Marx often discusses how capitalism destroys landholders, forcing them to become capitalists. He follows classical economics, but predicts greater and greater intensification of capital, coupled to ever worsening conditions for laborers. Ultimately, the ruling classes of the state and the cartels of capitalists will fall to a revolution of a universal class.

Where then is the *positive* possibility of German emancipation? Answer: In the formation of a class with *radical chains*, a class of civil society, which is not of civil society; an estate which is the dissolution of all estates; a sphere which possesses a universal character through its universal suffering; which claims no *specific rights*, because no *specific wrong* but rather *unqualified wrong* is perpetrated against it; which can no longer claim an *historical* title, but only a *human* one; which stands in no one-sided opposition to consequences, but in an all-sided opposition to the presuppositions of the German state; a sphere, finally, which cannot emancipate itself without emancipating itself from all remaining spheres of society and therewith emancipating all remaining spheres; which in a word, is the *complete loss* of humanity, and thus through which can win itself only through the *complete redemption of humanity.* This dissolution of society as a specific class is the *Proletariat.* (KH, 390/141–42)

The proletariat are the dispossessed laborers who have been all but cut out of the fabric of civil society. They will accomplish the revolution in which civil society will be overturned. They will be the universal class which will be opposed to class. In earlier society with immediate communities, class struggle resulted only in the realignment of classes, but since the dissolution of intermediary social structures, any class struggle now will result in the end of class structure. The very universality and totality of their oppression qualifies them not only to overthrow the capitalists and their state, but to stand against oppression in itself, to be the last revolutionaries. The radicality of their oppression (their chains) means that they can be expected to put an end to history, to social struggle. With the revolution, full sociality, the social humanity discussed at the outset, will arrive. In overcoming the state, the revolution will also overthrow capital and its central institution: private property.

Modern bourgeois private property is the final and most complete expression of the producing and appropriating of products that is based on class antagonisms, on the exploitation of one man by another.

In this sense, the theory of the Communists may be summed up in the single sentence: Abolition of private property. (MK, 475/23)

The proletariat, because they have no private property, will not revolt by demanding what others have, but will turn against the institution itself. And again, because civil society has taken oppression as far as it can go, it can be inverted, and we will now live in that full sociality without oppression, because all oppressive distinctions have been converted into that of property.

Economics Before and After the Revolution

Without delving into Marx's economic theories, I wish to make a few brief and fairly uncontroversial notes about Marx's view of capitalistic society. The focus in the earlier works is more on alienation, and less on quantitative economic analyses, although these are not necessarily independent, much less opposing, themes in Marx. Private property is the result of alienated labor. It is the hoarding of the workers' effort by the capitalist. Alienation in Marx focuses not simply on externalization of my will, but, specifically, on the expropriation of my labor. It is alienated labor that characterizes economics in the prerevolution world, for its is conserved by the structure of private property. Marx claims that the laborer becomes not only dissociated from his labor, but also from his fellow, and ultimately from himself. In a necessary cruel twist, landowners also become alienated from themselves and their tenants: their land comes to own them. The capitalist, too, becomes enslaved to his capital. Ultimately, the competition for the appropriation of things, for the accumulation of property, makes all human effort into a struggle for survival. Capital owns workers, landowners, even capitalists.

The expropriation of ourselves by our things, the replacement of labor's effort by capital's dominion, also results in worsening material conditions for the workers. For Marx, the injustice of capitalism is that people serve their commodities, that human faculties are reduced to a crude sort of animal materialism. Marx is not opposed to the material needs of humanity; but competition and commodification reduce them to the barest needs of survival.

And it is just this attack on the crude materialism of civil society that illuminates the reappropriation of materialism in terms of economics after the revolution. In the *1844 Manuscripts* Marx discusses how the human senses and character will be transformed by full sociality. Even perception will become humanized—by which I take him to mean we will no longer look at things only as a commodity with a price, but we will see it in relation to the human race, as a social product for social use. Our relation to objects will be changed, as objects will no longer be that in which we lose ourselves through our labor, but will now be what Levinas would call expressions of ourselves. The decisive difference in the two economies is that in civil society people are free individuals, free to pursue their own interest, but thus enslaved to the pursuit of property, while in the society to come, in a fully human society, human needs will become fully social. Each person's hunger will be that of his fellow, and so the satisfaction of those needs will be a social action. In civil society, the satisfaction is social, but only in the modes of oppression (the banker's profit on the farmer's loan is part of the cost of the bread we eat).

Communist Institutions

Without committing myself to outlining the altogether distressing and difficult issue of Marx's account of life after the revolution, I wish to take note of two important parallels with Levinas. What I am not doing is drawing together the few patchy comments about life after the revolution, starting with the absence of specified roles in the *German Ideology*, and continuing through the dictatorship of the proletariat as a means to the classless society in the *Communist Manifesto*, leading to the discussion of universal suffrage and decentralized communes in the *Civil War in France*. Ultimately, the radical nature of the revolution, as a revolution against classes and against the state, makes all speculation impossible. All current social forms partake of the oppression and alienation which will be universally overthrown by the new fully human society.

On the other hand, what is interesting is that Marx, like Levinas, finds: (1) that sexuality and the family form a positive image of sociality; but in his later thought he finds (2) that the rejection of the state becomes complicated and attenuated by recognizing the partial inescapability of the state. In the *1844 Manuscripts* Marx discusses how the relations of men and women can be used as a measure for the development of society. In the positive relation of fully social humanity, sexuality reveals the positive sense of our natural needs, for the other person becomes, as human, my need. The other is not a means to my satisfaction, but I have a social need, a need which can only be met by another human in her praxis as human. This is not the bourgeois family, which Marx interprets as prostitution, but it is a natural structure which can be embraced only in a universal society, where we are a fully social human race.

Nonetheless, Marx does not discuss this positive sexuality later in his works. And whatever the relationship of Lenin and later political developments may be to Marx's thought, still there is a temporary patience with a new state—the universal state which Marx calls the dictatorship of the proletariat. While Levinas must criticize the state and its politics precisely because it is universal and totalizing, and so abstracts from the originating infinite demand of the other, Marx rejects the state because it should become superfluous. The state is always a tool of the oppressing class. The modern state emerges as a separate power structure to serve the middle class against the classes of nobles and churchmen. The state will have no such function in communist society, because it is to be a classless society.

Marx does not develop the sort of dialectic of politics and ethics that Levinas does. Instead, we have a much more Hegelian total-state becoming a non-state. The Marxists, for their part, make different choices in interpreting these claims. For this paper, the interesting issue is how the full sociality, the communist society, has not only no need for the state, but similarly little or no need for social structures. Whatever the current social structures may be, they must function for oppression. Levinas, too, alerts us to this totalizing quality of social structures. Their respective positions against Hegel on the state take over a great deal from Hegel about society, even as both thinkers reject Hegel on the origin of sociality.

One marked difference in these parallel readings of these two thinkers should be noted here. While it is possible to follow a similar sequence of concepts in the two thinkers, the difference between the section on Levinas I titled "Economics Before and After the Face," and its counterpart in Marx—"Economics Before and After the Revolution"—provides a clue to their disagreement. For Marx, the practical action of revolution, of radical and even violent transformation of society, is the key to distinguishing two forms of society. For Levinas, it is a personal one-to-another experience that serves to distinguish the concepts. Levinas would object that the revolution does not put an end to totalizing social immorality and violence, while Marx would object that by focusing on the Face, Levinas has overlooked the need for radical transformation of society and its economic structures. Even bearing in mind that Levinas is not proposing a private relationship, we miss the call for refounding society, but similarly, we regret that Marx insists on a new totality and seems oblivious to the violent reduction of responsibility in any totality. Revolution or the Face? Or is social reform possible in a radical manner without totalizing?

3. Is it Jewish?

In this third and final part, I bring out a third perspective which helps to define a common ground for the two thinkers. Although few scholars have focused on Levinas's Jewishness, to make a claim for a Jewish conceptual context is not difficult. For Marx, the question is more complicated, although if we place him in the class of the 'non-Jewish' Jew, there is little difficulty in making the claim. Marx did reject religion in general, and his attack on Judaism, especially in the *Jewish Question*, is bitter. Yet I am hardly the first to suggest that Marx owes more than a little to his Jewish background or, even if that were too contentious, that Marx's agenda is a genuinely Jewish philosophical agenda despite his critique of Judaism. Thus what I propose below is not novel, nor unique, but sheds reciprocal light on the two thinkers in a context which they do share.

The greater problem is to define a Jewish context. Obviously, in a few pages I cannot argue that certain features are the essence of Judaism; all the more I cannot argue that a group of concepts have been held by all Jews in all times. For all that, I don't believe that what I will here identify as Jewish is idiosyncratic—rather it represents a main line of interpretation that can be traced back to the Bible, on through the sages, the medievals, and into modernity, even to some contemporary thinkers.

Still, more important is it to try to see what sort of relationship can obtain between these thinkers and Judaism—that is, what is the philosophical status of Jewish thought? I am not going to claim that any of the concepts here is uniquely Jewish, that only Jews have thought these ideas, or that non-Jews only think them by becoming Jewish. What is Jewish may well also be accessible to poets, artists, writers, philosophers, theologians, scientists, social critics, etc. who are not Jewish. Quite the opposite, I hope to suggest that what truth there is in the philosophical analyses of Levinas and Marx is accessible doubly, once through Judaism, but again through nonconfessional thought. The issue then devolves upon the benefit of comparing Jewish concepts with philosophical perspectives. While the discovery of a common ground for the two thinkers serves to cross-breed them, as it were, when we factor in this third perspective, we open up new possibilities.

The philosophers' analyses may help strengthen and clarify concepts of Jewish tradition, and similarly, lines of thought and practice from tradition may develop and extend the philosophic positions, providing ways of extending the positions which are consistent. In the first case, I would claim that the other-centered view of ethics is valuable for Jewish thought, and that the analyses of labor and needs also clarifies Jewish concepts. As for the latter (from Judaism to Philosophy), I believe that the emphasis on nontotalizing social structures (social but nonStatist) will enhance appreciation of both thinkers.

The Primacy of Ethics

The primary concern of both thinkers is the transformation of praxis, not the cognition of truth. By this I do not mean that truth is not also a goal, but it is a practical goal—even theory receives a practical justification. For each thinker, social ethics is the focus and indeed the fulcrum for their work. Whether the famous thesis on Feuerbach ("The philosophers have only interpreted the world in various ways; the point is to change it") or Levinas's claim that "Ethics is an optics," both philosophers firmly begin with the issues of practical reason.

The question of Jewishness is complex. Levinas clearly interprets Judaism as ethical, actually making the strong claims for ethics first in 'Hebrew' writings and then later in a philosophical context. And Marx seems to some to depend on this orientation of Judaism in his basic push. Again, I would not claim that all Jewish thought has always emphasized the practical as the context for theoretical reflection, but I would side with a view which centers on praxis. The emphasis on Law, on commandments, and on a pure heart, all form a baseline upon which the intellectual life constructs its schemas. It is pointedly true that Kant and Plato also emphasized what Kant calls the primacy of practical reason, but that does not make such an emphasis less Jewish—if we do not mean that Jewish is an exclusive term, reserved only for Jews. But in the cases of both Levinas and Marx, I would make the stronger argument that their elevation of praxis is derived from the Jewish tradition, and its emphasis on social practice.

Sociality not Individuality

The practice they make the fulcrum is social. Neither will tolerate an ethics which is private and individualistic. Neither accepts the cultivation of isolated virtue as an acceptable goal. Moreover, both thinkers reject the picture of society as a grouping of isolated individuals who each on their own use their freedom to enter a contract. They suspect that egoistic individuals cannot found society through their own freedom. Instead, they both argue that the individual is already social, prior to being free. Indeed, they both argue that by taking that prior sociality as a guide, a deeper and more ethical form of sociality can be realized. Even as both reject the view of society as a contract of egoistic individuals, they also reject the claim that society is a private immediate community. Each sees that the true society requires passage beyond the honeymoon: for Levinas, the entrance of the third, and so the recognition of all others in the face of the other; for Marx, the historical motion through civil society into a rational and universal human society.

The question of the Jewishness of this claim is at once obvious and elusive. The problem centers on the perennial problem of defining Jewish, either in terms of thought, or communal practice, or religion. Levinas claims unambiguously that this sociality is Jewish, as well as philosophical. The sources are as basic as being one's brother's keeper, and the discussion of doing before hearing at Sinai, as interpreted in the Babylonian Talmud (*Shabbat* 88a–b). The very concept of the chosen people is often interpreted as the excess of responsibility that marks the person as primordially social. Collective responsibility prior to contractual assent is one interpretation of what it means to belong to a people, to be chosen by God and not to choose God. If we reread Marx's description of the proletariat, can we avoid seeing that a substitution of Jewish people for the proletariat serves to give an almost traditional interpretation of the Jewish people ("a class with *radical chains*, a class of civil society, which is not of civil society," "a sphere which possesses a universal character through its universal suffering," "can win itself only through the *complete redemption of humanity*")?

In a parallel fashion, one can argue that Jewish communal solidarity was threatened by civil society and by Jewish assimilation into it; that Judaism, more than Christianity, required a particular community (as opposed to the destruction of communities that civil society represents); and therefore, that Jews in the modern world are keenly aware of the loss of a social dimension which cannot be recaptured by contracts of free individuals. Jews are the strongest advocates of sociality, and Marx as well as Levinas is trying to articulate a prior sociality which modern society obliterates.

Prophecy and Messianic Politics

Even if it were not commonplace now to assert that Marx's view of the communist revolution and the subsequent society are messianic, it would not be a difficult task to demonstrate the claim. The revolution to end revolutions, as well as classes and oppression—surely this is a paradigmatic statement of messianism. Moreover, the function of this messianic expectation is to justify the prophetic critique of existing society. The failure of civil society and its nation-state to establish the fully human society is the prophetic edge to the call for the coming of the messianic age. The issue of hurrying the coming of the kingdom, of human action bringing it about, is complex, but it is hardly unique among Jewish heretics.

As for Levinas, he makes several unveiled references to messianic politics, a politics which is no longer what Levinas calls politics, but which is the hoped-for rule of what he calls religion. His exploration of the discussions in the last chapter of *Sanhedrin* as well as his discussion of Rosenzweig display a more quietistic, but still profound, evocation of messianism (DL2, 89ff., 253f.). His prophetic critique, moreover, is much more pronounced. From the frontispiece to *Otherwise than Being*, with its quotations from Ezekiel, to his discussions of prophecy proper, Levinas maintains an almost prophetic, clearly moralistic, tone. Indeed, it is prophecy which best serves in his philosophical works as the category for his own discourse.

Levinas's important use of such a clearly religious category displays at once his dependence on Judaism and also the compatibility of philosophical thought and Judaism. More, I believe that the justification of speaking to others about ethical responsibilities that they have to others requires such a category. The very capacity for speech, for Levinas, has become prophecy, in that in every word I utter, there is also the apology, the availability of myself to the other. All speech is prophecy—and so all speech is a challenge in the name of God.

Resurrection and the Material World

The messianic age is also the preface to the resurrection of the body. Leaving aside the embarassment found in some medieval and modern Jewish thought, the resurrection of the body promises a new materialism. It is bound to a refusal to denigrate human physicality. One of the great similarities of Levinas and Marx is their insistence that ethics takes place in the world of material needs and is not a flight or repression of those needs in the name of some higher needs. Levinas quotes Chaim of Volozyn: "My neighbour's material needs are my spiritual needs." The very corporeality of Jewish observance is, in this light, an affirmation of the reality of others' material needs.

At this point, I can address Marx's notorious *Jewish Question*. Schwarzschild has discussed both the biographical context (his marriage to the daughter of establishment antisemitism) and more importantly the critique of Mammon and Jewish money-lending. What I wish to add is that Marx there critiques not the observant (the Sabbath) Jew, but the secular Jew. More important, what Marx loads on the secular Jew's shoulders is a crude materialism, a materialism which is simply the inversion of the predominant spiritualized Christianity. Disregarding the polemics and apologetics on the origin of the Jewish role as moneylender, I should point out that the social roles available to Jews in medieval Christian culture were stipulated largely by Christians. Economic life in Christian society required a class which would perform functions the Christian, spiritualized vision of society had precluded. The revulsion from the materiality of the economic world created an antispiritual role, which the Jews then served. Thus Marx's attack on Judaism is, more correctly, an attack on a crude materialistic social structure born of an antimaterial spiritualism. The result is that the critique does not touch the very concept of Judaism I am exploring here. Instead, the critique emerges not from an antisemitism, but rather from a normative idea of Judaism, and it lands its attack upon a social structure created by an antimaterial spiritualism.

The materialism of resurrection is not, therefore, an inversion of Christian spirituality, of other-worldliness in general. It is not pure hedonism, but it is precisely the materialism of sociality, the material needs of the others. Social ethics is not a renunciation of materiality for some higher form of reality, but it is a social and human relation to each other's material needs.

The Rejection of the State

Both Levinas and Marx criticize the universal, rational state of Hegel. Neither believes that it resolves the conflicts in society that it is supposed to. For Marx, that state is only a precursor of the stateless communist society. The totalization of power makes possible the sublating of all state power. For Levinas, the totalization of power in the state demands that we look away from the state to ethics for genuine sociality. In the earlier works, this can produce religion, which may include institutions based on the family, on ethics, while in the later works, we are saddled with a state, but one which always falls prey to the critique of ethics. Levinas is clear: neither nationalistic state power nor universalistic state power is free of a fundamental violence against individuals.

The question now is most important: To what extent are these rejections of states and national politics Jewish? In the Bible there is ambiguity about national politics: the desire for a king is criticized, but the reigns of David and especially Solomon are praised. In the Talmud there are similar ambiguities. However, the adaptation first to limited autonomy centered around the Temple priests in the Second Commonwealth, and then second to life in the diaspora after the

Roman destruction led to the fashioning of social institutions that did not involve national autonomy. However much the sages idealized both the reign of the earlier kings or the reign of a messianic king, their concrete work displays a remarkable absence of statism and of national politics. I am not claiming that the sages advocated power-lessness, but that power was concentrated in social institutions which stood without the support of national politics, and especially of a national army.

If Judaism could survive without an army, without a state—and indeed the lesson the sages discovered was that Judaism needed to abandon those forms of social structure in order to survive—then it depended on solidarity and a strengthening of sociality. Whether or not we have outgrown *galut*-Judaism, we cannot strip it of its genius: the creation of an enduring society without a state. The philosophical rejection of nationalism and the state in both Marx and Levinas is not based on any sectarian affirmation of 'Normative Judaism.' And yet, the very trade-off—sociality for national politics—is precisely the move that the sages made hundreds of years earlier. And that move formed the Jewish society that both thinkers were educated/formed in.

I realize that to invoke armiless and nonnationalistic Judaism is controversial. The claim I would like to make is that the social ethics that Marx and Levinas present and the reasoning that they use must be met if one wishes to defend nationalism and military power. The question I am broaching can partially be clarified by reference to the norms and arguments found in their writings.

Halakhah and Social Institutions

To turn to the sages, moreover, is to gain access to forms of reasoning and creativity that can serve as resources in envisioning a society based on social institutions without a nation-state. Both Levinas and Marx lack the very diversity and complexity of analyses of positive social structures, of institutions which can build sociality without requiring a state, that fill the two Talmudim and many other works in the Jewish tradition. If they are so indebted to Judaism, if they are repeating a Jewish preference for sociality in place of national politics, then where did the creativity, rigor, even casuistry of the sages in creating those institutions go? Why is it that both thinkers see social institutions only as alienating and oppressive, as a betrayal of ethical sociality?

The paradoxical answer is once again Hegel. While some might say that we should turn back from Levinas, or back from Marx, to Hegel in order to appreciate intermediary social institutions, I believe that such a route will always fail. Hegel espouses a logic of totality which recognizes the ambiguity of institutions only in order to sublate them into more universal, rational forms. Once Hegel's dialectic appears in social analyses, there is no stopping it. Thus all social institutions are swept up into total states. Ethical sociality requires partial forms, nonuniversalizing reasoning. Levinas is a genius in exploring a logic which does not totalize over unique individuals, but does not degenerate into the particularisms of fascism. But he fails to appropriate the sages' use of a similar logic in creating, defining, reconstructing, and defending social institutions. Having accepted Hegel's analysis of social institutions, Marx and Levinas had to discover ethical sociality prior to its institutionalization. But had they freed themselves from Hegel's analysis, they might be able to find social institutions which enhance and preserve ethical sociality.

I am not arguing that the sages' product is demanded as the correct answer to a philosophic discussion. An apology for the *Shulchan Arukh* is not my goal. But the sages could give lessons on how institutions foster sociality without allowing the state total power over individuals. Marx and Levinas pursue similar agenda, and what is common to both is in a profound way Jewish. Were they more sensitive to Halakhah, to the logic of rabbinic social institutions, they might have found yet greater insight into what is also in their cases genuinely philosophical thought. The distinct perspectives can be enhanced through the discovery and exploration of common ground, for each develops concepts held in common in a distinctive way, and so has something to offer to the other. Levinas and Marx can heighten our reflection on the priority of the other's material needs, while the Jewish tradition can broaden their view of social structures.

Appendix: Levinas on Marx

It may seem paradoxical to write a paper on two thinkers and relegate one's discussions of the other to an appendix. And so it would be, if only Levinas had not himself relegated Marx to a secondary or rather tertiary status. The references to Marx in Levinas's philosophical works can be counted on the fingers of one hand. My task in this appendix is to indicate the variety of not only those comments, but also of other comments scattered in interviews and Jewish writings.

There are several comments by Levinas about the failure of Marxism, particularly Stalinism. The sharpest identify the failure of communism as the ultimate refutation of attempting to found a society on love or charity (Poirié, 134). Levinas also criticizes the Sino-Soviet debate as displaying the re-emergence of nationalism—as an evil—in the midst of supposedly internationalist communism (DL1, 227). This leads him elsewhere to suggest that the nationalistic divisions represent further needs which threaten the totalizing, rational, universal society that communism is supposed to be (HAH, 36/87). This critique recurs in an essay about Khrushchev, where Marx is linked with Hegel (DL1, 223). Even though the socialist society is opposed to fascism, Levinas still sees the universality of Marx as totalizing and incapable of accommodating individual freedom. What unifies these critiques is not merely the malaise of the disappointment in 1968 with what Marxism could not deliver. Rather, the failure is traced back to the totalizing, rational society it proposed. Such a society, for Levinas, will always violate the responsibility of its members. Moreover, the confidence, even naiveté, of wanting a society to be based on charity, and not on justice, produces the temptation to totalize.

But if these various comments seem more like a critique of current events, the few substantial references to Marx in the philosophical works focus on the very positive notion of materialism discussed in this paper. Not only is there a long praise of Marx for recognizing the sincerity of desire, that economics can be a realm without ulterior motives and that hunger and thirst have good will (EE, 69/45), but also that happiness is in meeting our needs, in fulfilling our desires (TI, 120/146). Levinas also admits that materialism has a part which is eternally true: that the human will is expropriable in its works (TI, 204–05/229). With those three citations, we exhaust the references to Marx in the main works. What they point out is a respect for the analysis of desire and also for the alienation of will in works. What is lacking, however, is a serious discussion of the sociality that Marx proposed. Levinas seems content to regard it as merely universalized material desire for assimilation/consumption. This paper has tried to show that such a reading is not the best that Levinas's perspective can do—although the question of rational totalization is serious in Marx.

There are also two concluding passages and a footnote I wish to mention. The footnote occurs in the midst of a discussion of whether the messianic age will bring the end of social injustice. Levinas cites the saying of Yochanan: "All of the prophets prophesied only for the messianic age. But for the world to come: 'Eye has not seen, except for you, Lord, what you will do for those who await' " (*Sanhedrin*, 99a). He has his own interest in this passage, but he does say that this "singularly recalls the strange passages where Marx awaits the socialist society with its modifications of the human condition, baffling all anticipation in fact of their very revolutionary essence" (ADV, 218). Levinas locates Marx within a rabbinic argument, an argument about the need for politics and the persistence of suffering. But such a locating is in large measure one of praise.

The first passage is a still warmer affirmation of Marx's project, as the primacy of praxis. In an interview with Richard Kearney, Levinas states:

When I spoke of the overcoming of Western ontology as an "ethical and prophetic cry" in "God and Philosophy," I was in fact thinking of Marx's critique of Western idealism as a project to understand the world rather than to transform it. In Marx's critique we find an ethical conscience cutting through the ontological identification of truth with an ideal intelligibility and demanding that the theory be converted into a concrete praxis of concern for the other. It is this revelatory and prophetic cry that explains the extraordinary attraction that the Marxist utopia exerted over numerous generations. Marxism was, of course, utterly compromised by Stalinism. The 1968 Revolt in Paris was a revolt of sadness . . . (Kearney, 33)

Here is the appreciation of the primacy of praxis, as social praxis—'concern for the other.' Moreover, we find here the messianic echoes and prophetic critique identified in this paper. That Levinas could see this in Marx, and yet ignore him throughout his work, raises questions that I cannot begin to answer about Levinas's own reflections.

There is a second text to consider, indeed the only prolonged discussion of anything Marxian in Levinas's work: an essay "On Death in the Thought of Ernst Bloch" (DVI, 62f.). It represents for us exactly the point that Levinas is hardly unaware of or uninterested in Marxian thought. But he feels little compulsion to go back and study Marx as he studies Heidegger, or Buber, or even Montaigne and Pascal. His position is relative to Marx and his contemporary followers, but he has no philosophical interest either in the Marx of the sociality I have discussed, or in a more economic Marx. The task falls on those like me, who wish to consider how the two balance and counteract each other. And, not surprisingly, liberation theologians, the solidarity thinkers, and even French Marxists find that social thought needs a combination of the two.

References

All translations in the text are my own. The texts are cited by abbreviation, then in the original pagination followed by the English.

ADV   Levinas, *L'Au-delà du Verset.* Paris: Editions de Minuit, 1982.

AE   Levinas, *Autrement qu'être ou au-delà de L'Essence.* The Hague: Nijhoff, 1974. *Otherwise than Being or Beyond Essence,* trans. by Alphonso Lingis. The Hague: Nijhoff, 1981.

DL1   Levinas, *Difficile Liberté.* Paris: Editions Albin Michel, 1961.

DL2   _____, 2nd ed., 1976.

DVI   Levinas, *De Dieu qui Vient à l'Idée,* Paris: Vrin, 1982.

EE   Levinas, *De l'existance à l'existant.* Paris: Vrin, 1947 (3rd ed. 1981). *Existents and Existants,* trans. by Alphonso Lingis. The Hague: Nijhoff, 1978.

HAH   Levinas, *Humanisme de l'Autre Homme.* Paris: Fata Morgana, 1972. *Collected Philosophical Papers,* trans. by Alphonso Lingis. The Hague: Nijhoff, 1987.

KH   Marx, *Zur Kritik der Hegelischen Rechtsphilosophie.* In Marx and Engels, *Werke,* 1. Band. Berlin: Dietz Verlag, 1958, pp. 378–91. *Critique of Hegel's 'Philosophy of Right',* ed. by Joseph O'Malley. Cambridge: Cambridge University Press, 1972.

JF   Marx, *Zur Judenfrage.* In Marx and Engels, *Werke,* 1. Band. Berlin: Dietz Verlag, 1958, pp. 347–77. *Selected Writings,* ed. by David McLellan. Oxford: Oxford University Press, 1977.

MK   Marx and Engels, *Manifest der Kommunistischen Partei.* In Marx and Engels, *Werke,* 4. Band. Berlin: Dietz Verlag, 1964, pp. 459–94. *Communist Manifesto.* New York: International Publishers, Inc. 1948.

MS   Marx, *Ökonomisch-philosophische Manuskripte aus dem Jahre 1844.* In Marx and Engels, *Werke,* Ergänzungsband, Erster Teil. Berlin: Dietz Verlag,

1968. *Economic and Philosophic Manuscripts of 1844*, ed. by Dirk J. Struik, New York: International Publishers, Inc., 1964.

MT Levinas, "Le Moi et la Totalité." *Revue de Métaphysique et de Morale*, 59 (1954); 363–73.

SAS Levinas, *Du Sacré au Saint*. Paris: Les Editions de Minuit, 1977.

TI Levinas, *Totalité et Infini*. The Hague: Nijhoff, 1961, *Totality and Infinity*, trans. by Alphonso Lingis. Pittsburgh: Duquesne University Press, 1969.

Kearney (1986). Interview with Levinas. In *Face to Face with Levinas*, ed. by Richard A. Cohen. Albany: SUNY Press.

Poirié (1987). Entretien avec Levinas. In *Emmanuel Levinas: Qui êtes-vous?* Paris: La Manufacture.

Individual and Communal Forgiveness

Elliot N. Dorff

1. Afterward

This paper is an emotional minefield. It will inevitably offend many; parts of it even offend me at times. I apologize in advance for the distress and indignation it will cause. It is certainly not my goal to raise people's hackles; by nature, I continually try to avoid that. This paper also raises intricate, philosophical complexities.

In view of these problems, discretion would have dictated that I choose a much safer topic. I nevertheless feel the need to present this topic to those most concerned, for it is we who must begin to face the issue it addresses. At some point, the Jewish community will need clear thinking on this issue, grounded on familiarity with, and commitment to both philosophical and Jewish sources. However much we might prefer it otherwise, then, it seems to be that our philosophical and Jewish backgrounds impose an obligation upon us to deal with this topic.

2. The Issue

Since 1973, I have been part of the Priest-Rabbi Dialogue sponsored by the Los Angeles Archdiocese and the Board of Rabbis of Southern California. Over the course of the years we have produced brief readings to be read before the Lenten Reproaches in all Catholic churches in this region in order to eliminate the original, anti-Semitic intention of the readings and to apply them instead to the individual, Catholic parishioner hearing them, and we have together written papers explaining our commonalities and differences on the subjects of covenant, kingdom, and salvation/redemption. Another local, joint, Catholic-Jewish committee, consisting of clergy and laypeople, has produced papers on abortion, caring for the dying person, the single-parent family, the nuclear reality, allocation of health care, and chemical dependency. All of these have been published with the agreement of the Catholic cardinal and the Board of Rabbis.[1]

After this long history of dialogue, the priests in the Priest-Rabbi dialogue finally felt sufficiently secure in their relationships with us rabbis to raise one of the questions which certainly was in the back of all of our minds. It is no secret—to them as well as to us—that the Catholic Church historically has been anything but exemplary in its relationship with Jews. Recent Catholic statements, including a number from the Vatican itself, have moved in the direction of apologizing for past wrongs and condemning any current manifestations of anti-Semitism. The Church has not yet gone as far as we would like, in particular with regard to its relationships with the state of Israel, but even the most wary of Jews must acknowledge that it has made some radical changes in both word and deed since the Second Vatican Council promulgated *Nostra Aetate* in 1965.

The question which the Catholics are now asking us is this: With full recognition that the history of Catholic treatment of Jews has been bleak and that as recently as World War II officials of the Catholic Church were often obsequious to the Nazis, what would it take to put that history behind us? That is, what would it mean for the Catholic Church to warrant forgiveness and for the Jewish community to give it? Whether either community would *want* to engage in this process is, of course, another matter, but what would it mean to do so in the first place? How, in general, can groups engage in remorse, apology, and forgiveness—acts which we normally associate with individuals?

In our case, there is a further complication. The present generation of Jews is, by and large, not the people who were wronged. Conversely, the present generation of Catholics, while not totally free of anti-Semitism, is not responsible for perpetrating the atrocities for which we most often blame the Church. Can descendants act in any meaningful way in matters of regret and forgiveness on behalf of their ancestors?

One might seek to soften this philosophical question by noting that past wrongs continue to affect us now. So, for example, while the primary brunt of the Crusades and the Inquisition was surely borne by Jews of those times, contemporary Jews still suffer from the results of those acts. Our dispersion, our secondary political status in many countries, continued acts of anti-Semitism seen by the perpetrators (even if wrongly) as sanctioned by the Church, and our diminished number itself are all effects of past offenses. Jewish wariness of

Catholics in our time is, in no small measure, a function of having been burned—literally and figuratively—and of smarting still from the effects. The greater suffering, though, and the conceptually more difficult question relate to the Jews of previous generations, and it is forgiveness on behalf of them on which this paper will concentrate.

In this paper, then, I shall first briefly survey Jewish sources on individual and communal forgiveness. As we shall see, the tradition demands that we be most forthcoming in pardoning individuals who have wronged us, but its reaction to groups who have wronged Jews is anything but forgiving. With this as a background, I shall ask the philosophical questions described above concerning, first, the notion of group regret and forgiveness and, second, the issue of descendants' regretting and forgiving on behalf of their ancestors. After developing a secondary sense of forgiveness which can accommodate the realities of current Catholic-Jewish relations, I shall briefly explore why we might be interested in considering this in the first place—that is, what the Catholic Church has done in the past twenty-five years to warrant our considering this issue anew now—and, on the other hand, why we might still refuse to offer even a secondary form of forgiveness.

This preliminary outline should alert the reader that my interest in this paper is *not* to argue for or against forgiving the Catholic Church; it is rather to explore what such an act would mean. In the end, in other words, this is not a paper in Jewish public policy, but in philosophy.

3. God's Forgiveness of Individual Jews and the People Israel

The Jewish tradition is confident that God will forgive both individual Israelites and the people Israel as a whole. In the Torah, God Himself proclaims that He "forgives iniquity, transgression, and sin," and the rabbis maintained that God's forgiveness exceeds His wrath five hundred fold.[2] There are several reasons why God forgives. God is by nature a loving Father who, like any good parent, will punish transgression when necessary to correct our ways, but who always hopes that we will return to Him so that He can instead forgive.[3] After the Flood, God made a covenant with all children of Noah—and, indeed, with all living creatures—not to destroy the world again, however angry He gets.[4] Furthermore, as an expression of His special love for Israel, He has made a distinct covenant with Israel which obligates Him to forgive and sustain her even after fiercely punishing her for multiple and egregious transgressions.[5]

God remembers the merit of the patriarchs; the relationship He had with them and the promises He made them prompt Him to forgive their descendants.[6] Since failure to forgive Israel may lead others to underestimate the extent of God's power and goodness, God forgives Israel also to preserve and enhance His own reputation among the nations.[7]

God forgives, however, only when human beings sincerely seek to make amends in both mind and deed. It is not enough to hope and pray for pardon or to perform the rituals associated with it (animal sacrifices, weeping, fasting, rending one's clothes, donning sackcloth and ashes, etc.); people must humble themselves, acknowledge their wrongs, and resolve to depart from sin.[8] Moreover, inner contrition must be followed by the outward acts of ceasing to do evil and then, in its place, doing good.[9]

4. Human Forgiveness of Individuals

God's forgiveness, however extensive, only encompasses those sins which a person commits directly against Him; those in which an injury is caused to one's fellow human being are not forgiven, according to the rabbis, until the injured party has personally forgiven the perpetrator. Hence the custom of seeking forgiveness from those one may have wronged in the days before the Day of Atonement, without which proper atonement cannot be made.[10] The search for forgiveness and restoration of bonds with God and people, however, while the focus of the high holy day season, is not restricted to it. If one has physically injured another, Jewish law maintains that payment of compensatory payments is not sufficient; the assailant must also ask the victim's forgiveness.[11] It is not only the injury which must be repaired, but the relationship.

This imposes a reciprocal obligation upon the wronged party: he or she, when asked for forgiveness, must forgive. Injured parties who refuse to do so even when asked three times in the presence of others are, in turn, deemed to have sinned.[12] They are called cruel and are not regarded as descendants of Abraham; for ever since Abraham forgave Abimelech, forgiveness has been a distinguishing mark of Abraham's descendants, a special gift God bestowed upon them.[13] Such people also cannot expect divine forgiveness for their own sins: "All who act mercifully [forgivingly] toward their fellow creatures will be treated mercifully by Heaven, and all who do not act mercifully toward their fellow creatures will not be treated mercifully by Heaven."[14] Moreover, they have failed to imitate God, for just as God is forgiving, so we are supposed to be.[15]

This does not mean that people who have been wronged are supposed to squelch their feelings of anger. The Torah prohibits retaliatory action: "You shall not take vengeance or bear a grudge against your fellow. Love your neighbor as yourself." Nevertheless, in the verse immediately before this one, it sanctions and even commands that one express one's feelings of outrage after being wronged: "You shall not hate your kinsman in your heart. Reprove your neighbor, and incur no guilt because of him."[16] According to rabbinic interpretation, this even justified a student criticizing his teacher, and the rebuke could be repeated even one hundred times over—although another rabbinic dictum urges us to admonish only those who will listen. There was a dispute among the rabbis as to whether the censure could take the form of physically striking the offender, but all agreed that it could not include public embarrassment.[17] Biblical and rabbinic law did, however, stipulate in considerable detail the ingredients of a just punishment or compensation for the range of human transgressions of one person toward another.

It also stipulated the rules under which a community as a whole could punish its members. The communal court would impose these punishments. One of the clearest expressions of communal distaste for an act was the penalty of excommunication, for then the very essence of the punishment was that the community was asserting that person X was no longer fit to live with them—at least until he or she abided by the dictates of the court.

Once culprits paid the penalty, however, Jewish law required that the community take them back into the community wholly. "When the parties to a suit are standing before you," Judah, the son of Tabbai said, "you should regard them both as guilty; but when they have departed from you, you should regard them as innocent, for they have accepted the verdict."[18] Unlike American law, where a felon continues to suffer disabilities and embarrassment for the rest of his or her life, Jewish law demanded that the community's forgiveness be complete—even to the point of not mentioning the crime any longer.[19]

In sum, while wrongs are to be redressed and the emotions accompanying them assuaged, the ultimate goal is to mend human ties through forgiveness and reconciliation. As Hillel said: "Be among the disciples of Aaron, loving peace and pursuing peace, loving your fellow creatures and bringing them close to the Torah."[20]

5. God's Forgiveness of Nations

The Bible spares nothing in describing the fierce punishments for disobedience which God has in store for Israel. Because of the covenantal promises God made Israel, because of God's promises to, and the merit of, the patriarchs, and because of God's concern for His own reputation, however, God will not destroy Israel utterly. Twice in the Torah He wants to do so, and Moses must persuade Him not to, but ultimately God feels restrained from doing this. Jeremiah articulates God's resultant policy:

> "But you, have no fear, my servant Jacob," declares the Lord, "for I am with you. I shall make an end of all the nations among which I have banished you, but I will not make an end of you! I will not leave you unpunished, but I will chastise you in measure."[21]

When the Bible speaks of nations other than Israel, however, the tone changes drastically. What rings in the mind of every traditional Jew on this subject is God's words concerning Amalek:

> Remember what Amalek did to you on your journey, after you left Egypt—how, undeterred by fear of God, he surprised you on the march, when you were famished and weary, and cut down all the stragglers in your rear. Therefore, when the Lord your God grants you safety from all your enemies around you, in the land that the Lord your God is giving you as a hereditary portion, you shall blot out the memory of Amalek from under heaven. Do not forget![22]

The rabbinic tradition understood this literally and, one must say, enthusiastically: " 'Remember' means by word, 'Do not forget' means in the heart, for it is forbidden to forget to despise and hate him."[23] In the account of this in the Book of Exodus, it is not only Israel who is not supposed to forget: God Himself "will be at war with Amalek throughout the generations."[24]

In rabbinic and medieval literature, Amalek became the symbol of all oppressors of Israel, and that might account for the particular vilification of Amalek in the Jewish tradition. It is not only Amalek, however, for whom God rules out repentence and reconciliation. Already in God's promises to Abram, Egypt is to be punished and the nations of Canaan are to be driven out of their homeland for their sins. "You must doom them to destruction," the Israelites are later told; "grant them no terms and give them no quarter."[25] Destroying Amalek and the seven Canaanite nations becomes, in fact, a clearly commanded war, one which, in later Jewish law, requires no consultation of the *Urim ve-Tumim* and no confirmation by the Sanhedrin.[26] The tradition is so determined to avenge these wrongs that, particularly in the stories of Midian and Amalek, it raises difficult moral questions in ignoring the difference between soldiers and civilians.[27]

One might explain these cases as part of the tradition's attempt to make a strong case for Israel's right to the land inhabited by others, but the Bible's disdain for other nations does not stop there. It often excoriates non-Canaanite nations other than Amalek for the wrongs they have committed and warns them of the punishment to follow.[28] In these accounts, little, if any, mention is made of the possibility of repentance. The talmudic legend at the beginning of *Avodah Zarah* carries this further: it mocks other nations to the point of asserting that they could not even fulfill one "easy" commandment.[29]

One important exception to this, of course, is the Book of Jonah, wherein the entire story centers on the turning of the people of Nineveh away from their sins and the forgiveness which God therefore extends to them. This is one clear case in which God is willing to forgive not only individuals, but nations, and not only Israel, but others. The rabbis probably chose this book for reading on the Day of Atonement (Yom Kippur) for its assurance that repentance can procure God's mercy, but it is striking that the example of repentance is specifically a nation, and a non-Jewish one at that.

One is tempted to think that God refuses to forgive nations which attack Israel, but when a nation's sins are moral, sometimes God forgives (as in the case of Nineveh) and sometimes not (as in the case of the Canaanite nations). The Book of Jonah states clearly that God's judgment against the inhabitants of Nineveh was because "their wickedness has come before Me" (1:2), and the king's exhortation to his subjects is, "Let everyone turn back from his evil ways and from the injustice of which he is guilty" (3:8).

One must remember, though, that Nineveh was the capital of Assyria, which had destroyed the Northern Kingdom of Israel and had besieged Jerusalem. Indeed, in the Bible itself Zephaniah and

Nahum prophesy its destruction.[30] The case of Nineveh thus does not provide us with clear guidelines as to when God forgives nations and when not. Moreover, while the Torah treats Amalek, Ammon, and Moab harshly, it states that "You shall not abhor an Egyptian, for you were a stranger in his land"—even though Egypt never expressed regret for enslaving Israel.[31] Thus there are instances in which God has forgiven not only moral sins, but national ones, and other cases when He has rejected even the possibility of such forgiveness, with no clear indication of why some nations are treated in one way and some in another.

6. Human vs. Divine Forgiveness of Nations

There are other problems in trying to apply the example of Jonah to contemporary relations with the Catholic Church—or with any other group of people. The Book of Jonah, after all, speaks of *God's* forgiveness of a nation, while we are talking about what forgiveness extended by *us human beings* would look like.

This distinction has several implications. First, God presumably knows a nation's sins and can punish or forgive, as He chooses. The people Israel, in contrast, may know full well the brunt of another nation's disdain and wrath, but historically we seldom have been able to respond in kind. Are we, then, even in a position to forgive? Must one be the equal or the superior of the culprit for one's forgiveness to make any sense, or can one also forgive those whom one could not choose to punish? Of course, if those who have power over you force you to engage in some expression of forgiveness, one could say that there has been no forgiveness since the act was coerced and, on your part, insincere; but what if the culprit honestly means to apologize? Can you forgive in the full sense of the word when your only choice is to withhold forgiveness?

Another way in which the distinction between God and human beings affects forgiveness is in the identity of the party extending forgiveness. There are, of course, many philosophical problems inherent in justifying belief in the existence of God and in identifying the nature of God. If one believes in the existence of a personal God, however, one presumably understands what it would mean for God to forgive, basing one's conception largely on what it means for a person to forgive. What, though, does it mean for the people Israel to forgive? It has been centuries since a Sanhedrin could speak in the name of the Jewish people. Who, then, would have the right even to consider the question as to whether to forgive the Catholic Church, let alone extend such forgiveness?

7. The Proper Parties for Forgiveness and Regret

This problem is exacerbated by the lapse of time between the abuses inflicted upon our ancestors and ourselves. If, in response to the first philosophical issue mentioned above, we decide that it does make sense for an underling to forgive a powerful superior, a Jewish communal court at the time of an atrocity might have forgiven the perpetrators for the ravages inflicted upon the members of that specific community, but what legal or moral standing do we have to do that? Only the victims of the Crusades and Inquisition, it seems, would have that right. If we were to do this, it would seem to be adding insult to injury.

A corollary to this issue of time is the converse of the matter just discussed. Not only does it seem that the present Jewish community cannot rightfully forgive the sins of the past, but the present Catholic community cannot meaningfully regret the errors of their ancestors to justify such forgiveness.

Martin Golding[32] has identified three types of regret: (1) *intellectual* regret, in which the regret arises from a recognition of having misjudged the facts as they were or from a miscalculation of the future (e.g., "I regret having bet on the third horse"); (2) *moral* regret, which arises out of a recognition that one has done something wrong (e.g., "I regret having lied"); and (3) *other-oriented* regret, which one feels (and expresses) because one has wronged someone else ("I regret—I am sorry for—having stolen from you").

When one injures or otherwise wrongs someone else, one has put oneself *in debt* to that party, creating in him or her *justified resentment*. Outside parties might have, in contrast, *justified indignation*. Only other-oriented regret, together with adequate steps to make amends, constitute grounds for the victim's giving up this resentment and granting forgiveness.

Forgiveness does *not* entail that either the perpetrator or the victim forgets the wrongdoing. In the contrary, part of the moral regeneration required in justifying forgiveness is that the culprit recognizes the violation, vows to do otherwise, and remembers the incident and the vow later on, when the same situation arises again. The victim also remembers the hurt but manages to put it in its place in a longer perspective of the relationship (or the lack of one) so that resentment is no longer a factor in dealing with the wrongdoer.

What forgiveness accomplishes, then, is not the expunging of the memory of the injury (even though sometimes that is wished), but rather the removal of a continuing justification for resentment so that relations between the parties can return to an even keel. That, in fact, is the reason it is sought in the first place. Depending upon the previous relations of the parties, the culprit might want more than this minimum: he or she might want the victim to resume a positive attitude toward the perpetrator, not just a neutral one. Forgiveness, though, is the first step in reinstituting neutral relations so that positive ones might later develop.

This analysis helps to define both sides of the problem. As an outside party to the injury, the current Jewish community can only have justified indignation at past atrocities, not justified resentment. It therefore cannot remove the victims' resentment, even if it wanted to forgive. Only the victims can do that, and they are no longer alive. Conversely, the contemporary Catholic Church cannot have appropriate regret for acts committed centuries ago since it did not perpetrate them.

Along these lines, Golding points out that if the victim is no longer alive, the most a regretful perpetrator can do is to remove the justified indignation of outside parties through appropriate amends. Those parties cannot extend forgiveness, however, because that "would be to confuse indignation and resentment and to overlook the rather dependent or secondary character of the role that outside parties have in interpersonal forgiveness situations."[33]

8. The Possibility of Forgiveness as Part of an Ontological Entity

While that articulates the problem, it also points to the solution. Golding's analysis holds for the vast majority of cases, where the victim and the outside party on the one hand, and the perpetrator and the one seeking forgiveness on the other, are *separate* parties, however closely related. Then the current actors cannot perform the roles which the perpetrator and victim alone can.

Ours, however, is not the usual situation. What makes the request for forgiveness on the part of contemporary Catholics *meaningful* is that they see themselves as the current embodiment of the Church which extends back to the Apostle Peter, and they see us—as we see ourselves—as the current embodiment of the people Israel which extends back to the Exodus, if not to the patriarchs and matriarchs. Therefore, it is *the same* party who committed the wrong that is now seeking forgiveness, and it is *the same* party who suffered the wrong who is being asked to forgive.

Since we normally think of ourselves in European Enlightenment terms as individuals, it is appropriate to remind ourselves how much that differs from the way the Jewish tradition understands us. My participation in the people Israel, in the eyes of the tradition, is not simply a voluntary act, which I can retract at will. It is rather part of my very being, which no act on my part can change. Even if I convert to another religion, I continue to bear the obligations of being a Jew.[34] That is why Hillel's comment, "If I am here, then everyone is here,"[35] is not just metaphorical (or egotistical!): We are all part of the same ontological entity, the Jewish people, and that entity is present in every one of us.[36]

Religious Jews have felt this ontological tie to the people Israel—past, present, and future—throughout time. It is probably part of what led the tradition to define Jewish identity in biological terms.[37] Even secular Jews in our postmodern age, I would argue, feel much of the same thing. They may not accept the religious underpinnings of Jewish identity, but few would deny their Jewishness, and many would take umbrage at any offense against Jews. Sometimes, when the attack against Jews is extreme, as it was before and during the Six Day War, these Jews "come out of the woodwork," as it were, to defend the people of whom they still feel a part.

Our ability to forgive Catholics as part of our membership in the ontological reality of the people Israel over time does not, of course, mean that contemporary Jews *should* extend the hand of forgiveness to Catholics. That is a matter of judgment which we have yet to consider. My argument so far has been only that the request is *logically meaningful*, for it is the party which committed the act (or, at least, an extension of that party) who is asking for forgiveness, and the party which suffered the act (or, at least, an extension of that party) who is being asked.

The problem, of course, is that, even with this ontological perspective in mind, contemporary Catholics and Jews are not the perpetrators and the victims themselves, respectively, but only extensions of them. As a result, even though we are, in the eyes of both our traditions, ontologically related to our ancestors, our regret and forgiveness cannot be nearly as forceful as if the Church had asked forgiveness immediately after perpetrating the atrocities (or, better yet, had taken steps to prevent them in the first place!). This is, in other words, a *secondary* sense of regret and forgiveness that I am developing, one which we might call "reconciliation" or "acceptance." In this form, the regret and forgiveness are not extended by the parties themselves but, on the other hand, not, in Golding's terms, by strictly "outside" parties either. It is rather extensions of the parties involved in the original acts who are now called upon to decide whether to engage in the process of forgiveness, and that, it seems to me, is a meaningful extension of our primary notions of regret and forgiveness. As such, it is logically appropriate for the contemporary Church to seek forgiveness and for the current Jewish community to consider whether to grant it.

There is, though, one other problem in imagining how Jews might forgive Catholics for past offenses: presumably the Vatican would represent Catholics, but who would represent Jews? The state of Israel? the presidents of major American Jewish organizations? the World Jewish Congress? Clearly, no one body—not even the state of Israel—speaks for world Jewry as the Vatican does for Catholics. As a result, Jewish reconciliation with Catholics, if deemed appropriate, will more likely take place on the interpersonal and local levels first—that is, through friendships and joint activities of individual Jews and Catholics and through united, local initiatives to tackle common problems. If and when trust builds, national Jewish organizations in North America and elsewhere may, at some point, acknowledge progress in Catholic-Jewish relations through resolutions of reconciliation. Because of our disorganization, this process will not be as neat as we might like it, but the lack of a single, worldwide Jewish representative does not make reconciliation logically or practically impossible.

One feature of forgiveness—both the primary forgiveness of the victim toward the culprit and the extended kind of forgiveness which I have been describing—should be made clear at this point. We have already seen that forgiveness does not expunge memory of the event; it also does not eliminate moral culpability. In ancient times, people could literally "wipe clean" (*kapper*) their sins through animal sacrifices. God may still do that (perhaps now motivated by prayer, repentance, and good deeds, as the high holy day liturgy maintains), but human beings do not. When one human being forgives another, the victim agrees to engage in present and future relationships with the perpetrator *despite* the wrong committed; the act itself continues to be considered wrong by the victim—and, if the process of repentance works, by the perpetrator too. If one member of a couple cheats on the other, for example, the latter may agree to forgive the former and be reconciled to him or her, but neither party condones the adultery. Similarly here, if Jews decide to forgive Catholics or Germans (the cases are clearly different), neither the memory nor the moral culpability of the abuses is at stake; the question is only whether to be reconciled despite the past wrongs.

9. An Argument against Forgiveness Granted by Descendants

In a recent article entitled "Why I Won't Go to Germany," Cynthia Ozick has argued against something like the secondary kind of forgiveness that I have been describing. She says that Jews from America and elsewhere who go to Germany to explore reconciliation with the Germans permit the Germans to hide from the fullness of their sin. Germans must, she says, repent for their actions in the absence of Jews—"the absence of Jews in contemporary Germany being precisely the point." Current Jews—especially those from abroad—only becloud the issue when they go to such meetings because they permit the Germans to believe that we have the right or power to act in the victims' stead.

> This principle of surrogacy is conceived in profound error. Who will dare to suggest that any living Jew can offer reconciliation—or even simple human presence—on behalf of the murdered? . . . Americans [who visit Germany to explore reconciliation] are confusing the question by abetting the tragic and degrading falsehood of human interchangeability.

What should happen instead, according to Ozick, is that Germans of goodwill should deal with the German national conscience on their own:

> The German task is, after all, a kind of 'liberation' (of conscience into history), or emancipation, and the only genuine emancipation—as we know from many other national, social, and cultural contexts—is auto-emancipation. . . . Patriotism . . . is something you do for yourself, by yourself, out of obligation to the moral improvement of your country; . . . it is, above all, a dream of self-transformation.[38]

It is, of course, true that no living Jew can morally represent any victim of the Holocaust or, for that matter, of any past persecution. It is also true that much of the process of *teshuvah*, whether individual or national, is the act of recognizing the sin and admitting it—both of which only the sinner can do.

I differ with Ozick, however, on two counts. First, as Jewish sources specify, repentance cannot be achieved by the sinner alone. After recognizing the sin, admitting guilt for it, and expressing remorse, one must seek forgiveness from the wronged parties. Since that is the teaching of our own tradition as well as the psychological reality, we must surely understand that German or Catholic repentance cannot be limited to the acts of the Germans or the Church alone. At some point, they will need evidence of reacceptance by someone.

Second, contemporary Jews, it seems to me, are not totally incapable of filling that role. The problem, of course, is that the parties who would be in the best position to offer forgiveness—the victims themselves—no longer can. Ozick thinks that the Germans should just have to live with the inability to make full repentance and the guilt and shame this incurs; it is simply, in her view, part of the gravity of their crime and its just punishment. I agree that only the victims can offer *full* forgiveness, but, based on the corporate reasoning I have been advancing, it seems to me that the descendants can offer some lesser form of it.

Moreover, one might argue that we should. After all, by and large, in the case of the Germans, we are no longer talking about those who perpetrated or even acquiesced in the crime, and this is all the more true for the past persecution our people has suffered at the hands of the Catholic Church. Furthermore, by and large, the vast majority of Jews living today are not the ones who were directly abused by either party. Therefore, although we cannot forgive what our ancestors suffered, contemporary members of the Jewish community can, in the name of the community, judge whether current members of the German or Catholic community have done their best to prevent future conduct of that sort and whether we should consequently extend to them the hand of acceptance and perhaps even friendship. This would not be forgiveness in its pristine form; that, only the victims can give. It would, however, be a lesser form of forgiveness—what I have called "reconciliation" or "acceptance"—which would enable the communities involved to get beyond the negatives of the past and build a better future.

10. Precedents for Reconciliation

It is interesting that the Talmud anticipated a form of extended forgiveness somewhat similar to what I am proposing. It raises the question of what a person should do if the victim of his or her act has died before forgiveness can be sought. It prescribes that the perpetrator should bring ten people to the victim's grave and say before them: "I have sinned to the Lord, God of Israel, and to so-and-so, for thus I have done to him." Furthermore, if the perpetrator owes the victim money, says the Talmud, he or she must pay it to the victim's heirs. If the perpetrator does not know whether the victim has any heirs, he or she must leave the money in the hands of the court and go through the process of admission described above.[39]

Here, as in our case, the aggrieved party, the one who alone can offer forgiveness in the full sense of the word, can no longer even be asked, let alone decide whether to do so. Even so, the perpetrator *can* achieve a secondary form of forgiveness by making public amends at the deceased person's grave, provided that he or she first repairs the damage itself for the heirs. The community and the heirs, in other words, are taken to be extensions of the deceased party—sufficient, at any rate, to receive the regret and grant the forgiveness.

Our case, of course, is different from the Talmud's in that it is not the perpetrator who is asking for forgiveness; with contemporary Catholics and Jews, neither the perpetrators nor the victims are alive. This makes the case both stronger and weaker: stronger, in that living Catholics did not commit the crimes and so bear none of the guilt which would obstruct a repair in relations; but weaker, in that current Jews did not suffer the violence and therefore cannot offer full forgiveness. Nevertheless, the Talmud's case does provide a precedent for stretching the concept of forgiveness to include secondary, extended forms of it when one or both parties are no longer alive.

Moreover, there is at least one case in which a nation forgave another nation. After World War II, the United States, through the Marshall Plan and other allocations, spent considerable sums of money to rebuild not only allies like France and the Netherlands, but also West Germany and Japan, the defeated enemies. The purpose of doing so was not to seek reconciliation with those countries but rather to rebuild them so that they would not fall prey to Communism, and hence the language used to convince the American people to adopt and to implement this program was not that of altruism but of pragmatic value. Nevertheless, Americans did not see this as a crass political act; in fact, Marshall Plan aid was even offered to the Soviet Union and the countries of Eastern Europe. In the minds of most Americans, this was rather an attempt to undo the damage of the war and to help Europe and Japan get back on their feet. This was a clear—and costly—example of reconciliation in deed, if not in word.[40]

11. Whether to Forgive: The Factors Against

While contemporary Jews *can* take steps toward reconciliation, it is not necessarily what we *ought* to do. That depends upon the degree to which we think the repentance is real. Here I would suggest that we use the same criteria for judging nations which the Jewish tradition applied to individuals—specifically, evidence of recognition of the act as a violation, admission of guilt, remorse, efforts to seek forgiveness, and steps to insure that the act will not happen again.[41] In that way, our policy for dealing with the repentance of nations will not be based on the general biblical response to national violation, but rather on the lesson of the Book of Jonah, as solitary as it is. We will thus be shaping our tradition in the way it always has been shaped—by the conscious or unconscious choice of some parts of the tradition over others for purposes of emphasis and development.[42]

Why, then, do we hesitate to engage in this process of improving relations? Why are we wary?

Part of the reason is that the Church continues to do things which aggravate us. Almost everything it does regarding the state of Israel falls into this category, including its supercilious pronouncements on Israeli actions, the meetings between the Pope and Arafat, and, especially, the Vatican's formal refusal to recognize the state of Israel. The Pope's meetings with Waldheim and the delay in removing the Carmelite monastery at Auschwitz minimally indicate that the Church does not recognize the depth of Jews' sensitivity to Holocaust issues and, as a result, makes some Jews doubt the sincerity of the Church in making amends on this issue.

Another part of Jewish misgivings is the reticence of the Church to admit it was wrong in the past. It has certainly condemned anti-Semitism in the strongest of terms, but it has never said in an official document that the Church itself was ever guilty of it, neither during the middle ages nor in more recent times. One has the suspicion that the Church's condemnation of anti-Semitism is directed to the current and future Church; that in itself is good, but repentance also requires admission of guilt for the past.

Then, of course, there is the long history of persecution. Even if the Church were openly to admit its past sins, the pain they caused does not go away easily. In this situation as in all others, readiness to forgive is, in part, a function of the extent of damage done. The Germans have been quite forthcoming in admitting guilt for the Holocaust and in expressing remorse in both word and deed, and yet many Jews, like Ozick, would never step foot in Germany, let alone condone resuming relations with the Germans, due to the enormity of the violence they committed against us. The Catholic Church may even have had a hand in this in permitting and fostering anti-Semitism for so long, as well as in what it did or failed to do during World War II; but even its sharpest critics would not compare its abuse of Jews to that of the Nazis. Nevertheless, it was considerable, and our people's memory of it makes forgiveness—or even steps toward it—difficult.

The most nagging issue, however, is that we have no right to forgive that which was done to our ancestors. That, of course, is true, and, as I have argued, this feeling is magnified by our deeply ingrained Enlightenment individualism. Nevertheless, if we see ourselves as the tradition sees us, as part of an extended corporate entity known as the Jewish people, then we, as its present members, do have the right (indeed, the responsibility) to act on behalf of the group—present, past, and future—in this issue as in all others. Neither the Church's present amends nor our forgiveness would be nearly as meaningful as those of the perpetrators and victims, and we may, in the end, choose not to forgive; but it is logically and morally possible and does carry meaning for present and future relations.

12. Whether to Forgive: The Factors For

What, though, has the Church done to warrant that we even consider extending this lesser form of forgiveness? Beginning with *Nostra Aetate* in 1965, the Vatican has engaged in a number of efforts to repair relations with Jews. Its Commission for Religious Relations with the Jews has produced two further official documents to amplify the themes of *Nostra Aetate* and to put its commitments into practice—*Guidelines and Suggestions for Implementing the Conciliar Declaration "Nostra Aetate" (no. 4)* in December 1974 and *Notes on the Cor-*

rect Way to Present Jews and Judaism in Preaching and Catechesis in the Roman Catholic Church in June 1985. These documents have not addressed all of our concerns to our satisfaction—in particular, with regard to the state of Israel—but they have come a long way.[43]

The Second Vatican Council itself admonished Catholics not to hold Jews responsible for Jesus' death, and it condemned anti-Semitism in the strongest of terms. "Jews should not be presented as rejected or accursed by God, as if this followed from the Holy Scriptures," it said, and the Council "decries hatred, persecutions, displays of anti-Semitism, directed against Jews at any time and by anyone."

Aside from acting to remove the negative in this way, the Church also has tried to create ideological and institutional structures to build positive ties between Catholics and Jews. Catholics must, according to *Guidelines*, recognize that the Old Testament "retains its own perpetual value" and "has not been cancelled by the later interpretation of the New Testament." Christians, of course, still maintain that "the New Testament brings out the full meaning of the Old, while both the Old and the New illumine each other," but we would make the same claim for rabbinic literature's relationship to the Hebrew Bible. To counteract the general impression of Christians that Judaism was only a prelude to Christianity, *Guidelines* proclaimed that "Christians . . . must strive to learn by what essential traits the Jews define themselves in the light of their own religious experience." Catholics are to study not only the religion of the Bible, but "the faith and religious life of the Jewish people as they are professed and practised still today."

The Church has been ambivalent, as one can understand, in trying to balance its mission "to proclaim Jesus Christ to the world" and at the same time to maintain "the strictest respect for religious liberty in line with the teaching of the Second Vatican Council," and it has not yet openly abandoned missionizing among Jews. The fact, though, that *both* of these commitments were published in adjoining paragraphs in *Notes* indicates that the Church on the highest levels at least sees this as a problem with which it must grapple.

Even regarding the state of Israel there has been some progress. Both *Nostra Aetate* and the *Guidelines* omitted any mention of the state of Israel, and the Vatican has yet to extend diplomatic recognition to Israel. These are both serious affronts to Jews. *Notes*, however, includes two paragraphs on the land and state of Israel—to my knowledge, the first time such references have appeared in official Vatican documents of doctrine. The document points to the unbroken attachment in both memory and hope that Jews have with the land of Israel as the land of their forefathers and bids Catholics "understand this religious attachment which finds its roots in biblical tradition, without however making their own particular religious interpretation of this relationship." Instead, "the existence of the state of Israel and its political options should be envisaged not in a perspective which is in itself religious, but in their reference to the common principles of international law."

One can hear all kinds of hesitation here, and one wonders what the simple meaning of some of this phraseology is. What is clear, though, is that the Vatican feels that it must respond to Jewish pressure to deal with the state of Israel, if it wants to build better relations with us, and that would not have happened if we had self-righteously closed off communication with them since 1965.

Given the sharp changes in policy these documents express, one would expect that it would take some time to implement them and that the degree of activity along these lines would vary by region. That, indeed, has happened. The pattern seems to be that in this matter, as in others, what the Church does depends upon local conditions and upon the priorities of the local leadership. The Polish cardinal of Krakow, for example, whose family hid Jews during World War II, held a conference in Krakow in April 1988 of rabbis and other Jewish leaders from around the world (including some from Poland) to expose all of the seminary professors in his region to living Judaism and Jews so that they would make their charges sensitive to the sentiments expressed in these Vatican documents. The cardinal of Warsaw, on the other hand, refused to participate. Cardinal Manning of Los Angeles, generally a conservative, appointed a priest with the specific portfolio of stimulating Catholic-Jewish dialogue and joint action. The cardinal's participation in the Second Vatican Council and the large Jewish population in Los Angeles were undoubtedly factors in this, but clearly his own values played a role too, since he could have put all of this "on the back burner." On the other hand, in Sao Paulo, Brazil the initiative for Catholic-Jewish dialogue and joint action has come from the local rabbinic leadership.

At this point, then, the effect of the Vatican documents depends upon local conditions, and it will take time to see how much the Church can and will translate the contents and intentions of these documents into concrete results. Still, one must, in fairness, note that the Church has not buried *Nostra Aetate*; indeed, in some areas of the

world the extent to which steps have been taken to reflect its principles has been remarkable.

Beyond all this, there is a practical point which must not be for-
gotten. For better or for worse, the Roman Catholic Church represents
more than half of Christendom and is the largest single religion in the
world.[44] It is therefore undoubtedly in the best interests of Jews to foster good relations with the contemporary Church. "Good relations"
does not mean that we suppress our memories of past wrongs or our
anger at present ones, but it does mean coming to some understanding that we are going to get along *despite* past atrocities.

In *The Periodic Table*, Primo Levi, a chemist by profession,
describes contacts he had after World War II with a Dr. Muller, the
German in charge of the chemical laboratory in which Levi worked as
a Jewish prisoner during the war. Muller had arranged for him to
have a second shave each week and a new pair of shoes, and so he
was not a stereotypical, unabashed Nazi; if anything, he seemed sur-
prised at the vile treatment of the prisoners. At the same time, he was
a member of the Nazi party and did work to further its war efforts.
After the war, Muller worked for a chemical company in Germany
which supplied resin for the varnish company in Italy for which Levi
worked. Coincidentally, it was the self-same Muller who wrote on
behalf of his company in response to a complaint about a shipment of
defective resin to Levi's company, and it was Levi who received
Muller's letter. In subsequent correspondence, Levi identified himself
to Muller and sent him his book describing the horrors of his experiences during the war. When Muller wrote to Levi after some time, he
was neither completely repentant nor completely defensive; he was
somewhere in between. He did, however, seek to meet with Levi to
"overcome the past." Levi writes:

> I did not feel capable of representing the dead of Auschwitz, nor
> did it seem to me sensible to see in Muller the representative of
> the butchers.
>
> . . . if this story were invented, I would have been able to
> introduce only two kinds of letters: a humble, warm, Christian
> letter from a redeemed German; a ribald, proud, glacial letter
> from an obdurate Nazi. Now this story is not invented, and real-
> ity is always more complex than invention: less kempt, cruder,
> less rounded out. It rarely lies on one level. . . . The Muller char-
> acter . . . [was] neither infamous nor a hero: after filtering off the
> rhetoric and the lies in good or bad faith, there remained a typi-

cally gray human specimen, one of the not so few one-eyed men in the kingdom of the blind. . . .

I made a draft: I thanked him for having taken me into the lab; I declared myself ready to forgive my enemies, and perhaps even to love them, but only when they showed certain signs of repentance, that is, when they ceased being enemies. In the opposite case, that of the enemy who remains an enemy, who perseveres in his desire to inflict suffering, it is certain that one must not forgive him: one can try to salvage him, one can (one must!) discuss with him, but it is our duty to judge him, not to forgive him. . . .[45]

The relationship between contemporary Jews and Catholics bears some striking resemblances to Levi's situation, but it is different in at least one important way. Like Levi, contemporary Jews are reticent to assume the moral burden of judging whether or not to forgive the perpetrators of past atrocities—or their descendants. Like Muller, the Catholic Church has recognized the immorality of its previous actions, but it has not renounced them or atoned for them in words or deeds quite as forthrightly as we would have hoped. The record, instead, is mixed, as most human records are. Muller, however, died before Levi had to face the prospect of meeting him face to face; Catholics, in contrast, are still very much alive, and Jews must decide how to deal with them as honestly and productively as possible.

If we do decide that reconciliation is warranted, our efforts to seek better relations with Catholics would be motivated not only by such practical factors, but also by ideological commitments. Our tradition has not spared its contempt for nations which have attacked Israel, but it has also praised those who have sought to repair relationships. It knows quite well that sometimes human beings wrong others, and it goes to great lengths to specify what justice demands in such circumstances. But it also prescribes that we not only accept evidence of remorse in others, but actively seek to achieve a world of peace.

"Seek peace and pursue it" (Psalms 34:15). The Law does not order you to seek or pursue the other commandments, but only to fulfill them on the appropriate occasion. But peace you must seek in your own place and pursue it even to another place.[46]

13. The Bottom Line

Shall we forgive? That is a matter the Jewish community must still discuss. It will depend, in large measure, upon continued evidence of a Catholic desire to repent. A positive Jewish response to this will probably not take place in one single moment or be universally offered by Jews. Forgiveness will rather be achieved little by little, through joint word and action, just as personal forgiveness usually is. Over a period of time we will test the degree of the Church's appropriate regret and get used to working together, rather than at odds, with one another. Ultimately we may apply the tradition's embrace of forgiveness with regard to individuals to the Catholic community as a whole.

Whether we will remains to be seen. This paper has demonstrated, though, that, at least in a secondary form of forgiveness, it is logically possible for us to do so.

Notes

In all of the following, M. = Mishnah; T. = Tosefta; B. = Babylonian Talmud; J. = Jerusalem Talmud; M.T. = *Mishneh Torah* (by Maimonides, 1177); and S.A. = *Shulchan Arukh* (by Joseph Karo, 1563).

1. These statements have been reproduced in Vadikan and Wolf 1989.

2. Exodus 34:7; T. *Sotah* 1:4; cf. M.T. *Laws of Repentance* 1:3–4 and 7:1–8, qualified, however, in 3:6ff. God thus forgives *almost* everyone and everything, with, however, some notable exceptions.

In this section and the next, where I am briefly reviewing the rudiments of the traditional view of divine and human forgiveness extended to individuals, I shall only cite a few sources for each of the components of the doctrines, although in most cases many, many more could be cited. Since these doctrines derive from the very roots of Judaism, I shall generally cite biblical or rabbinic sources rather than later, medieval forms of the doctrine.

When quoting classical sources, I have left their male language for God intact, simply because that is how they read. I use inclusive language for God (and human beings!), however, when expressing my own views.

3. That God will discipline us: Deuteronomy 8:5. That God hopes that we will return to Him so that He can forgive: e.g., Jeremiah 3:14, 22.

4. Genesis 9:8–17.

5. Leviticus 26:44–45; Psalms 106:45.

6. God's relationship with the patriarchs as a motive for forgiveness: Deuteronomy 9:27. God's promises to the patriarchs as a motive for forgiveness: Exodus 32:13.

7. Exodus 32:12; Numbers 14:13–20; Deuteronomy 32:26–27; Psalms 79:8–9.

8. 1 Kings 21:27–29; Isaiah 1:10–20; 29:13; Joel 2:13; etc.

9. Isaiah 1:15–17; 33:14–15; 58:3ff.; Jeremiah 7:3ff.; 26:13; Amos 5:14–15; etc.

10. M. *Yoma* 8:9.

11. M. *Bava Kamma* 8:7; B. *Yoma* 85b, 87b; M.T. *Laws of Repentance* 2:9–10.

12. B. *Bava Kamma* 92a; Tanchuma, *Chukkat* 19; M.T. *Laws of Forgiveness* 2:10.

13. Genesis 20:17; B. *Betzah* 32b; B. *Yevamot* 79a; *Numbers Rabbah* 8:4.

14. B. *Shabbat* 151b.

15. B. *Shabbat* 133b.

16. Leviticus 19:17–18.

17. Even a student should rebuke his teacher, and even a hundred times over: B. *Bava Metzia* 31a. Some (Rab) include permission to strike the offender, and some (the Baraita toward the top of the page and, probably, Samuel) do not, but all agree that one may not publicly embarrass the offender: B. *Arakhin* 16b. Scold only those who will probably listen: B. *Yevamot* 65b, and Rashi there.

18. M. *Avot* 1:8.

19. M. *Bava Metzia* 4:10; B. *Kiddushin* 40b; cf. M.T. *Laws of Repentance* 1:3.

20. M. *Avot* 1:12.

21. The longest and fiercest expositions of the punishments God has in store for Israel are in Leviticus 26 and Deuteronomy 28. That God, even after those punishments, will not utterly destroy Israel is made clear in Leviticus 26:44–45. The times when God wanted to obliterate Israel but was restrained from doing so: Exodus 32:1–14; Numbers 14:11–45. The passage cited is from Jeremiah 46:28.

22. Deuteronomy 25:17–19.

23. B. *Megillah* 18a; *Sifre*, "Ki Tetze," par. 296; cf. M.T. *Laws of Kings* 5:5.

24. Exodus 17:16.

25. Genesis 15:13–21; Deuteronomy 7:1–11.

26. M. *Sotah* 8:7 (44b); M.T. *Laws of Kings* 5:1–5. For general discussions of this topic, cf. Bleich 1983 and Dorff 1987.

27. Numbers 31; 1 Samuel 15.

28. For example, Amos 1:3 – 2:5; Jeremiah 46–51.

29. B. *Avodah Zarah* 2aff.; the nations are asked to build a *sukkah*, specifically because it is an "easy commandment" to fulfill, as indicated at the bottom of p. 3a.

30. 2 Kings 17–19; Zephaniah 2:13ff.; Nachum 1:1 – 3:19 (entire book).

31. The cited verse is Deuteronomy 23:8. On Ammon and Moab, cf. Deuteronomy 23:4–7.

32. Golding 1984–1985, pp. 121–37.

33. ibid., p. 133.

34. B. *Sanhedrin* 44a and the codes on that passage. Cf. also Nachmanides' comment on Deuteronomy 29:14, where he explains this as a result of the fact that we were all at Sinai, including even "those who are not with us here today"—presumably later generations of Jews as well as converts. A good summary of these laws can be found in "Apostasy," *Encyclopedia Judaica* 3: 211–14.

35. B. *Sukkah* 53a.

36. A good discussion of these differing views of the individual and their legal implications for American Jews can be found in Konvitz 1978, ch. 5.

37. The fact that Jews, through most of their history, have been scattered worldwide rather than inhabiting one geographic space also, of course, was a factor. It is interesting, though, that cognitive or moral commitments, or even actions in accordance with the commandments, were not chosen as the defining factors. This is not entirely fortunate; cf. Wyschogrod 1983 and my review of it (Dorff 1986).

38. Ozick 1988.

39. B. *Yoma* 87a; cf. M.T. *Laws of Forgiveness* 2:11.

40. Between 1947 and 1951, the United States spent more on aid to Europe than it had in the entire federal budgets of the last prewar years, 1937 and 1938. In addition, between 1945 and 1951, it spent nearly two billion dollars on aid for Japan. Cf. Bragdon and McCutchen 1958, pp. 657, 661.

41. Maimonides, as usual, gives a good summary of the tradition's view of this process: M.T. *Laws of Repentance*, chapter 2.

42. Louis Jacobs describes this process well in Jacobs 1957, chapter eight, especially pp. 90–92. As he points out, this is, after all, simply the doctrine of the oral Torah.

43. I have analyzed the implications of these documents for Catholic-Jewish relations more fully in Dorff 1988.

44. *Columbia Encyclopedia* 19:5814.

45. Levi 1984, pp. 218, 221–223. I am indebted to Lenn Goodman for this reference.

46. J. *Pe'ah* 1:1. Alan Udoff has discussed the theological underpinnings of mutual tolerance for one another—leading, in some cases, to friendship—in Udoff 1987.

References

Bleich, J. David. Spring, 1983. "Preemptive War in Jewish Law." *Tradition* 21.1: 7–14.

Bragdon, Henry W. and McCutchen, Samuel P. 1958. *History of a Free People.* New York: Macmillan.

Dorff, Elliot N. 1986. Review of Wyschogrod, 1983. *The Journal of Reform Judaism* 33.1: 95–97.

———. 1987. " 'A Time for War and a Time for Peace:' A Jewish Perspective on the Ethics of International Intervention." *University Papers* 6.3: 1–20.

———. September, 1988. "Catholic/Jewish Dialogue: A Jewish Perspective on Vatican Documents." *Ecumenical Trends* 17.8: 116–20.

Golding, Martin. 1984–85. "Forgiveness and Regret." *The Philosophical Forum* 16.1/2: 121–37.

Jacobs, Louis. 1957, 1965. *We Have Reason To Believe.* London: Vallentine, Mitchell.

Konvitz, Milton. *Judaism and the American Idea.* New York: Schocken Books.

Levi, Primo. 1984. *The Periodic Table.* New York: Schocken Books.

Ozick, Cynthia. 1988. Untitled. *The Quarterly: The Magazine of New American Writing* 8: 175–81. Reprinted as "Why I Won't Go to Germany" in *The Jewish Journal of Greater Los Angeles,* 7–13 April 1989, pp. 19, 21.

Udoff, Alan. 1987. "Tolerance." In *Contemporary Jewish Religious Thought,* ed. by Arthur A. Cohen and Paul Mendes-Flohr. New York: Scribner's, pp. 989–94.

Vadikan, Royale M. and Wolf, Alfred, eds. 1989. *A Journey of Discovery: A Resource Manual for Jewish-Catholic Dialogue.* Valencia, California: Tabor Publishing.

Wyschogrod, Michael. 1983. *The Body of Faith: Judaism as Corporeal Election.* New York: Seabury Press.

Contributors

Eugene B. Borowitz is the Sigmund L. Falk Distinguished Professor of Education and Jewish Religious Thought at Hebrew Union College–Jewish Institute of Religion (New York). He is the author of twelve books, most recently *Exploring Jewish Ethics* (1990) and *Renewing the Covenant: A Theology for the Postmodern Jew* (1991). He has been the editor of *Sh'ma, a Journal of Jewish Responsibility* since founding it in 1970.

Elliot N. Dorff is Provost and Professor of Philosophy at the University of Judaism (Los Angeles). He is the author of numerous articles on Jewish law, ethics, and theology and of four books, among which are *Jewish Law and Modern Ideology* (1971) and (with Arthur Rosett) *A Living Tree: The Roots and Growth of Jewish Law* (1988).

Daniel H. Frank is Associate Professor of Philosophy at the University of Kentucky. He has published in the areas of classical philosophy and of medieval Islamic and Jewish philosophy. He is the author of *The Arguments "From the Sciences" in Aristotle's Peri Ideon* (1984) and is editor (with Oliver Leaman) of *The Routledge History of Jewish Philosophy* (in preparation).

Robert Gibbs is Assistant Professor of Religion at Princeton University. His book, *Correlations: Rosenzweig and Levinas*, is forthcoming. His current research focuses on social ethics.

Lenn E. Goodman is Professor of Philosophy at the University of Hawaii. A specialist in medieval Islamic and Jewish Philosophy, he has published studies of most of the major Muslim philosophers as well as of such Jewish thinkers as Maimonides and Saadiah. His most recent books are a translation with philosophic commentary of Saadiah Gaon's *Book of Theodicy* (1988) and a philosophic study, *On Justice* (1991).

Ze'ev Levy is Professor of Jewish Thought at the University of Haifa. He is the author of numerous articles and of eight books, among which are *Between Yafeth and Shem: On the Relationship between Jewish and General Philosophy* (1982) and *Baruch or Benedict: On Some Jewish Aspects of Spinoza's Philosophy* (1989).

Kenneth Seeskin is Professor and Chair of the Department of Philosophy at Northwestern University and Director of its Jewish Studies Program. He is the author of many articles in classical philosophy and in Jewish philosophy and of three books, *Dialogue and Discovery: A Study in Socratic Method* (1987), *Jewish Philosophy in a Secular Age* (1990), and *Maimonides: A Guide for Today's Perplexed* (1991).

Martin D. Yaffe is Associate Professor of Philosophy at the University of North Texas. He has published in the areas of classical political philosophy and of Jewish thought. He is co-author of a translation of Aquinas' *Literal Exposition on Job* (1989), and is currently cotranslating Hermann Cohen's *The Dramatic Idea in Mozart's Opera Texts* and editing a volume of critical essays on the Jewish historian, Ellis Rivkin.

Subject Index

Absolute spirit, 11
Abstract Right, 176
Academy (later), 37n.7
activity: contemplative, 2, 4; political, 16. *See also* politics
action, moral and political, 2. *See also* morality; politics
aesthetics, 12
afterlife, 90
alienation, 48-53, 163, 176, 179, 189
anarchy, 35, 88
antinomianism, 22
anti-Semitism, 194–195, 208–210
apocalypse, 78
aporia. See perplexity
appearance, and reality, 25
articles of faith, 48
asceticism, 102
atomization, of individual, 4, 5
authority: of community, 10, 18; of individual, 10, 13, 18, 19; political, 151–153; supramoral, 155
autonomy: ambiguity of term, 21; and community, 72, 149–150; economic, 72–74, 104; and morality, 4, 24; national, 187; primary of, 11; and Sabbath, 74–75; why believe in, 33–37

Bar (or Bat) Mitzvah, 15
Bereira, 17
Bible: as authority of God, 100; interpretation of, 49–50
brotherhood, universal, 91

calendar (Jewish), 16

capital punishment, 77, 101
capitalism, 11, 177, 179
categorical imperative, 144, 145
cause: natural, 31; spontaneous, 30
Chasidic movement, 62
Christianity, 48, 70, 72, 184–185. *See also* Roman Catholic Church
chosen people, concept of, 184
Cities of Refuge, 77
class struggle, 178
"commanding presence," 33
commandments, 21, 27, 28, 29, 32, 33–34, 36–37, 101–102
communism, 175–181, 189, 207–208. *See also* revolution, communist
community: and individual, 1, 2, 4, 92; political, 4, 150–151
confirmation (ceremony), 15
conscience, 10, 11, 12, 14, 16, 17, 18, 22, 23, 62–63
Constitution, of United States, 32
Copernican Revolution (Kant's), 22
cosmopolitanism, 4, 146
covenant, 20, 22, 35, 78, 92–93, 195–196, 198
Crusades, 194, 201
Cushites, 78
creation (of world), 27, 28, 111n.51
Cynics, 110n.48

Day of Atonement. *See* Yom Kippur
deists, 72
democracy, 10, 13, 14, 15–16
desire, 24, 25, 26
determinism, 28, 31, 37n.13, 46
dialogue, Catholic-Jewish, 193, 211
Diaspora, 61

Name Index